PIC'n Up The Pace

PIC16/17 MICROCONTROLLER
APPLICATIONS GUIDE

FROM

DAVID BENSON

VERSION 1.0

NOTICE

TRADEMARKS

PIC is a registered trademark of Microchip Technology Inc. in the U.S.A.
PICmicro is a registered trademark of Microchip Technology, Inc.
PIC16/17 is a registered trademark of Microchip Technology, Inc.
MPLAB is a registered trademark of Microchip Technology, Inc.
MPASM is a registered trademark of Microchip Technology, Inc.
PICSTART is a registered trademark of Microchip Technology, Inc.

ISBN 0-9654162-1-6

PUBLISHER

```
Square 1 Electronics
P.O. Box 501
Kelseyville,CA  95451  U.S.A.

Voice   (707)279-8881
FAX     (707)279-8883
EMAIL   sqone@pacific.net
http://www.sq-1.com
```

PIC16/17 MICROCONTROLLER
APPLICATIONS GUIDE
FROM

INTRODUCTION

"PIC'n Up The Pace" begins where "Easy PIC'n" ends. I am assuming you know all the beginner information included in "Easy PIC'n" either from using the book or from other experience. There will be very little overlap.

The programs included in this book are examples to help you learn. My hope is that you will study the examples in this book and write your own borrowing from what you see here. That way, you will know what's in your code because you created it. If you want to borrow from the code in this book, it is currently available for downloading at the Square 1 website (no charge) or on disk.

Include files are not used in this book because if you use someone else's include file (this includes those provided by Microchip), you won't know precisely what's in it and will spend a lot of time scratching your head because your program isn't working because you didn't pay attention to what the author of the include file had in mind.

If you write the code, you know what's in it and what it does.

Use of macros and most assembler directives is avoided because they confuse people who are learning more often than not. If you end up doing a lot of "PIC'n", you may find them useful.

Reluctantly, I have chosen to use file register bank switching rather than use the TRIS and OPTION instructions for the majority of examples in this book. This will prepare you for situations where things can't be done otherwise plus it will foster understanding of other's code such as the examples in Microchip's "Embedded Control Handbook".

Destination designator equates are used in "Easy PIC'n" because the version(s) of MPASM(tm) available at the time it was written would not accept "w" and "f". The version of MPASM contained in MPLAB(tm) will accept "w" and "f", so destination designator equates are not included in the program listings in this book. If the version of MPASM you use requires them, you can easily add them.

I think you will particularly enjoy the serial LCD module project. It can be incorporated in your future projects and can use used as test equipment to troubleshoot your own PIC16 applications as you develop them. It can provide a "window" into what is happening as a PIC16 program is executed and a way to display results. It can take the place of the LED's used in the examples in this book. When you create your own applications, those pins will be busy controlling your widget instead of LED's and won't be available for display purposes. With the serial LCD module, 1 pin = 1 wire will allow you to display whatever your choose.

Where programs used previously in the book are combined for use in a more exotic application, I did not rewrite the code to achieve double duty (shared) use of file registers. This is particularly true in the LCD chapter.

HEXADECIMAL NUMBERS vs. MPASM ASSEMBLER

The use of hexadecimal numbers with PIC16/17's is full of inconsistencies! You will see this when you look through program listings from other sources. For example port B may be equated to the file address hexadecimal 06 in the following ways:

```
portb    equ        6
                    06
                    06h
                    h'06'
                    0x06
```

The MOVLW instruction is used to load the W register with hexadecimal literals as follows:

```
         movlw      00
                    00h
                    h'00'
                    0x00
                    0f
                    ff         ;won't work
                    ffh        ;won't work
                    h'ff'
                    0xff
```

If 00 and 0f work, why doesn't ff work? It looks like the same form to me. The important thing is to be aware of the inconsistencies and use a format that always works.

The first character in the literal expression must be "0" or "h" for the assembler to work.

Sooooo .... to make things manageable we will settle on a standard/uniform way of doing things for the examples in this book.

Single hex digits by themselves will be used for:

Equates	bits 0 → 7
Instructions	bit designator b 0 → 7

Hex addresses will be in the following form:

File registers = data memory	0xXX
Program memory	0xXXX

Hex numbers in literal instructions will be in the following form:

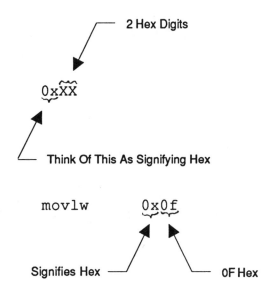

The programs in this book are written using these conventions.

All references to hexadecimal numbers in the text of the book will use the 0x notation.

BINARY AND DECIMAL NUMBERS vs. MPASM ASSEMBLER

Binary and decimal literals may be written as shown:

```
movlw   b'00001111' ;binary
movlw   d'16'       ;decimal
```

Note that the ' is the apostrophe on the same key as " on the keyboard. Some listings I have seen appear to have the literal bracketed in ` '. Only ' ' works with MPASM.

ASCII CHARACTERS vs. MPASM ASSEMBLER

Most ASCII characters may be included in a program by doing the following:

```
movlw   'A'             ;ascii capital A
```

PARTS IS PARTS

As the Microchip microcontroller product line grows, and I am glad that it is, the part numbering conventions/system seems to be getting a bit involved. Microchip is going to do what it will. You and I, however, need a way to keep things straight between us.

The PIC16/17 (tm) designation is used because of a trademark conflict in Germany which prevents Microchip from using "PIC" by itself.

What about 12/14/16/17? Hmmm ...... We will use PIC16 for lack of anything better to do and because I sell books in Germany. I notice that Microchip is using PICmicro (tm) on some of their latest stuff. I guess I could use that but you wouldn't recognize it (yet anyway).

Microchip is now publishing a Product Line Card revised quarterly which will tell you what's new and what's current. I find it to be very useful.

The real key to sanity here is to recognize that there are three fundamental product groups in terms of how they function and, to some extent, how program code must be written for them. The three product groups have 12-bit, 14-bit and 16-bit cores. We don't really care how many bits are in an instruction word. We just need to know which set of rules and features apply when writing code for a selected chip. "Easy PIC'n" and this book talk only about the 12-bit core base-line and 14-bit core mid-range parts. Here are some popular examples:

```
Device          Core Size    Pins
-------------------------------------
PIC12C508          12           8
     12C671        14           8
     16C54         12          18
     16C554        14          18
     16C62         14          28
     16C71         14          18
     16C74         14          40
     16C84         14          18
     16F84         14          18
```

In days gone by, the 12CXXX parts had 12-bit cores, the PIC16C5 whatever parts had 12-bit cores, etc. But no more. Forget the part numbering scheme and look at the data book or summary for core size.

The PIC16C554 is pin-for-pin compatible with the very popular PIC16C54 and PIC16C54A and currently sells for the same price! The PIC16C554 has a 14-bit core and the features that go with it such as interrupts and an 8-level stack, plus 2.5 times the number of file registers. I would guess that the 14-bit core parts will eventually (long term) replace the 12-bit core parts.

As an aside, notice that the PIC16C556, PIC16C558 or PIC16C621 might be useful as a OTP version of the PIC16C84 or PIC16F84, less the EEPROM data memory. Food for thought.

The PIC16C84 is being replaced over time by the PIC16CF84 which, for our purposes, is essentially the same part. The "C" part is very popular and well known. The "F" part will be.

PROGRAMMING STYLE

One thing I have learned about myself is that when designing programs for PIC16's, I tend to lay them out the way I think (do this, then do that). PIC16's don't always work the way I think or visualize a sequence of functions should flow. There are often better/shorter/faster ways for PIC16's to do things. For example, let's take a situation where we want to test one bit and then make the second bit the same (1 or 0) as the one tested.

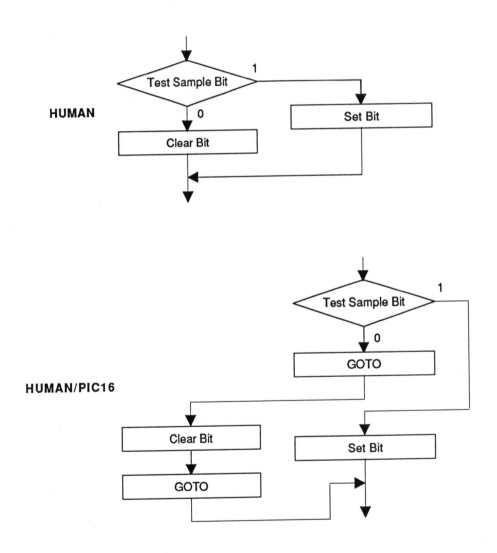

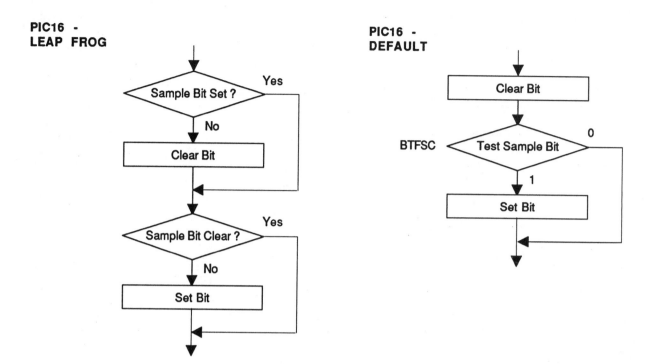

The most efficient way to code this is to use the default method. The bit to be altered is first cleared by default. If the bit tested is clear, fine. If not, the bit to be altered is set.

Since I am a "visual" person, I find it convenient to keep a "cheat-sheet" handy which has flow charts for some standard operations. You may find the following useful:

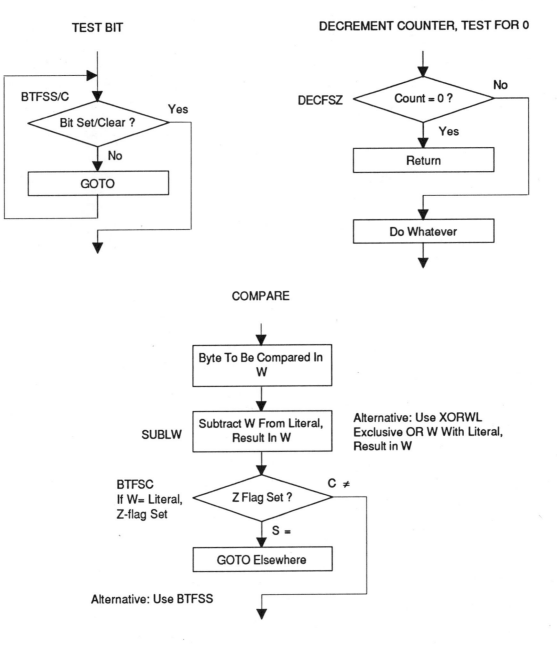

Code may be optimized for speed, for minimizing use of program memory space, or so you can understand it. How these considerations are traded off depends on the learning stage you are in at the moment and the demands of the application you are working on.

CIRCUIT MODULE FOR EXPERIMENTS

'84 ON A BOARD

A simple circuit may be assembled for use in most of the experiments in this book. It includes a PIC16C84 with clock oscillator, reset, power supply decoupling capacitor, and port pullup resistors. These items are required in or are common to almost all of the experiments. The pullup resistors are used in the experiments primarily for the purpose of preventing unused inputs from floating. There are pullups on port B built into the PIC16C84. I decided not to use them because they just add confusion to the program examples and detract from explanation of the applications themselves. So...... if you use the circuit, remember to activate (via DIP switches) pullup resistors on all unused port lines (input or output). You can save refinements for later.

I recommend connecting the port lines to a DIP socket. A 16-conductor ribbon cable terminated with DIP plugs may then be used to connect the '84 on a board to a solderless breadboard for many of the experiments. The wiring done on the solderless breadboard is minimal and chances are you won't want to preserve the specialized part of the circuit after you have done the experiment anyway (on to better things).

If you are of a mind to, I would definitely consider use of a ZIF socket for the '84.

The same circuit module may be used for the PIC16C71 A/D experiment by substituting a PIC16C71 in the microcontroller socket.

Two '84 on a board modules are needed for the PIC-to-PIC serial communication experiment.

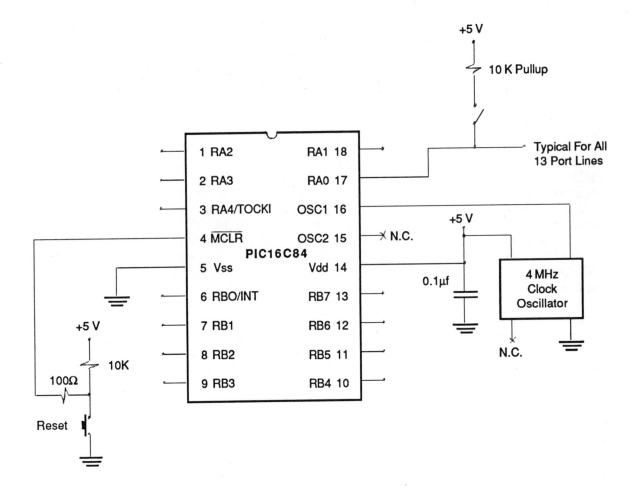

USING OP-AMPS

Op-amps will be used in several applications in this book. A complete dissertation on the care and feeding of op-amps is beyond the scope of this book and lots of reference material is already available. I have chosen three op-amps for use in the circuit examples as follows:

```
------------------------------------------------------------------
          Application              Op-amp and Power Supply(s)
------------------------------------------------------------------
Offset and scale, 3 op-amps        741C   +/-9V
Offset and scale, single op-amp    MAX406, +5V
A/D - DIY 1-pin, V in, Z transform LM358, +9V or MAX406, +5V
D/A - R ladder w/buffer            LM358, +9V or MAX406, +5V
D/A - PWM filter w/buffer          LM358, +9V or MAX406, +5V

MAX406BCPA is full part number
```

Offset and scale with the 3 op-amp design requires handling both positive and negative voltages. The 741C operates using both positive and negative power supplies and was chosen because of it's availability and low price.

Offset and scale can also be accomplished using one single power supply op-amp. The MAX406 was selected because it operates from a single power supply and it can accept input voltages ranging from ground potential to the power supply voltage (rail-to-rail).

The remaining three applications require processing input (with respect to the op-amp) signals ranging between 0 and +5 volts with unity gain. An LM358 may be used at the cost of an additional power supply with higher voltage such as +9 volts (or maybe a charge pump circuit). The LM358 is inexpensive and readily available. My alternate choice is the MAX406BCPA which will operate from a single +5V supply and from rail-to-rail. It costs more and is a little harder to find. Life is full of trade-offs as usual.

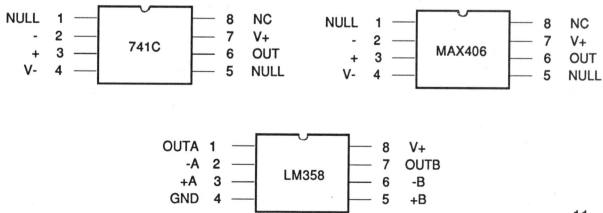

SERIAL COMMUNICATION

Since PIC16's have few pins, serial communication is, more often than not, the best way for the microcontroller to communicate with peripheral chips on the same board, or between one PIC16 and another via a short cable. Communication between a PIC16-controlled device and the outside world is typically done serially (via RS-232 for example).

If you have not been exposed to serial communication, it involves taking data which is in a parallel format, converting it to serial format for transmission down a single (data) wire and converting the data back to parallel format at the receiving end. Sending 8 bits of data in parallel requires 8 wires for data. Sending 8 bits serially requires 1 wire for data.

Serial communication involves varying numbers of wires for the various functions. Usually the count does not include ground. In this book, we will not worry about the number of wires and we won't use anyone's protocol or standard. We will just concentrate on understanding what's going on and getting the job done.

The next chapter covers shift registers. They come in two flavors--serial-in, parallel-out and parallel in, serial-out. Getting a PIC16C84 to talk to each type is a good way to get started with serial communication.

The following chapter involves interfacing a PIC16C84 and 93C46 serial EEPROM. This is another form of serial communication, the design of which is dictated by the 93C46's pin compliment and internal workings.

Next, we'll get one PIC16C84 talking to another PIC16C84. Several other examples will follow. By the time you finish, you should feel comfortable with simple serial communication.

Note that the clock signal in the examples is irregular. Timing diagrams for the serial peripheral devices used as examples show a nice symmetrical clock signal. This is not required. It also is not possible in many applications.

SHIFT REGISTERS

Shift registers are used to convert serial data to parallel or vice versa. "Talking" to shift registers is a good way to get started learning about serial communication. Shift registers are useful as parallel output and input ports which may be interfaced with a PIC16 serially.

For our first example, we will use a 74HC164 which is a serial in, parallel out shift register. The "in" vs. "out" designations are with respect to the shift register. The object is to create and send 8 bits of data to the shift register serially and look at its outputs via DVM, LED's or whatever to see if the byte got there successfully.

The PIC16C84 will be used in this example.

The data to be sent from the PIC16C84 is initially defined and stored in a file register as 8 bits in parallel format. In order to convert them to serial format, the 8 bits in the file register are shifted left (RLF) one at a time. Bit 7 of the file register is sent on its way via a single output port line after each shift. The most significant bit is sent first because that is what the 74HC164 expects.

Example:

Initial 8 Bits

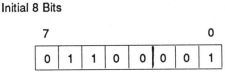

Shift Left (RLF) First Time

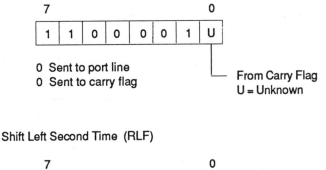

Shift Left Second Time (RLF)

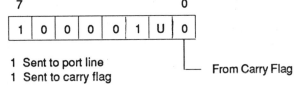

The 8 bits are marched out one at a time in succession.

SERIAL IN, PARALLEL OUT SHIFT REGISTER - 74HC164

Let's talk about the hardware.

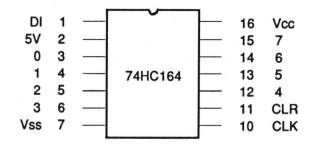

Notice the 74HC164 has three control lines.

- Serial Input
- Clear   ⊓̅   Clears outputs to 0's (normally HI)
- Clock   ⌐_   Shifts data through bit 0 toward bit 7

To move data into the shift register, the first data bit is presented to the input. Then it is shifted in. The second bit is presented and shifted, and so on. Simple!

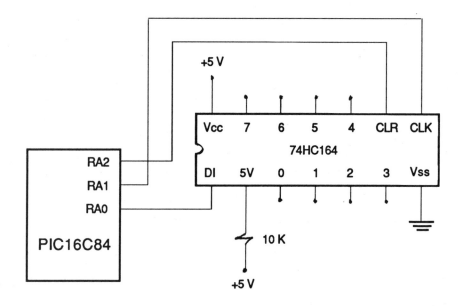

Here is how the complete process of sending one byte of data works:

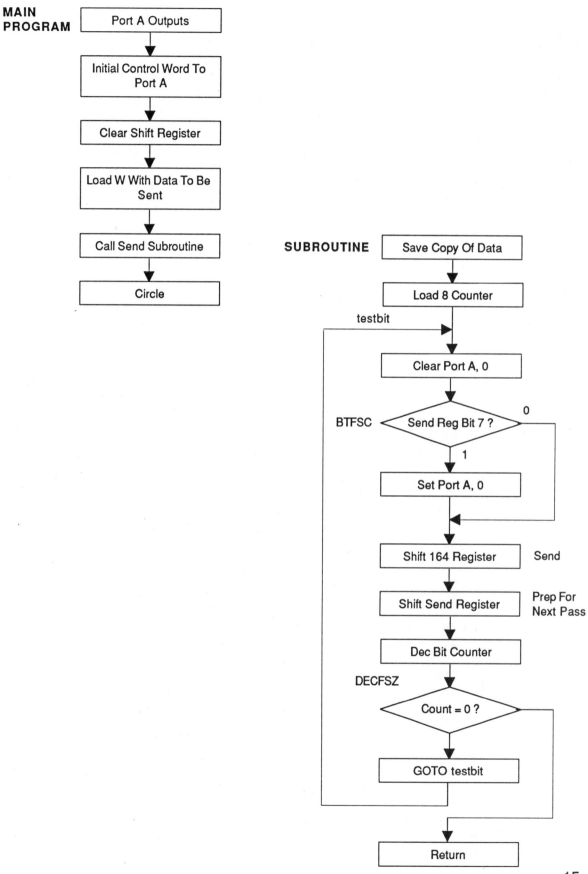

15

The shift register outputs are cleared on initialization as part of the power-on reset housekeeping so that all outputs will be low to start with.

The assembly language program for doing all this is a subroutine (ser_out). It is a code module which may be modified, if necessary, to reflect port pin assignment, etc. and used for your own future projects.

```
;=======74HC164.ASM================================4/25/97==
        list    p=16c84
        radix   hex
;-----------------------------------------------------------
;       cpu equates (memory map)
porta   equ     0x05
status  equ     0x03
sendreg equ     0x0c
count   equ     0x0d
trisa   equ     0x85
;-----------------------------------------------------------
;       bit equates
rp0     equ     5
;-----------------------------------------------------------
        org     0x000
;
start   bsf     status,rp0   ;switch to bank 1
        movlw   b'00000000'  ;outputs
        movwf   trisa
        bcf     status,rp0   ;switch back to bank 0
        movlw   0x04         ;0000 0100
        movwf   porta        ;control word
        bcf     porta,2      ;clear shift register
        bsf     porta,2
        movlw   0x80         ;number to be sent
        call    ser_out      ;to serial out subroutine
circle  goto    circle       ;done
;-----------------------------------------------------------
ser_out movwf   sendreg      ;save copy of number
        movlw   0x08         ;init 8 counter
        movwf   count
testbit bcf     porta,0      ;default
        btfsc   sendreg,7    ;test number bit 7
        bsf     porta,0      ;bit is set
shift   bsf     porta,1      ;shift register
        bcf     porta,1
rotlft  rlf     sendreg,f    ;shift number left
        decfsz  count,f      ;decrement bit counter
        goto    testbit      ;next bit
        return               ;done
;-----------------------------------------------------------
        end
;-----------------------------------------------------------
;at blast time, select:
;       memory unprotected
;       watchdog timer disabled (default is enabled)
```

```
;          standard crystal (using 4 MHz osc for test) XT
;          power-up timer on
;==============================================================
```

PARALLEL IN, SERIAL OUT SHIFT REGISTER - 74HC165

Bringing 8 bits of data into a PIC16 serially is done in a similar way. We will use a 74HC165 parallel in, serial out shift register.

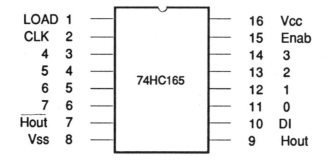

Notice the 74HC165 has three control lines.

```
•    Serial Output
•    Load          ⊔    Loads 8 bits into shift register
•    Clock         ⌐    Shifts data MS bit first
```

The 8 bits of data presented to the shift register are latched in using the load control line. This must be done so that if the input lines are changing state with time, only the data latched in at one instant in time will be transmitted to the PIC16. The 8 data bits are shifted out most significant bit first.

Again, one PIC16C84 port pin is used for serial in. It is convenient to use bit 0 for serial input. The program looks at the port as a whole, rotates bit "0" into the carry flag, and rotates the contents of the carry flag into the least significant bit of the file register assigned to receive the incoming data. This process is carried out for each of the 8 bits. Notice that the first bit is available at the serial output line immediately after the data is latched. Shifting 7 times (not 8) is required to access the remaining bits.

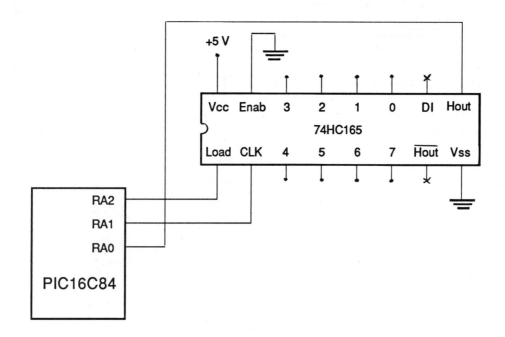

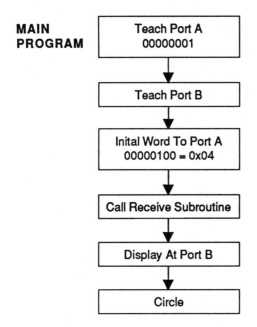

MAIN PROGRAM

- Teach Port A
  00000001
- Teach Port B
- Inital Word To Port A
  00000100 = 0x04
- Call Receive Subroutine
- Display At Port B
- Circle

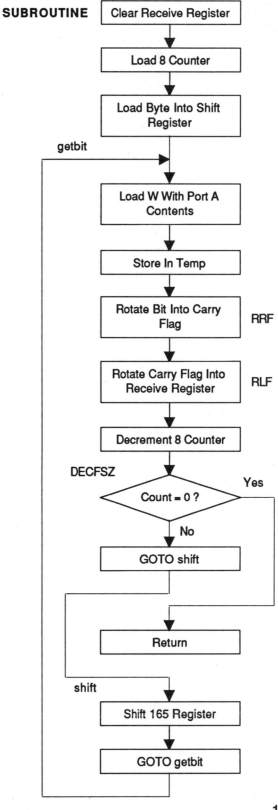

SUBROUTINE

- Clear Receive Register
- Load 8 Counter
- Load Byte Into Shift Register

getbit

- Load W With Port A Contents
- Store In Temp
- Rotate Bit Into Carry Flag   RRF
- Rotate Carry Flag Into Receive Register   RLF
- Decrement 8 Counter

DECFSZ

- Count = 0 ? — Yes
- No
- GOTO shift
- Return

shift

- Shift 165 Register
- GOTO getbit

Again, this is code includes a subroutine which you may use in the future.

```
;=======74HC165.ASM===============================4/25/97==
        list    p=16c84
        radix   hex
;-------------------------------------------------------------
;       cpu equates (memory map)
porta   equ     0x05
portb   equ     0x06
status  equ     0x03
rcvreg  equ     0x0c
count   equ     0x0d
temp    equ     0x0e
trisa   equ     0x85
trisb   equ     0x86
;-------------------------------------------------------------
;       bit equates
rp0     equ     5
;-------------------------------------------------------------
        org     0x000
;
start   bsf     status,rp0  ;switch to bank 1
        movlw   b'00000001' ;bit 0 = input
        movwf   trisa
        movlw   b'00000000' ;outputs
        movwf   trisb
        bcf     status,rp0  ;switch back to bank 0
        movlw   0x04        ;0000 0100
        movwf   porta       ;control word
        call    ser_in      ;to serial input subroutine
        movf    rcvreg,w    ;get data
        movwf   portb       ;display data via LED's
circle  goto    circle      ;done
;-------------------------------------------------------------
ser_in  clrf    rcvreg      ;clear receive register
        movlw   0x08        ;init 8 counter
        movwf   count
        bcf     porta,2     ;load shift register
        bsf     porta,2
getbit  movf    porta,w     ;read port A
        movwf   temp        ;store copy
        rrf     temp,f      ;rotate bit into carry flag
        rlf     rcvreg,f    ;rotate carry flag into rcvreg
        decfsz  count,f     ;decrement counter
        goto    shift
        return              ;done
shift   bsf     porta,1     ;shift 1 bit
        bcf     porta,1
        goto    getbit      ;again
;-------------------------------------------------------------
        end
;-------------------------------------------------------------
;note: the 74HC165 gets shifted 7 times
```

```
;----------------------------------------------------------------
;at blast time, select:
;       memory unprotected
;       watchdog timer disabled (default is enabled)
;       standard crystal (using 4 MHz osc for test) XT
;       power-up timer on
;================================================================
```

SERIAL IN, PARALLEL OUT - 74HC595

The 74HC595 is similar to the 74HC164. The 8 outputs of the 74HC164 will change state as data is shifted in. If the chip is being used as a parallel output port, this will not be a good thing. The 74HC595 has latches which hold the data presented at the output lines. New data may be shifted in while the outputs remain stable. Then the new data is latched in. This, of course, requires a 4th control line to latch data.

```
  1  1  ─────┐      ┌─────  16  Vcc
  2  2  ─────┤      ├─────  15  0
  3  3  ─────┤      ├─────  14  DI
  4  4  ─────┤      ├─────  13  G̅
  5  5  ─────┤74HC595├─────  12  LAT
  6  6  ─────┤      ├─────  11  CLK
  7  7  ─────┤      ├─────  10  C̅L̅R̅
Vss  8  ─────┘      └─────   9  Q'H
```

The 74HC595 has four control lines.

- Serial Input
- Latch   ⎍   Shift register contents to latches
- Clock   ⎍   Shifts data MS bit first
- Clear   ⎍   Clears shift register

Data is shifted in most significant bit first.

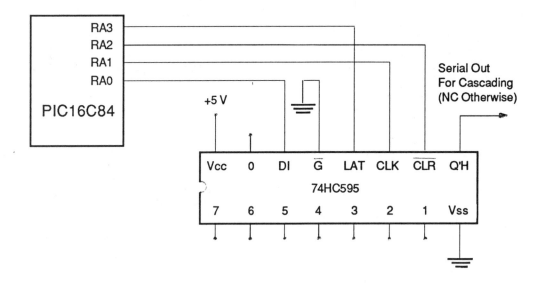

The 74HC595 has an output line designed for cascading two or more chips. 74HC595's may be cascaded by:

- Q'H serial output of first chip connected to serial input of second chip
- Connect shift register clear lines together
- Connect shift clock lines together
- Connect latch data lines together

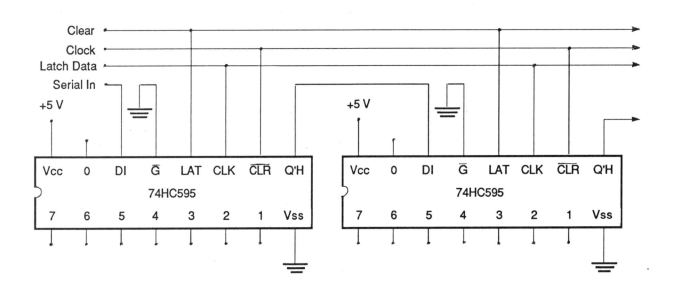

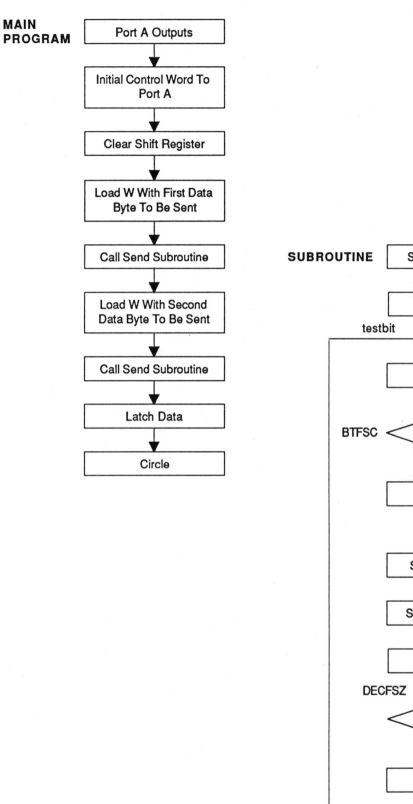

MAIN PROGRAM

- Port A Outputs
- Initial Control Word To Port A
- Clear Shift Register
- Load W With First Data Byte To Be Sent
- Call Send Subroutine
- Load W With Second Data Byte To Be Sent
- Call Send Subroutine
- Latch Data
- Circle

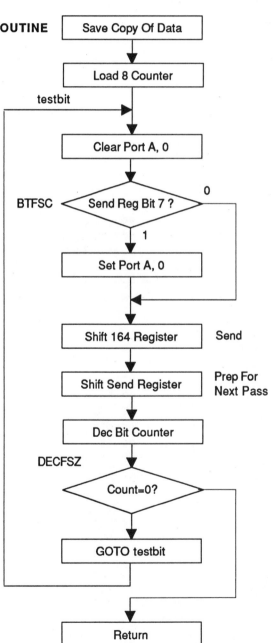

SUBROUTINE

- Save Copy Of Data
- Load 8 Counter
- testbit → Clear Port A, 0
- BTFSC — Send Reg Bit 7 ? — 0
- 1 → Set Port A, 0
- Shift 164 Register — Send
- Shift Send Register — Prep For Next Pass
- Dec Bit Counter
- DECFSZ — Count=0?
- GOTO testbit
- Return

23

```
;=======74HC595.ASM===================================4/25/97==
          list      p=16c84
          radix     hex
;--------------------------------------------------------------
;         cpu equates (memory map)
porta     equ       0x05
status    equ       0x03
sendreg   equ       0x0c
count     equ       0x0d
trisa     equ       0x85
;--------------------------------------------------------------
;         bit equates
rp0       equ       5
;--------------------------------------------------------------
          org       0x000
;
start     bsf       status,rp0  ;switch to bank 1
          movlw     b'00000000' ;outputs
          movwf     trisa
          bcf       status,rp0  ;switch back to bank 0
          movlw     0x04        ;0000 0100
          movwf     porta       ;control word
          bcf       porta,2     ;clear shift register
          bsf       porta,2
          movlw     0x80        ;first number to be sent
          call      ser_out     ;to serial out subroutine
          movlw     0x0f        ;second number to be sent
          call      ser_out     ;to serial out subroutine
          bsf       porta,3     ;register contents to latches
          bcf       porta,3
circle    goto      circle      ;done
;--------------------------------------------------------------
ser_out   movwf     sendreg     ;save copy of number
          movlw     0x08        ;init 8 counter
          movwf     count
testbit   bcf       porta,0     ;default
          btfsc     sendreg,7   ;test number bit 7
          bsf       porta,0     ;bit is set
shift     bsf       porta,1     ;shift register
          bcf       porta,1
rotlft    rlf       sendreg,f   ;shift number left
          decfsz    count,f     ;decrement bit counter
          goto      testbit     ;next bit
          return                ;done
;--------------------------------------------------------------
          end
;--------------------------------------------------------------
;at blast time, select:
;         memory unprotected
;         watchdog timer disabled (default is enabled)
;         standard crystal (using 4 MHz osc for test) XT
;         power-up timer on
;==============================================================
```

SERIAL EEPROMS

Serial EEPROMs come in three main flavors and a variety of sizes. The 93XXX devices are the easiest to interface to PIC16's (in my humble opinion). We will use the 93C46 (by Microchip and others) as an example.

The 93C46 is a small non-volatile memory peripheral chip. It is organized as 64 registers of 16 bits each. The programming voltage and write timing are developed on-chip. The self-timed write cycle takes about 10 milliseconds.

All communication with the 93C46 begins with sending 9 instruction bits. The first bit (MSB) is a logic "1" start bit. The remaining 8 bits may be an op code or an op code and address combination. If the operation is a write operation, 16 data bits follow the instruction bits, MSB first.

The 93C46 is available in an 8-pin DIP.

```
         CS   1 ──┤           ├── 8  Vcc
         CLK  2 ──┤           ├── 7  NC
                  │   93C46   │
         DI   3 ──┤           ├── 6  NC
         DO   4 ──┤           ├── 5  Vss
```

The control lines are:

- Serial data in
- Serial data out
- Clock
- Chip select

Some use rules are:

1) A register must be erased (all 1's) before it can be written to. The chip has a built-in auto erase cycle which takes place when a write is called for.

2) The chip select pin (CS) must be brought low for a minimum of 1 microsecond between consecutive instruction cycles to synchronize the internal logic of the device.

3) For read operations, a dummy "0" precedes the 16 data bits. Data is shifted out MSB first.

4) Completion of an erase cycle or write cycle to an individual memory location takes about 10 milliseconds. The serial data output (D_0) pin may also be used as a status pin during the self-timing phase of these operations to indicate the status of the device. On completion of erase or write, CS is brought low briefly. After that, D_0 will be low until the operation is complete. When D_0 goes high again, the device is no longer busy and is accessible for other operations.

The instructions are:

- Read a register
- Write to a register
- Erase a register
- Erase/Write enable (EWEN)
- Erase/Write disable (EWDS)
- Erase all registers (ERAL)
- Write all registers (WRAL) (with same data)

I haven't figured out why anyone would want to write the same data to all registers, but maybe you will.

There are 6 address bits (to definite 64 register locations) contained in the instruction words that need them.

Operation	Start Bit	Op Code		More Op Code or Address					
Read	1	1	0	A5	A4	A3	A2	A1	A0
Write	1	0	1	A5	A4	A3	A2	A1	A0
Erase	1	1	1	A5	A4	A3	A2	A1	A0
EWEN	1	0	0	1	1	X	X	X	X
EWDS	1	0	0	0	0	X	X	X	X
ERAL	1	0	0	1	0	X	X	X	X
WRAL	1	0	0	0	1	X	X	X	X

X = Don't care

Now we need to digest all this and figure out how to write some code to make the thing work.

One way to write a program to communicate with the 93C46 is to send the start bit as a separate operation which precedes sending the remaining 8 bits. Then the remaining 8 bits will fit into a file register. This file register is used as a working register to cook up instruction words:

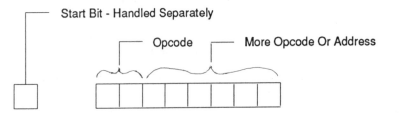

Start Bit - Handled Separately

Opcode   More Opcode Or Address

The next consideration is what to do with the "X's", i.e., don't cares. Let's make them "0's". Now the instruction table looks like this:

Operation	Hex Op Code	Op Code		More Op Code or Address					
Read		1	0	A5	A4	A3	A2	A1	A0
Write		0	1	A5	A4	A3	A2	A1	A0
Erase		1	1	A5	A4	A3	A2	A1	A0
EWEN	0x30	0	0	1	1	0	0	0	0
EWDS	0x00	0	0	0	0	0	0	0	0
ERAL	0x20	0	0	1	0	0	0	0	0
WRAL	0x10	0	0	0	1	0	0	0	0

This method of putting "0s" in place of "X's" makes the instruction table look less intimidating. Further, there are now four hex opcodes we can use for four of the instructions to make life easier.

Next we need to deal with addresses in individual register operations. Perhaps the easiest thing to do is to dedicate a file register for holding the address prior to executing our serial routine. The routine can grab the address from there and move it to the working register (labeled "cook"). Don't worry about the upper 2 bits in the address register For the address 00 0000 (binary), use 0x00. The range is 0x00 to 0x3F. In the "cook" register we can modify the upper 2 bits to make them an erase, read, or write op code. At that point, we have cooked up the complete instruction for the operation.

This example EEPROM serial communication program will be modular meaning a main program will call subroutines such as "read one register" or "write one register" which will, in turn, call other subroutines as needed.

To get started, we will need an erase one register subroutine, a write to one register subroutine, and a read one register subroutine. We will need to precede erase and write with an erase/write enable (EWEN) and follow with an erase/write disable (EWDS).

Notice that the start bit is sent as part of the code as needed (requiring 2 instructions) and that 8 bits of op code/address/data are sent at a time directly out of the "cook" register.

You can write an "erase all registers" routine on your own if you find a need for one.

These routines may be modified and used in your own programs.

DEMO CIRCUIT

This circuit will be used to demonstrate interfacing a PIC16 to a 93C46 serial EEPROM:

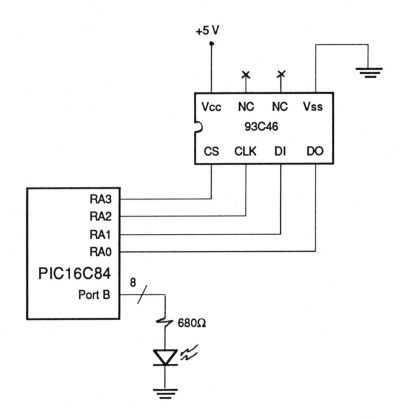

MAIN PROGRAM - INITIAL TEST

The main program will make use of subroutines. It will enable and disable operations, write to a register, and read back 16 bits of data from a register. If we can make this work, we can do anything we want with the 93C46.

An erase the contents of a register subroutine is also shown.

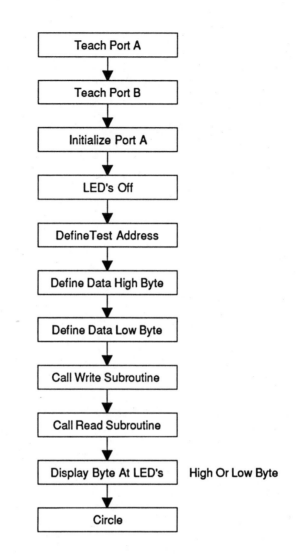

High Or Low Byte

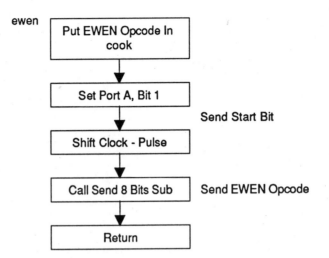

ewen

Put EWEN Opcode In cook

Set Port A, Bit 1 — Send Start Bit

Shift Clock - Pulse

Call Send 8 Bits Sub — Send EWEN Opcode

Return

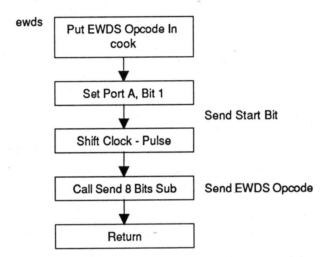

ewds

Put EWDS Opcode In cook

Set Port A, Bit 1 — Send Start Bit

Shift Clock - Pulse

Call Send 8 Bits Sub — Send EWDS Opcode

Return

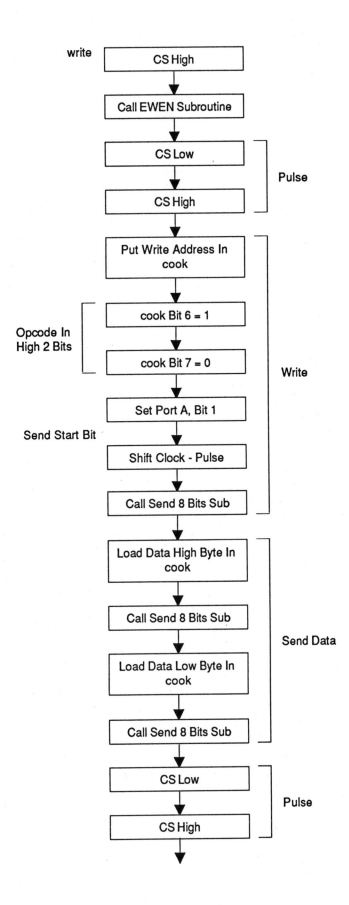

write

CS High

Call EWEN Subroutine

CS Low ⎫
CS High ⎬ Pulse

Put Write Address In cook ⎫

Opcode In High 2 Bits {
cook Bit 6 = 1
cook Bit 7 = 0

Set Port A, Bit 1

Send Start Bit
Shift Clock - Pulse

Call Send 8 Bits Sub ⎬ Write

Load Data High Byte In cook

Call Send 8 Bits Sub

Load Data Low Byte In cook ⎬ Send Data

Call Send 8 Bits Sub

CS Low ⎫
CS High ⎬ Pulse

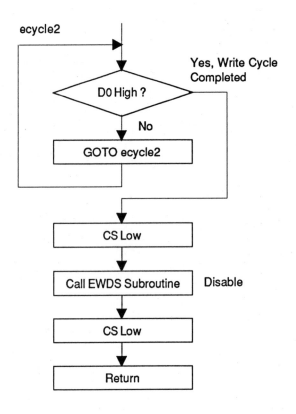

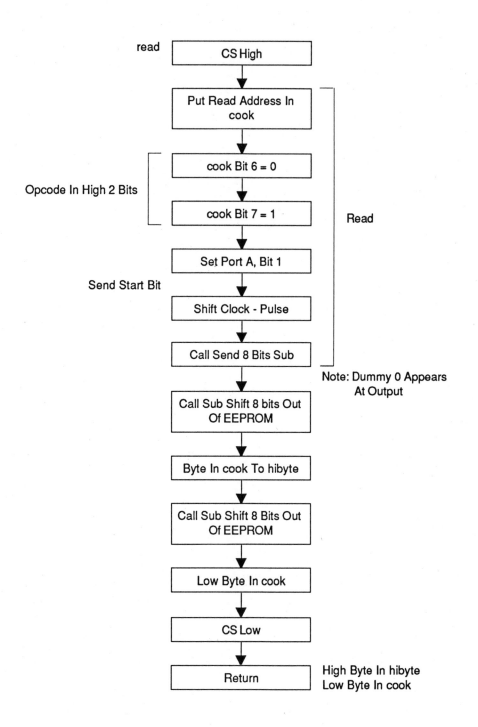

read

CS High

Put Read Address In cook

Opcode In High 2 Bits

cook Bit 6 = 0

cook Bit 7 = 1

Read

Set Port A, Bit 1

Send Start Bit

Shift Clock - Pulse

Call Send 8 Bits Sub

Note: Dummy 0 Appears At Output

Call Sub Shift 8 bits Out Of EEPROM

Byte In cook To hibyte

Call Sub Shift 8 Bits Out Of EEPROM

Low Byte In cook

CS Low

Return

High Byte In hibyte
Low Byte In cook

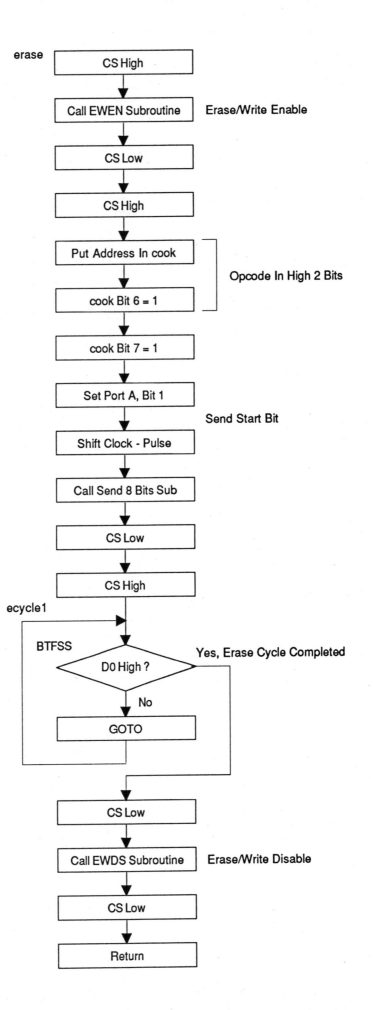

erase

CS High

Call EWEN Subroutine — Erase/Write Enable

CS Low

CS High

Put Address In cook ⎤
cook Bit 6 = 1 ⎦ Opcode In High 2 Bits

cook Bit 7 = 1

Set Port A, Bit 1

Send Start Bit

Shift Clock - Pulse

Call Send 8 Bits Sub

CS Low

CS High

ecycle1

BTFSS

D0 High ? → Yes, Erase Cycle Completed

No

GOTO

CS Low

Call EWDS Subroutine — Erase/Write Disable

CS Low

Return

34

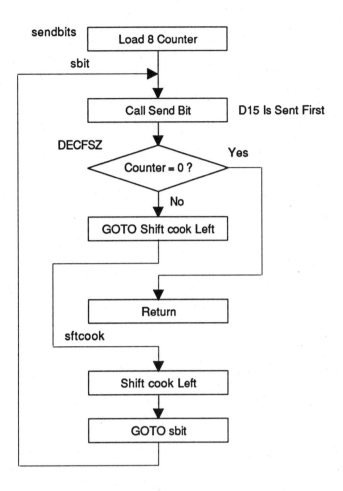

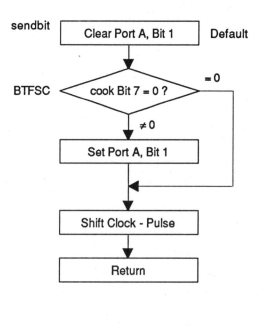

sendbit → Clear Port A, Bit 1 — Default

BTFSC — cook Bit 7 = 0 ? — = 0

≠ 0

Set Port A, Bit 1

Shift Clock - Pulse

Return

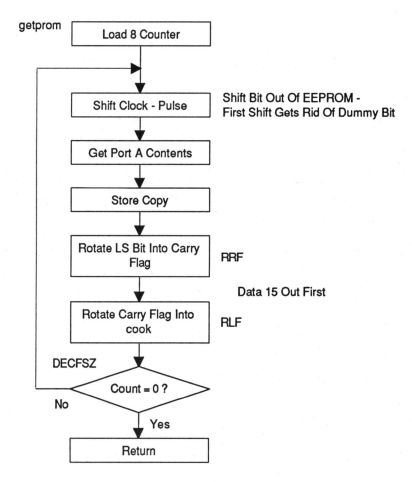

getprom → Load 8 Counter

Shift Clock - Pulse — Shift Bit Out Of EEPROM - First Shift Gets Rid Of Dummy Bit

Get Port A Contents

Store Copy

Rotate LS Bit Into Carry Flag — RRF

Data 15 Out First

Rotate Carry Flag Into cook — RLF

DECFSZ — Count = 0 ?

No

Yes

Return

36

```
;=======93C46.ASM===================================4/26/97==
          list      p=16c84
          radix     hex
;------------------------------------------------------------
;         cpu equates (memory map)
status    equ       0x03
porta     equ       0x05
portb     equ       0x06
cook      equ       0x0c
hibyte    equ       0x0d
count     equ       0x0e
address   equ       0x0f
data_hi   equ       0x10
data_lo   equ       0x11
temp      equ       0x12
trisa     equ       0x85
trisb     equ       0x86
;------------------------------------------------------------
;         bit equates
rp0       equ       5
;------------------------------------------------------------
          org       0x000
;
start     bsf       status,rp0   ;switch to bank 1
          movlw     b'00000001'  ;bit 0 = input
          movwf     trisa
          movlw     b'00000000'  ;outputs
          movwf     trisb
          bcf       status,rp0   ;switch back to bank 0
          bcf       porta,1      ;initialize
          bcf       porta,2      ;initialize
          bcf       porta,3      ;initialize
          movlw     0x00         ;00000000
          movwf     portb        ;LED's off
          movlw     0x00         ;define test address
          movwf     address
          movlw     0x80         ;define test hi byte
          movwf     data_hi
          movlw     0x0f         ;define test lo byte
          movwf     data_lo
          call      write        ;write subroutine
          call      read         ;read subroutine
          movf      cook,w       ;get lo byte
          movwf     portb        ;display via LED's
circle    goto      circle       ;done
;------------------------------------------------------------
ewen      movlw     0x30         ;ewen op code
          movwf     cook         ;to cook
          bsf       porta,1      ;send start bit
          bsf       porta,2      ;shift
          bcf       porta,2
          call      sendbits     ;send ewen op code
          return
```

```
;------------------------------------------------------------
ewds    movlw   0x00        ;ewds op code
        movwf   cook        ;to cook
        bsf     porta,1     ;send start bit
        bsf     porta,2     ;shift
        bcf     porta,2
        call    sendbits    ;send ewds op code
        return
;------------------------------------------------------------
write   bsf     porta,3     ;cs high
        call    ewen        ;erase/write enable
        bcf     porta,3     ;cs low
        nop                 ;1 microsecond min
        bsf     porta,3     ;cs high
        movf    address,w   ;get address
        movwf   cook        ;store in cook
        bcf     cook,7      ;op code
        bsf     cook,6      ;ms 2 bits
        bsf     porta,1     ;send start bit
        bsf     porta,2     ;shift
        bcf     porta,2
        call    sendbits    ;send address
        movf    data_hi,w   ;get data hi
        movwf   cook
        call    sendbits    ;send data hi
        movf    data_lo,w   ;get data lo
        movwf   cook
        call    sendbits    ;send data lo
        bcf     porta,3     ;cs low
        nop                 ;1 microsecond min
        bsf     porta,3     ;cs high
ecycle2 btfss   porta,0     ;write cycle complete?
        goto    ecycle2     ;not yet
        bcf     porta,3     ;cs low
        nop                 ;1 microsecond min
        bsf     porta,3     ;cs high
        call    ewds        ;yes, erase/write disable
        bcf     porta,3     ;cs low
        nop                 ;1 microsecond min
        return
;------------------------------------------------------------
read    bsf     porta,3     ;cs high
        movf    address,w   ;get address
        movwf   cook
        bsf     cook,7      ;op code
        bcf     cook,6      ;ms 2 bits
        bsf     porta,1     ;send start bit
        bsf     porta,2     ;shift
        bcf     porta,2
        call    sendbits    ;send address
        call    getprom     ;shift hi 8 bits out of eeprom
        movf    cook,w      ;hi byte result in hibyte
        movwf   hibyte
        call    getprom     ;shift lo 8 bits out of eeprom
```

```
        bcf     porta,3         ;cs low
        nop                     ;1microsecond min
        return                  ;exit sub with lo byte in cook
;-------------------------------------------------------------
sendbits movlw  0x08            ;count=8
        movwf   count
sbit    call    sendbit         ;send 1 bit
        decfsz  count,f         ;done?
        goto    sftcook         ;no
        return                  ;yes
sftcook rlf     cook,f          ;shift cook left
        goto    sbit            ;again
;-------------------------------------------------------------
sendbit bcf     porta,1         ;default
        btfsc   cook,7          ;test cook bit 7
        bsf     porta,1         ;bit is set
shift1  bsf     porta,2         ;shift
        bcf     porta,2
        return
;-------------------------------------------------------------
getprom movlw  0x08            ;count=8
        movwf   count
shift2  bsf     porta,2         ;shift
        bcf     porta,2
        movf    porta,w         ;read port A
        movwf   temp            ;store copy
        rrf     temp,f          ;rotate bit into carry flag
        rlf     cook,f          ;rotate carry flag into cook
        decfsz  count,f         ;decrement counter
        goto    shift2
        return                  ;done
;-------------------------------------------------------------
        end
;-------------------------------------------------------------
;at blast time, select:
;       memory unprotected
;       watchdog timer disabled (default is enabled)
;       standard crystal (using 4 MHz osc for test) XT
;       power-up timer on
;=============================================================


;-------------------------------------------------------------
erase   bsf     porta,3         ;cs high
        call    ewen            ;erase/write enable
        bcf     porta,3         ;cs low
        nop                     ;1 microsecond min
        bsf     porta,3         ;cs high
        movf    address,w       ;get address
        movwf   cook            ;store in cook
        bsf     cook,7          ;op code
        bsf     cook,6          ;ms 2 bits
        bsf     porta,1         ;send start bit
        bsf     porta,2         ;shift
```

```
        bcf     porta,2
        call    sendbits        ;send address
        bcf     porta,3         ;cs low
        nop                     ;1 microsecond min
        bsf     porta,3         ;cs high
ecycle1 btfss   porta,0         ;erase cycle complete?
        goto    ecycle1         ;not yet
        bcf     porta,3         ;cs low
        nop                     ;1 microsecond min
        bsf     porta,3         ;cs high
        call    ewds            ;yes, erase/write disable
        bcf     porta,3         ;cs low
        nop                     ;1 microsecond min
        return
```

NOPs are used to insure that the 93C46 chip's timing requirements are met.

PIC-TO-PIC SERIAL COMMUNICATION

In an effort to expand our serial communication capabilities, we will get a couple of PIC16's to talk to each other. Actually, we'll do part of the job by getting one PIC16 to talk while the other listens. We'll see if the listener understood what the talker said. We will set this up so you can continue on your own by sending more than one word and by interchanging the talk/listen roles (two-way communication).

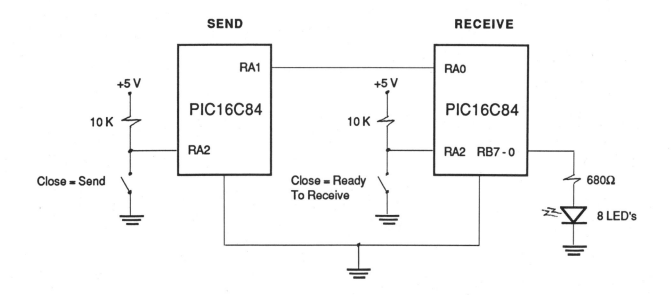

Two '84 on a board modules may be used for this experiment.

Both PIC16's are PIC16C84's with 4.0 MHz clock oscillators. For the transmitting chip, port A, bit 1 is used to transmit. The receiver uses port A, bit 0 is used to receive. We will choose the bit time interval as 256 internal clock (1 MHz) cycles. Both transmitter and receiver will use TMR0 for timing.

When the transmit data (TD) line is high, the condition is known as "mark". When TD is low, the condition is known as "space." The terminology comes from the old teletype days.

When one word (8 bits) is sent, the TD line output vs. time will look like this:

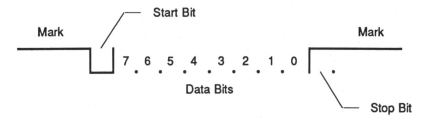

The TD line sits at mark = logic "1" until the word is sent. It drops to "0" first. This is the start bit which tells the receiver PIC16 that an 8-bit word is coming.

The transmitter transmits bits at some rate (bits per second = baud rate). The receiver must be set up to receive bits at the same rate. When the receiving PIC16's receive program is running, it sits in a loop looking for a start bit (high-to-low transition on the receive data (RD) line. When that transition takes place, the receiver's program waits for a time equal to half the width of the start bit. It looks at the RD line to see if it is still low. If not, a false start occurred and the program goes back to looking at the RD line. If the RD line is low, valid data follows and the program starts TMR0 (free-running mode) for a time interval equal to the width of a bit. Then it looks at the RD line to see if a "0" or a "1" is present. It grabs that bit and shifts it into a file register (shifting left, MSB received first). The program waits a bit-width (to middle of second bit, bit 6) and grabs it and stores it. This process is repeated until all 8 data bits have been received. The 8-bit word received is then displayed at the port B LED's so you can see if the correct data was received.

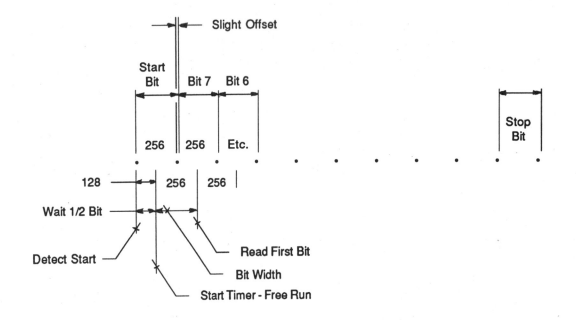

The use of TMR0 is explained in **Easy** PIC'n.

The default method for bit testing is used in the send program. The output bit may be cleared when it should be set, but it gets cleared right after that. It doesn't matter because the receiver samples the bit in the center. What goes on at the beginning or end will have no effect.

Flow charts and code for this simple example follow. The technique will be used for the serial LCD interface in the next chapter.

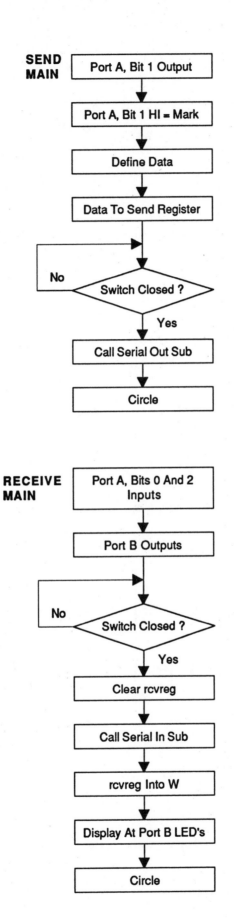

SEND MAIN

Port A, Bit 1 Output

↓

Port A, Bit 1 HI = Mark

↓

Define Data

↓

Data To Send Register

↓

Switch Closed ? — No (loops back)

↓ Yes

Call Serial Out Sub

↓

Circle

RECEIVE MAIN

Port A, Bits 0 And 2 Inputs

↓

Port B Outputs

↓

Switch Closed ? — No (loops back)

↓ Yes

Clear rcvreg

↓

Call Serial In Sub

↓

rcvreg Into W

↓

Display At Port B LED's

↓

Circle

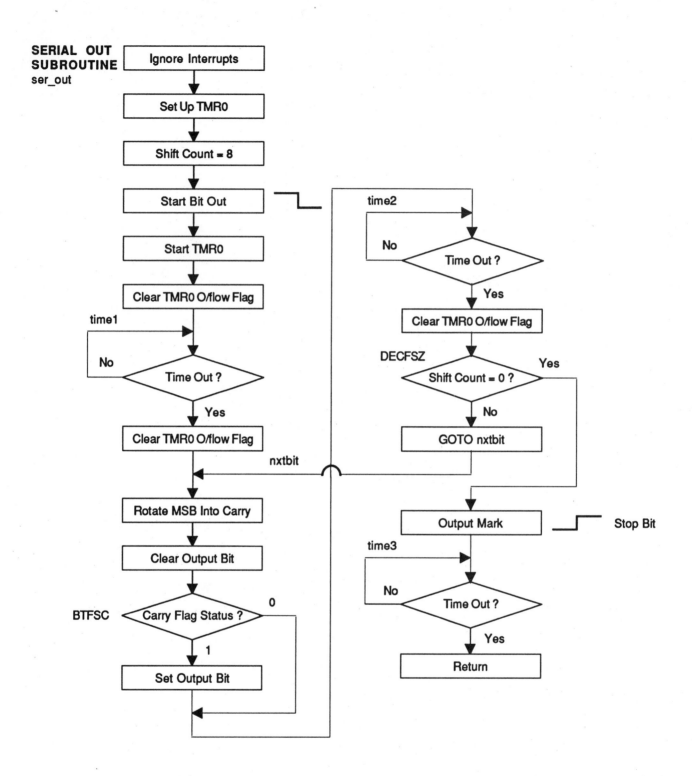

SERIAL OUT
SUBROUTINE
ser_out

Ignore Interrupts

Set Up TMR0

Shift Count = 8

Start Bit Out

Start TMR0

Clear TMR0 O/flow Flag

time1

Time Out ?

No

Yes

Clear TMR0 O/flow Flag

nxtbit

Rotate MSB Into Carry

Clear Output Bit

BTFSC   Carry Flag Status ?   0

1

Set Output Bit

time2

Time Out ?

No

Yes

Clear TMR0 O/flow Flag

DECFSZ

Shift Count = 0 ?   Yes

No

GOTO nxtbit

Output Mark   Stop Bit

time3

Time Out ?

No

Yes

Return

44

```
;=======P2PSEND.ASM==================================4/29/97==
        list    p=16c84
        radix   hex
;--------------------------------------------------------------
;       cpu equates (memory map)
tmr0    equ     0x01
status  equ     0x03
porta   equ     0x05
intcon  equ     0x0b
sendreg equ     0x0c
count   equ     0x0d
optreg  equ     0x81
trisa   equ     0x85
;--------------------------------------------------------------
;       bit equates
c       equ     0
rp0     equ     5
;--------------------------------------------------------------
        org     0x000
;
start   bsf     status,rp0      ;switch to bank 1
        movlw   b'00000100'     ;port A inputs/outputs
        movwf   trisa
        bcf     status,rp0      ;switch back to bank 0
        bsf     porta,1         ;output mark, bit 1
        movlw   0x80            ;number to be sent
        movwf   sendreg         ;store
switch  btfsc   porta,2         ;start send?
        goto    switch          ;not yet
        call    ser_out         ;to serial out subroutine
circle  goto    circle          ;done
;--------------------------------------------------------------
ser_out bcf     intcon,5        ;disable tmr0 interrupts
        bcf     intcon,7        ;disable global interrupts
        clrf    tmr0            ;clear timer/counter
        clrwdt                  ;clear wdt prep prescaler assign
        bsf     status,rp0      ;to page 1
        movlw   b'11011000'     ;set up timer/counter
        movwf   optreg
        bcf     status,rp0      ;back to page 0
        movlw   0x08            ;init shift counter
        movwf   count
        bcf     porta,1         ;start bit
        clrf    tmr0            ;start timer/counter
        bcf     intcon,2        ;clear tmr0 overflow flag
time1   btfss   intcon,2        ;timer overflow?
        goto    time1           ;no
        bcf     intcon,2        ;yes, clear overflow flag
nxtbit  rlf     sendreg,f       ;rotate msb into carry flag
        bcf     porta,1         ;clear port A, bit 1
        btfsc   status,c        ;test carry flag
        bsf     porta,1         ;bit is set
time2   btfss   intcon,2        ;timer overflow?
```

```
        goto    time2       ;no
        bcf     intcon,2    ;clear overflow flag
        decfsz  count,f     ;shifted 8?
        goto    nxtbit      ;no
        bsf     porta,1     ;yes, output mark
time3   btfss   intcon,2    ;timer overflow?
        goto    time3       ;no
        return              ;done
;-------------------------------------------------------------
        end
;-------------------------------------------------------------
;at blast time, select:
;       memory unprotected
;       watchdog timer disabled (default is enabled)
;       standard crystal (using 4 MHz osc for test) XT
;       power-up timer on
;=============================================================
```

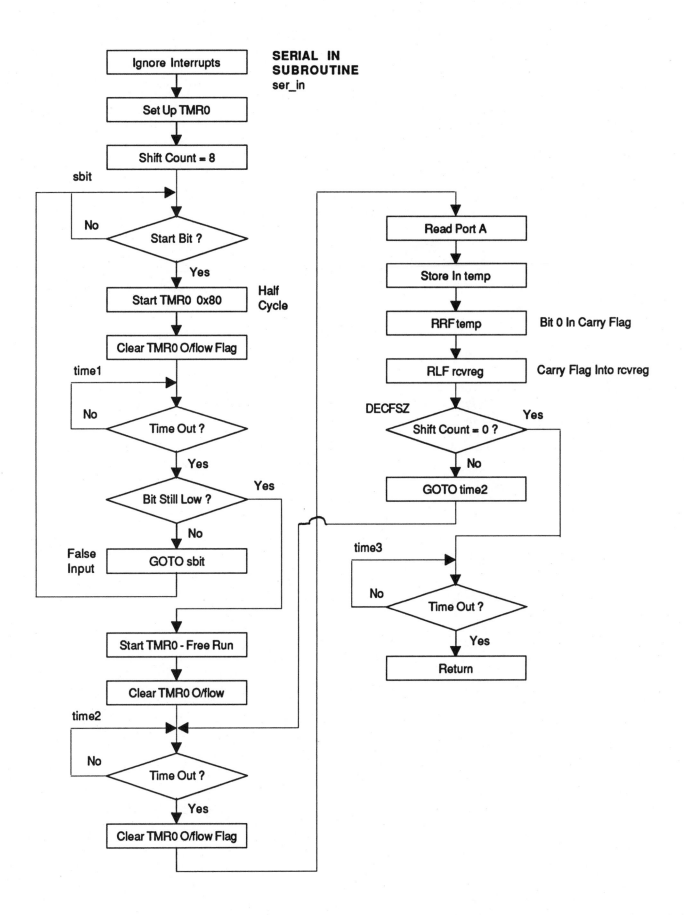

SERIAL IN
SUBROUTINE
ser_in

Ignore Interrupts

Set Up TMR0

Shift Count = 8

sbit

No

Start Bit ?

Yes

Start TMR0 0x80   Half Cycle

Clear TMR0 O/flow Flag

time1

No

Time Out ?

Yes

Bit Still Low ?   Yes

No

False Input   GOTO sbit

Start TMR0 - Free Run

Clear TMR0 O/flow

time2

No

Time Out ?

Yes

Clear TMR0 O/flow Flag

Read Port A

Store In temp

RRF temp   Bit 0 In Carry Flag

RLF rcvreg   Carry Flag Into rcvreg

DECFSZ   Yes

Shift Count = 0 ?

No

GOTO time2

time3

No

Time Out ?

Yes

Return

```
;======P2PRCV.ASM===================================4/29/97==
        list    p=16c84
        radix   hex
;-------------------------------------------------------------
;       cpu equates (memory map)
tmr0    equ     0x01
status  equ     0x03
porta   equ     0x05
portb   equ     0x06
intcon  equ     0x0b
rcvreg  equ     0x0c
count   equ     0x0d
temp    equ     0x0e
optreg  equ     0x81
trisa   equ     0x85
trisb   equ     0x86
;-------------------------------------------------------------
;       bit equates
rp0     equ     5
;-------------------------------------------------------------
        org     0x000
;
start   bsf     status,rp0  ;switch to bank 1
        movlw   b'00000101' ;port A inputs/outputs
        movwf   trisa
        movlw   b'00000000' ;port B outputs
        movwf   trisb
        bcf     status,rp0  ;back to bank 0
        clrf    portb
        clrf    rcvreg
switch  btfsc   porta,2     ;operator ready to receive?
        goto    switch      ;no
        call    ser_in      ;yes, to serial in subroutine
        movf    rcvreg,w    ;get byte received
        movwf   portb       ;display via LED's
circle  goto    circle      ;done
;-------------------------------------------------------------
ser_in  bcf     intcon,5    ;disable tmr0 interrupts
        bcf     intcon,7    ;disable global interrupts
        clrf    tmr0        ;clear timer/counter
        clrwdt              ;clear wdt prep prescaler assign
        bsf     status,rp0  ;to page 1
        movlw   b'11011000' ;set up timer/counter
        movwf   optreg
        bcf     status,rp0  ;back to page 0
        movlw   0x08        ;init shift counter
        movwf   count
sbit    btfsc   porta,0     ;look for start bit
        goto    sbit        ;mark
        movlw   0x80        ;start bit received, half bit time
        movwf   tmr0        ;load and start timer/counter
        bcf     intcon,2    ;clear tmr0 overflow flag
time1   btfss   intcon,2    ;timer overflow?
        goto    time1       ;no
```

48

```
        btfsc   porta,0     ;start bit still low?
        goto    sbit        ;false start, go back
        clrf    tmr0        ;yes, half bit time - start timer/ctr
        bcf     intcon,2    ;clear tmr0 overflow flag
time2   btfss   intcon,2    ;timer overflow?
        goto    time2       ;no
        bcf     intcon,2    ;yes, clear tmr0 overflow flag
        movf    porta,w     ;read port A
        movwf   temp        ;store
        rrf     temp,f      ;rotate bit 0 into carry flag
        rlf     rcvreg,f    ;rotate carry into rcvreg bit 0
        decfsz  count,f     ;shifted 8?
        goto    time2       ;no
time3   btfss   intcon,2    ;timer overflow?
        goto    time3       ;no
        return              ;yes, byte received
;-----------------------------------------------------------
        end
;-----------------------------------------------------------
;at blast time, select:
;       memory unprotected
;       watchdog timer disabled (default is enabled)
;       standard crystal (using 4 MHz osc for test) XT
;       power-up timer on
;===========================================================
```

To run the programs:

Run "send" first with switch off (RA2) - establish proper level on TD = mark.
Run receive second with switch off (RA2) - get ready to receive.
        Stabilize, then switch on = ready.
Send switch on.

Multiple bytes may be transmitted from the file registers by using the FSR and indirect addressing and a counter. Multiple bytes may be transmitted from a table in program memory by using relative addressing and a counter. Examples of both will be shown in the LCD Interface chapter.

LIQUID CRYSTAL DISPLAY INTERFACE

LIQUID CRYSTAL DISPLAY OVERVIEW

Liquid crystal displays (LCD) are now available which are inexpensive, display alphanumeric characters, require only 14 wires for connection and are simple to use. They come 16 to as many as 40 characters wide and 1, 2, or 4 lines high. We will use a 1 line x 16 character LCD.

1 X 16 LCD

The 1 line by 16 character display (Hitachi LM020L, Optrex DMC-16117A, Optrex DMC-16117AN or equivalent) is controlled by a Hitachi HD44780 LCD controller chip which is surface mounted on the back side of the display module's printed circuit board. The HD44780 display controller is commonly used in a variety of liquid crystal displays made by manufacturers such as Hitachi, Optrex, Amperex, Densitron and Epson. The following description will apply in a general way to similar displays made by these manufacturers.

Pins And Functions

```
 1    GND
 2    +5V
 3    GND
 4    RS
 5    R/W̄ - GND for simplicity
 6    E
 7    D₀
 8    D₁
 9    D₂
10    D₃
11    D₄
12    D₅
13    D₆
14    D₇
```

Note: Pin 3 may be used to control brightness. Merely
      wiring it to ground is adequate for most applications
      and doing so simplifies the circuit.

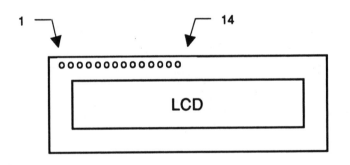

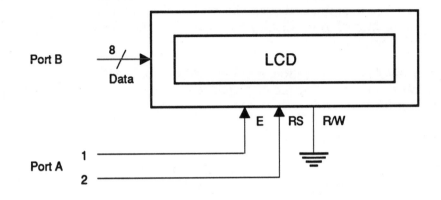

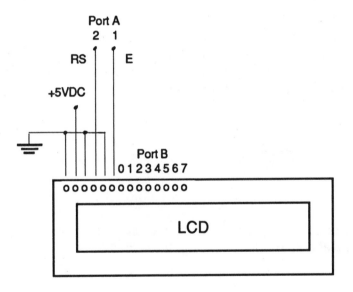

The display module has three control lines. RS makes the selection of instructions vs data and may be thought of as an address line which selects either the control register or the data register. The R/$\overline{W}$ line sets up for read vs. write. For our applications, the display will be written to only, so the R/$\overline{W}$ line is wired to ground. If used, the read mode would be used to read the contents of some RAM locations internal to the display module. E enables the display registers for a write operation when HI (logic 1).

Using the display involves initialization, sending control words and sending data. Two output ports will be involved in controlling the display, one for display data and display instruction words and the other for E and RS.

```
------------------------------------
Port    Bit(s)              Function
------------------------------------
 B      0 - 7               Data
 A       2                  RS
 A       1                  E
```

Data vs Instruction

There are two ports and some timing involved in controlling the display. The display control lines are set up before sending either an instruction word or a data word. The RS line is asserted 0 for sending an instruction or 1 for sending data.

```
                    RS
-----------------------
Instruction          0
Data                 1
```

This must be done in advance of pulsing the enable line HI. Also, the data or instruction byte must be stable at port B prior to pulsing the enable line HI.

Display Control

Instruction words are sent to the display to tell it what mode to operate in.

```
--------------------------------------------------------------------
Operation      Instruction Word        Function
--------------------------------------------------------------------
Function Set     0x38          8-Bit, 5x7
                               Used At Initialization Only

Display On/Off   0x0C          Display On, No Cursor
                 0x0F          Display On, Cursor Blink At Left

Clear Display    0x01          Clear Display = Blanks

Entry Mode Set   0x06          Increment Mode
```

These instruction words are sent to the display as part of the display initialization routine. Details follow.

Character Addresses

Each of the 16 display characters has an address. This tells the display controller where to put the next character data byte.

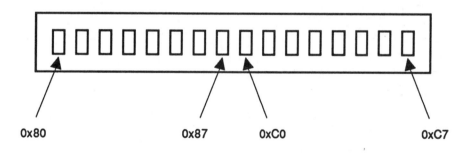

```
0x80                    0x87    0xC0                0xC7
```

Detailed information about the operation of the display follows.

LCD OPERATION

PIC/LCD Circuit

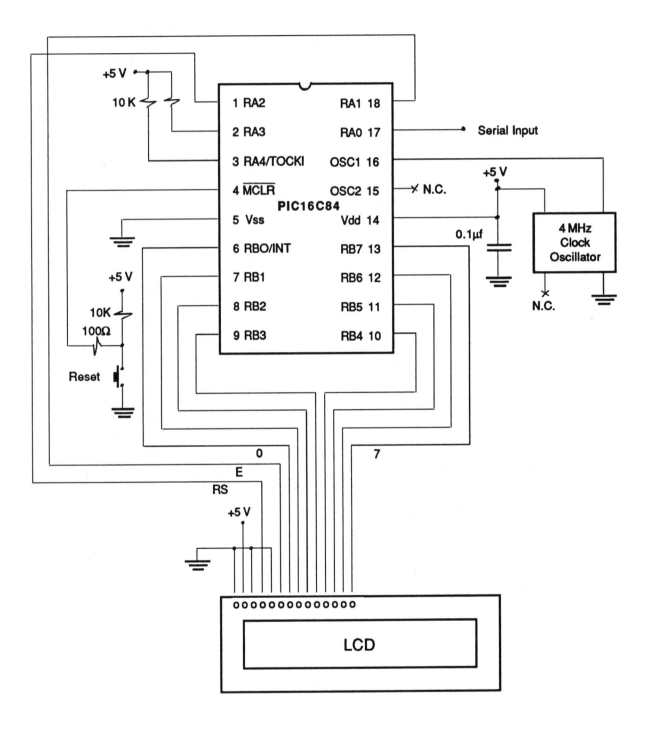

We will need some code to initialize the display to test the demonstration circuit. This will consist of a short main program which delays 5 milliseconds to allow the LCD microcontroller time to get itself organized after power-on reset (essential), an initialization routine for sending the LCD its operating mode instructions, and a second 5 millisecond delay (not needed here but useful later). Two time delay subroutines are included along with a subroutine for pulsing the display module to send each word.

For this example, the LCD module will run in the 8-bit mode meaning 8 parallel lines are used to transmit instructions and data to the display.

```
;=======LCDTST.ASM================================5/5/97==
        list    p=16c84
        radix   hex
;---------------------------------------------------------
;       cpu equates (memory map)
status  equ     0x03
porta   equ     0x05
portb   equ     0x06
count1  equ     0x0c
count2  equ     0c0d
trisa   equ     0x85
trisb   equ     0x86
;---------------------------------------------------------
;       bit equates
rp0     equ     5
;---------------------------------------------------------
        org     0x000
;
start   bsf     status,rp0   ;switch to bank 1
        movlw   b'00000000'  ;outputs
        movwf   trisa
        movwf   trisb
        bcf     status,rp0   ;switch back to bank 0
        movlw   b'00000000'  ;all outputs low
        movwf   porta
        movwf   portb
        call    del_5        ;allow lcd time to initialize itself
        call    initlcd      ;initialize display
circle  goto    circle       ;done
;---------------------------------------------------------
initlcd bcf     porta,1      ;E line low
        bcf     porta,2      ;RS line low, set up for control
        call    del_125      ;delay 125 microseconds
        movlw   0x38         ;8-bit, 5X7
        movwf   portb        ;0011 1000
        call    pulse        ;pulse and delay
        movlw   0x0f         ;display on, cursor blinking
        movwf   portb        ;0000 1111
        call    pulse
        movlw   0x01         ;clear display
        movwf   portb        ;0000 0001
        call    pulse
        call    del_5        ;delay 5 milliseconds after init
```

```
        return
;-------------------------------------------------------------
```

Timing And Pulsing

Four subroutines are used for timing and for pulsing or strobing instruction or data words into the display. The applications for the 5 millisecond time delay subroutine were explained previously.

The process of sending either an instruction or data word involves:

> 1) Setting up the RS line (0 or 1)
> 2) Delay 125 microseconds
> 3) Sending the control or data word to the output port
> 4) Raising the E line HI momentarily to enable the display to
>   receive the byte and then LO again
> 5) Delay 125 microseconds

5 Millisecond Delay

```
del_5   movlw   0x29        ;decimal 40
        movwf   count2      ;to counter
delay   call    del_125     ;delay 125 microseconds
        decfsz  count2,f    ;do it 40 times = 5 milliseconds
        goto    delay
        return              ;counter 0, ends delay
```

125 Microsecond Delay

```
del_125 movlw   0x2a        ;approx 42x3 cycles (decimal)
        movwf   count1      ;load counter
repeat  decfsz  count1,f    ;decrement counter
        goto    repeat      ;not 0
        return              ;counter 0, ends delay
```

Pulse Subroutine

```
pulse   bsf     porta,1     ;pulse E line
        nop                 ;delay
        bcf     porta,1
        call    del_125     ;delay 125 microseconds
        return
```

Testing The Circuit

The complete assembly source code for testing the display demo circuit follows. The display should have a blinking cursor at the left position and all other characters should be blank. This demonstrates that the circuit and LCD module are operating properly.

```
;=======LCDTST.ASM==============================5/5/97==
        list    p=16c84
        radix   hex
;-----------------------------------------------------
;       cpu equates (memory map)
status  equ     0x03
porta   equ     0x05
portb   equ     0x06
count1  equ     0x0c
count2  equ     0c0d
trisa   equ     0x85
trisb   equ     0x86
;-----------------------------------------------------
;       bit equates
rp0     equ     5
;-----------------------------------------------------
        org     0x000
;
start   bsf     status,rp0  ;switch to bank 1
        movlw   b'00000000' ;outputs
        movwf   trisa
        movwf   trisb
        bcf     status,rp0  ;switch back to bank 0
        movlw   b'00000000' ;all outputs low
        movwf   porta
        movwf   portb
        call    del_5       ;allow lcd time to initialize itself
        call    initlcd     ;initialize display
circle  goto    circle      ;done
;-----------------------------------------------------
initlcd bcf     porta,1     ;E line low
        bcf     porta,2     ;RS line low, set up for control
        call    del_125     ;delay 125 microseconds
        movlw   0x38        ;8-bit, 5X7
        movwf   portb       ;0011 1000
        call    pulse       ;pulse and delay
        movlw   0x0f        ;display on, cursor blinking
        movwf   portb       ;0000 1111
        call    pulse
        movlw   0x01        ;clear display
        movwf   portb       ;0000 0001
        call    pulse
        call    del_5       ;delay 5 milliseconds after init
        return
;-----------------------------------------------------
del_125 movlw   0x2a        ;approx 42x3 cycles (decimal)
        movwf   count1      ;load counter
```

```
repeat   decfsz   count1,f     ;decrement counter
         goto     repeat       ;not 0
         return                ;counter 0, ends delay
;--------------------------------------------------------------
del_5    movlw    0x29         ;decimal 40
         movwf    count2       ;to counter
delay    call     del_125      ;delay 125 microseconds
         decfsz   count2,f     ;do it 40 times = 5 milliseconds
         goto     delay
         return                ;counter 0, ends delay
;--------------------------------------------------------------
pulse    bsf      porta,1      ;pulse E line
         nop                   ;delay
         bcf      porta,1
         call     del_125      ;delay 125 microseconds
         return
;--------------------------------------------------------------
         end
;--------------------------------------------------------------
;at blast time, select:
;        memory unprotected
;        watchdog timer disabled (default is enabled)
;        standard crystal (using 4 MHz osc for test) XT
;        power-up timer on
;==============================================================
```

Display RAM

For the experiments in this book which involve sending characters to an LCD, we will use 20 file registers as display RAM. The addresses are 0x20 through 0x2F.

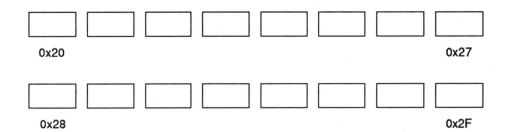

0x20   0x27

0x28   0x2F

The display RAM will be filled with the ASCII characters to be displayed including blanks. A subroutine will be used to send the contents of display RAM to the display one character at a time in sequence beginning with location 0x20. This involves the use of indirect addressing (explained in **Easy** PIC'n). The File Select Register (FSR) will be loaded with the address of the first character to be sent to the display, 0x20. After the first character has been sent, the FSR will be incremented to point to the next display RAM location (0x21) in preparation for sending the second character.

The program instruction says to load the W register with the contents of location 0x00. This location does not exist. What really happens is the contents of the FSR is used as the address. The example code which follows may be examined to see how this works.

Initialization

The operating mode of the display is determined by the initialization instructions which are sent to it prior to use. These instructions control data word length (4 or 8 bits - we will use 8 for now), display on/off, cursor on/off, display clear, character font (5 x 7 or 5 by 10 - we will use 5 x 7). The details are omitted here. The useful instructions are:

```
-----------------------------------------------------------------
Operation      Control Word          Function               Delay
-----------------------------------------------------------------
Function Set   0x38        8-Bit, 5x7                      125 µsec
                           Used At Initialization Only

Display On/Off 0x0C        Display On, No Cursor           125 µsec
               0x0F        Display On, Cursor Blink At Left

Clear Display  0x01        Clear Display = Blanks          5 msec

Entry Mode Set 0x06        Increment Mode                  125 µsec
```

These control words are used in the display initialization routines.

An example initialization routine follows. The first two instructions select the display's control register so that control words may be sent. This is followed by a time delay (125 microseconds) to allow time for the display controller to set up to receive the control words. The next instructions tell the LCD module that data will be send in 8 bit format and that the character format is 5 x 7 dots. The next instructions turn the display on and the cursor off. The final instructions select increment mode with no shift. Details of LCD operation are available in the manufacturer's data book. This is all you need to know for now.

Notice that a time delay subroutine (125 microseconds) is called after each control word is sent. This is essential and allows the LCD controller time to perform each operation before the next one is called for.

A longer delay (5 milliseconds) is required between power-on reset and initializing the display (1st use), after clearing the display (should you choose to use this instruction in one of your own applications), and after initialization is complete.

ASCII

The LCD displays ASCII characters. A large variety of characters may be displayed including upper and lower case letters, punctuation marks, special symbols and more. You can even create your own graphic elements which requires writing to the display's RAM (beyond the scope of this book.)

Most ASCII characters may be defined in MPASM using the MOVLW instruction.

```
        movlw    'A'           ;defines capital "A"
```

EXAMPLE ROUTINES FOR LCD

The techniques just described may be combined in a program which sets up and controls the display and which displays the word "HELLO". The characters (including blanks) will be stored in 16 consecutive file register or RAM locations. An initialization routine will set up the display and fill the display RAM with blanks on reset. The subroutines we will need are:

Display RAM
    Fill with blanks
    Fill with "HELLO"
LCD initialization (reset)
Send 16 characters from display RAM to display
Control
    125 microsecond delay
    5 millisecond delay
    Pulse Subroutine

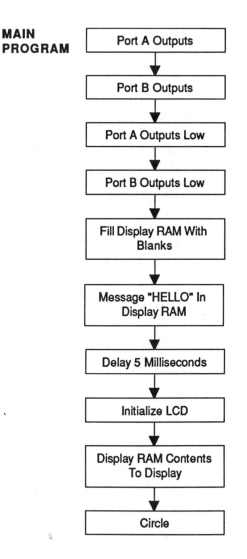

MAIN PROGRAM

Port A Outputs

Port B Outputs

Port A Outputs Low

Port B Outputs Low

Fill Display RAM With Blanks

Message "HELLO" In Display RAM

Delay 5 Milliseconds

Initialize LCD

Display RAM Contents To Display

Circle

```
;=======LCD8.ASM=====================================5/5/97==
        list    p=16c84
        radix   hex
;------------------------------------------------------------
;       cpu equates (memory map)
indf    equ     0x00
status  equ     0x03
fsr     equ     0x04
porta   equ     0x05
portb   equ     0x06
count1  equ     0x0c
count2  equ     0x0d
trisa   equ     0x85
trisb   equ     0x86
;------------------------------------------------------------
;       bit equates
z       equ     2
rp0     equ     5
;------------------------------------------------------------
        org     0x000
;
start   bsf     status,rp0   ;switch to bank 1
        movlw   b'00000000'  ;outputs
        movwf   trisa
        movwf   trisb
        bcf     status,rp0   ;switch back to bank 0
        movlw   b'00000000'  ;all outputs low
        movwf   porta
        movwf   portb
        call    blanks       ;fill display RAM with blanks
        call    hello        ;create message in display RAM
        call    del_5        ;allow lcd time to initialize itself
        call    initlcd      ;initialize display
        call    disp16       ;send 16 characters to display
circle  goto    circle       ;done
;------------------------------------------------------------
```

Fill Display With Blanks

Filling the display with blanks can be done using a clear instruction designed for this purpose. Instead, we will fill the display RAM with blanks and send them to the display. This way, a character or two in the display ram can be changed while the rest remains as is, including blanks. Then all 16 characters are sent at once. The whole display message including blanks does not have to be created each time.

The fill the display RAM with ASCII blanks routine works as follows:

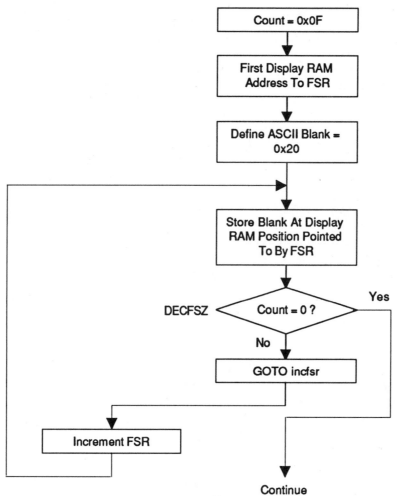

```
blanks   movlw   0x10          ;count=16
         movwf   count1
         movlw   0x20          ;first display RAM address
         movwf   fsr           ;indirect addressing
         movlw   0x20          ;ascii blank
store    movwf   indf          ;store in display RAM location
;                                  pointed to by file select register
         decfsz  count1,f      ;16?
         goto    incfsr        ;no
         return                ;yes, done
incfsr   incf    fsr,f         ;increment file select register
         goto    store
```

Notice the use of indirect addressing. The file select register (FSR) is loaded with 0x20, the address of the first display RAM location. Then the contents of the FSR is incremented 16 times to step through the 16 display RAM locations.

Display "HELLO"

Displaying the word "HELLO" may be used to indicate that the microcontroller has been reset and has control of the display. The five required ASCII characters are stored in the five most significant character positions in RAM.

```
hello    movlw    'H'
         movwf    0x20
         movlw    'E'
         movwf    0x21
         movlw    'L'
         movwf    0x22
         movwf    0x23
         movlw    'O'
         movwf    0x24
         return
```

LCD Initialization

The initialization subroutine sets up the display for use followed by a long time delay. No cursor is used.

```
initlcd bcf     porta,1       ;E line low
        bcf     porta,2       ;RS line low, set up for control
        call    del_125       ;delay 125 microseconds
        movlw   0x38          ;8-bit, 5X7
        movwf   portb         ;0011 1000
        call    pulse         ;pulse and delay
        movlw   0x0c          ;display on, cursor off
        movwf   portb         ;0000 1100
        call    pulse
        movlw   0x06          ;increment mode, no display shift
        movwf   portb         ;0000 0110
        call    pulse
        call    del_5         ;delay 5 milliseconds - required
                                  before sending data
;
        return
```

Character Addresses

Each of the 16 display characters has an address. This tells the display controller where to put the next character data byte.

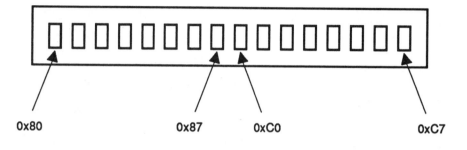

The display controller thinks of these addresses more as instruction words. Sending 0x80 tells the controller that display data is about to be sent which is to be placed starting at the most significant display location (extreme left). Following digits will be placed in sequence moving to the right.

Note that the 16 display characters are grouped in two blocks of 8 addresses which are <u>not</u> adjacent in memory (0x80 to 87 and 0xC0 to C7). To send all sixteen characters, 0x80 is sent as a control word or address prior to sending the first eight characters. 0xC0 is sent prior to sending the second group of eight characters.

Display 16 Characters

For displaying addresses and data, we will store the information in display RAM and then send all 16 characters to the display.

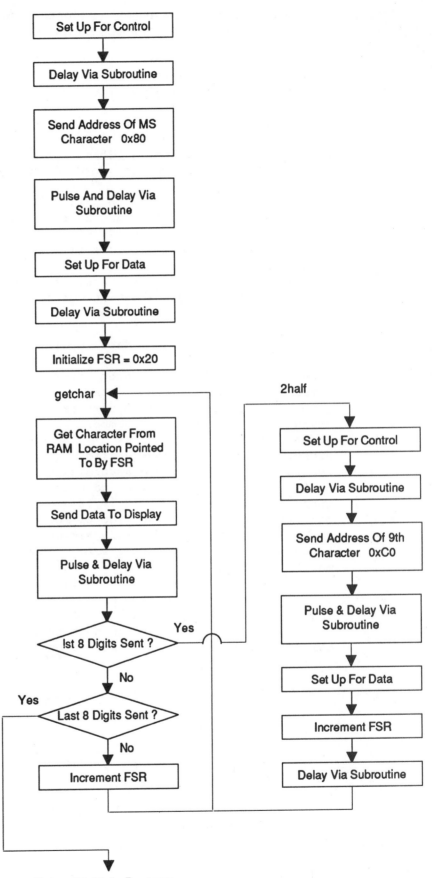

Return To Main Program

Notice that the first character address must be sent for each block of 8 characters. Moving the next character address in sequence is automatic except for the jump between the two blocks of 8 characters.

The subroutine uses 0x20 to 0x2F as display RAM.

```
disp16   bcf      porta,1     ;E line low
         bcf      porta,2     ;RS line low, set up for control
         call     del_125     ;delay 125 microseconds
         movlw    0x80        ;control word = address first half
         movwf    portb
         call     pulse       ;pulse and delay
         bsf      porta,2     ;RS=1, set up for data
         call     del_125     ;delay 125 microseconds
         movlw    0x20        ;initialize file select register
         movwf    fsr
getchar  movf     0x00,w      ;get character from display RAM
;                                 location pointed to by file select
;                                 register
         movwf    portb
         call     pulse       ;send data to display
         movlw    0x27        ;8th character sent?
         subwf    fsr,w       ;subtract w from fsr
         btfsc    status,z    ;test z flag
         goto     half        ;set up for last 8 characters
         movlw    2f          ;test number
         subwf    fsr,w
         btfsc    status,z    ;test z flag
         return               ;16 characters sent to lcd
         incf     fsr,f       ;move to next character location
         goto     getchar
half     bcf      porta,2     ;RS=0, set up for control
         call     del_125     ;delay 125 microseconds
         movlw    0xc0        ;control word = address second half
         movwf    portb
         call     pulse       ;pulse and delay
         bsf      porta,2     ;RS=1, set up for data
         incf     fsr,f       ;increment file select register to
;                                 select next character
         call     del_125     ;delay 125 microseconds
         goto     getchar
```

Finally, the del_5, del_125 and pulse subroutines as used in the LCD test program are needed.

The complete program listing follows:

```
;=======LCD8.ASM==================================5/5/97==
        list    p=16c84
        radix   hex
;------------------------------------------------------------
;       cpu equates (memory map)
indf    equ     0x00
status  equ     0x03
fsr     equ     0x04
porta   equ     0x05
portb   equ     0x06
count1  equ     0x0c
count2  equ     0x0d
trisa   equ     0x85
trisb   equ     0x86
;------------------------------------------------------------
;       bit equates
z       equ     2
rp0     equ     5
;------------------------------------------------------------
        org     0x000
;
start   bsf     status,rp0  ;switch to bank 1
        movlw   b'00000000' ;outputs
        movwf   trisa
        movwf   trisb
        bcf     status,rp0  ;switch back to bank 0
        movlw   b'00000000' ;all outputs low
        movwf   porta
        movwf   portb
        call    blanks      ;fill display RAM with blanks
        call    hello       ;create message in display RAM
        call    del_5       ;allow lcd time to initialize itself
        call    initlcd     ;initialize display
        call    disp16      ;send 16 characters to display
circle  goto    circle      ;done
;------------------------------------------------------------
blanks  movlw   0x10        ;count=16
        movwf   count1
        movlw   0x20        ;first display RAM address
        movwf   fsr         ;indirect addressing
        movlw   0x20        ;ascii blank
store   movwf   indf        ;store in display RAM location
;                               pointed to by file select register
        decfsz  count1,f    ;16?
        goto    incfsr      ;no
        return              ;yes, done
incfsr  incf    fsr,f       ;increment file select register
        goto    store
;------------------------------------------------------------
hello   movlw   'H'
        movwf   0x20
        movlw   'E'
        movwf   0x21
        movlw   'L'
```

```
        movwf    0x22
        movwf    0x23
        movlw    'O'
        movwf    0x24
        return
;--------------------------------------------------------------
initlcd bcf      porta,1      ;E line low
        bcf      porta,2      ;RS line low, set up for control
        call     del_125      ;delay 125 microseconds
        movlw    0x38         ;8-bit, 5X7
        movwf    portb        ;0011 1000
        call     pulse        ;pulse and delay
        movlw    0x0c         ;display on, cursor off
        movwf    portb        ;0000 1100
        call     pulse
        movlw    0x06         ;increment mode, no display shift
        movwf    portb        ;0000 0110
        call     pulse
        call     del_5        ;delay 5 milliseconds - required
;                                  before sending data
        return
;--------------------------------------------------------------
disp16  bcf      porta,1      ;E line low
        bcf      porta,2      ;RS line low, set up for control
        call     del_125      ;delay 125 microseconds
        movlw    0x80         ;control word = address first half
        movwf    portb
        call     pulse        ;pulse and delay
        bsf      porta,2      ;RS=1, set up for data
        call     del_125      ;delay 125 microseconds
        movlw    0x20         ;initialize file select register
        movwf    fsr
getchar movf     0x00,w       ;get character from display RAM
;                                  location pointed to by file select
;                                  register
        movwf    portb
        call     pulse        ;send data to display
        movlw    0x27         ;8th character sent?
        subwf    fsr,w        ;subtract w from fsr
        btfsc    status,z     ;test z flag
        goto     half         ;set up for last 8 characters
        movlw    2f           ;test number
        subwf    fsr,w
        btfsc    status,z     ;test z flag
        return                ;16 characters sent to lcd
        incf     fsr,f        ;move to next character location
        goto     getchar
half    bcf      porta,2      ;RS=0, set up for control
        call     del_125      ;delay 125 microseconds
        movlw    0xc0         ;control word = address second half
        movwf    portb
        call     pulse        ;pulse and delay
        bsf      porta,2      ;RS=1, set up for data
        incf     fsr,f        ;increment file select register to
```

```
;                              select next character
          call     del_125     ;delay 125 microseconds
          goto     getchar
;-------------------------------------------------------------------
del_125 movlw     0x2a         ;approx 42x3 cycles (decimal)
          movwf    count1      ;load counter
repeat   decfsz    count1,f    ;decrement counter
          goto     repeat      ;not 0
          return               ;counter 0, ends delay
;-------------------------------------------------------------------
del_5    movlw     0x29        ;decimal 40
          movwf    count2      ;to counter
delay    call     del_125      ;delay 125 microseconds
          decfsz   count2,f    ;do it 40 times = 5 milliseconds
          goto     delay
          return               ;counter 0, ends delay
;-------------------------------------------------------------------
pulse    bsf      porta,1      ;pulse E line
          nop                  ;delay
          bcf      porta,1
          call     del_125     ;delay 125 microseconds
          return
;-------------------------------------------------------------------
          end
;-------------------------------------------------------------------
;at blast time, select:
;        memory unprotected
;        watchdog timer disabled (default is enabled)
;        standard crystal (using 4 MHz osc for test) XT
;        power-up timer on
;===================================================================
```

DISPLAY HEX BYTE SUBROUTINE

The display hex byte subroutine takes the byte passed to it via the W register and prepares it for display by the LCD along with the corresponding bit pattern. Some blank locations remain at the right end of the LCD for a future application. The subroutine ends with the display RAM loaded and ready for the contents to be sent to the LCD.

Main

The main program defines the hex byte to be converted for display and calls the display hex byte subroutine which does the real work.

```
;======DISPLHEX.ASM==============================5/9/97==
          list     p=16c84
          radix    hex
;-------------------------------------------------------------------
;        cpu equates (memory map)
indf     equ      0x00
pc       equ      0x02
```

```
status    equ     0x03
fsr       equ     0x04
hexbyte   equ     0x0c
ms_dig    equ     0x0d
ls_dig    equ     0x0e
hold      equ     0x0f
sa        equ     0x10
sb        equ     0x11
sc        equ     0x12
sd        equ     0x13
count1    equ     0x14
;-----------------------------------------------------------
;         bit equates
c         equ     0
;-----------------------------------------------------------
;note: this works in MPSIM, not in chip
          org     0x000
;
start     movlw   0x01        ;load w with 0x__, test byte
          call    disphex     ;call display hex byte sub
;                             returns with display RAM filled
circle    goto    circle      ;done
;-----------------------------------------------------------
```

Display Hex Byte

The user's program ends by loading the W register with the byte to be displayed and calling the subroutine described below.

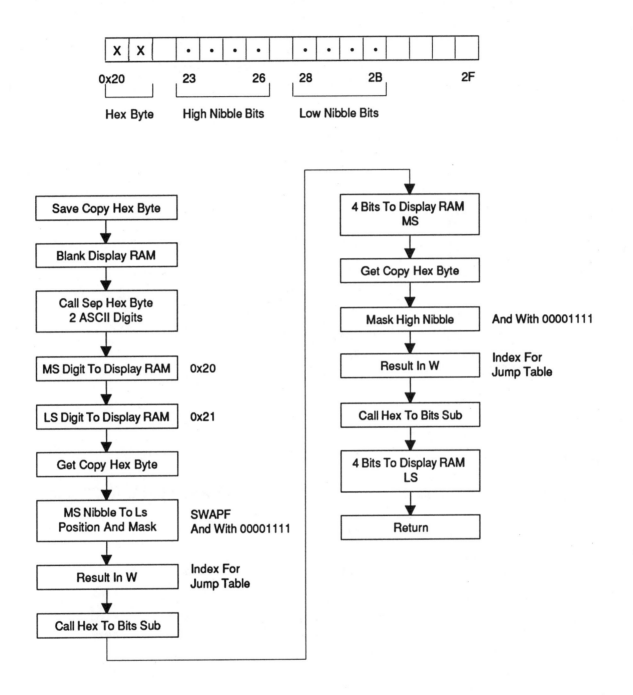

```
disphex  movwf   hexbyte       ;store copy of hex byte
         call    blanks        ;fill display RAM with blanks
         call    sephex        ;separate hex byte into 2 ASCII digits
         movf    ms_dig,w      ;get MS digit
         movwf   0x20          ;to display RAM
         movf    ls_dig,w      ;get LS digit
         movwf   0x21          ;to display RAM
         swapf   hexbyte,w     ;get copy of hex byte, swap MS/LS
         andlw   0x0f          ;mask HI nibble
         call    hexbits       ;call hex to bits
         movf    sa,w          ;get first bit
         movwf   0x23          ;to display RAM
         movf    sb,w          ;get second bit
         movwf   0x24          ;to display RAM
         movf    sc,w          ;etc.
         movwf   0x25
         movf    sd,w
         movwf   0x26
         movf    hexbyte,w     ;get copy of hex byte
         andlw   0x0f          ;mask HI nibble
         call    hexbits       ;call hex to bits
         movf    sa,w          ;get first bit
         movwf   0x28          ;to display RAM
         movf    sb,w          ;get second bit
         movwf   0x29          ;to display RAM
         movf    sc,w          ;etc.
         movwf   0x2a
         movf    sd,w
         movwf   0x2b
         return
```

Blanks

The blanks subroutine fills the 16 display RAM locations with ASCII blanks (0x20) using
indirect addressing.

```
blanks   movlw   0x10          ;count=16
         movwf   count1
         movlw   0x20          ;first display RAM address
         movwf   fsr           ;indexed addressing
         movlw   0x20          ;ascii blank
store    movwf   indf          ;store in display RAM location
;                                   pointed to by file select register
         decfsz  count1,f      ;16?
         goto    incfsr        ;no
         return                ;yes, done
incfsr   incf    fsr,f         ;increment file select register
         goto    store
```

Separate A Hex Byte Into Two ASCII Digits

In programs involving displaying hexadecimal data it will be necessary to separate a hex byte (2 hex digits) into two ASCII digits.

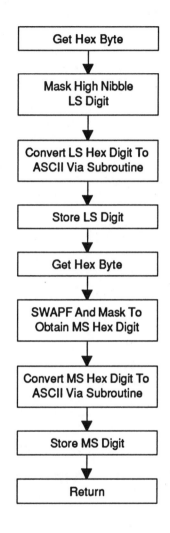

```
sephex   movf    hexbyte,w      ;get copy of hex byte
         andlw   0x0f           ;mask hi nibble
         call    hex2asc        ;hex to ASCII conversion
         movwf   ls_dig         ;store
         swapf   hexbyte,w      ;get copy of hex byte, swap MS/LS
         andlw   0x0f           ;mask hi nibble
         call    hex2asc        ;hex to ASCII conversion
         movwf   ms_dig         ;store
         return
```

The routine expects to find the byte to be separated in location hexbyte and stores the most significant digit at ms_dig and the least significant digit at ls_dig.

Hex Digit To ASCII Digit Conversion

Notice that hex characters are represented by four bits (nibble) and ASCII characters require eight bits (byte). To display a hex character, it must first be converted to ASCII using a conversion routine. The conversion process involves determining whether the hex digit is in the range 0x0 to 0x9 or 0xA to 0xF. Conversion is simply a matter of adding 0x37 to the digit if it falls in the lower range or adding 0x30 if it falls in the upper range.

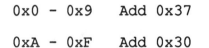

```
0x0 - 0x9    Add 0x37

0xA - 0xF    Add 0x30
```

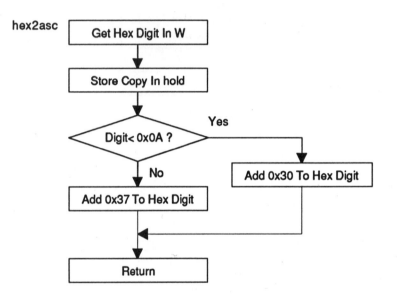

The routine tests for the contents of W ≥ 0x0A by subtracting the hex digit to be tested from one less than 0x0A (0x09) followed by testing the carry flag. The details of how comparisons are done are described in **Easy PIC'n**.

```
hex2asc  movwf    hold        ;store copy of hex digit
         sublw    0x09        ;subtract w from 1 less than 0x0a
         btfss    status,c    ;carry flag set if w < 0x0a
         goto     add37
         goto     add30
add37    movf     hold,w      ;get hex digit
         addlw    0x37
         return               ;return with ascii in w
add30    movf     hold,w      ;get hex digit
         addlw    0x30
         return               ;return with ascii in w
```

Hex To Bits Subroutine

Displaying the bit pattern corresponding to the hex byte is tricky. The work is done one nibble at the time. Four RAM locations are used as a scratch pad.

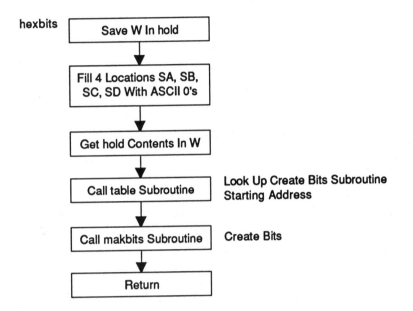

First, the scratch pad is filled with 0's. Then a jump table is used to direct activity to one-of-sixteen subroutines, one for each possible hex digit. The hex digit itself is used as the index for the jump table. If the hex digit is 0x0, the contents of the four scratch pad locations (0000) are then sent directly to display RAM. If two or three 0's are required, one or two 0's are changed to 1's. If the digit is 0xF, the scratch pad is filled with 1's. If three 1's are required, the scratch pad is changed to all 1's followed by changing one 1 to a 0. Then the contents of the scratch pad is sent to display RAM.

The short subroutines for filling the RAM scratch pad with 1's and 0's vary in length. Relative addressing works only in consecutive one address increments. The easiest method for getting around this is to:

- Store the subroutines (variable length) one after the other in the same 256 address segment of memory.

- Use a jump table to access the routines.

First, all the subroutines are written and laid out in hex digit order in sequential memory locations. Second, the distance of each subroutine from the beginning of the group of subroutines is then put in a table one address apart.

```
table    addwf    pc,f         ;add offset to program counter
         retlw    0x00         ;0
         retlw    0x01         ;1
         retlw    0x04         ;2
         retlw    0x07         ;3
         retlw    0x0b         ;4
         retlw    0x0e         ;5
         retlw    0x12         ;6
         retlw    0x16         ;7
         retlw    0x1a         ;8
         retlw    0x1d         ;9
         retlw    0x21         ;a
         retlw    0x25         ;b
         retlw    0x29         ;c
         retlw    0x2d         ;d
         retlw    0x31         ;e
         retlw    0x35         ;f
```

The subroutine starting addresses are now in a table which may be accessed by adding the value of the hex digit to be converted to the program counter to go to the proper location in the table. The return from subroutine takes place with the starting address of the bits routine in the W register.

```
hexbits  movwf    hold         ;save copy of hex digit
         movlw    0x30         ;fill with ascii 0's
         movwf    sa
         movwf    sb
         movwf    sc
         movwf    sd
         movf     hold,w       ;get hex digit, use as offset
         call     table        ;get 2nd offset for subroutine table
         call     makbits      ;to appropriate create bits sub
         return
```

Create Bits Subroutines

```
makbits  addwf    pc,f         ;add offset to program counter
         return                ;0x0    0000    leave as is
         movlw    0x31         ;0x1    0001
         movwf    sd
         return
         movlw    0x31         ;0x2    0010
         movwf    sc
         return
         movlw    0x31         ;0x3    0011
         movwf    sc
         movwf    sd
         return
         movlw    0x31         ;0x4    0100
         movwf    sb
         return
         movlw    0x31         ;0x5    0101
```

```
        movwf    sb
        movwf    sd
        return
        movlw    0x31        ;0x6    0110
        movwf    sb
        movwf    sc
        return
        call     fill1s      ;0x7    0111    fill with 1,s
        movlw    0x30
        movwf    sa
        return
        movlw    0x31        ;0x8    1000
        movwf    sa
        return
        movlw    0x31        ;0x9    1001
        movwf    sa
        movwf    sd
        return
        movlw    0x31        ;0xa    1010
        movwf    sa
        movwf    sc
        return
        call     fill1s      ;0xb    1011    fill with 1,s
        movlw    0x30
        movwf    sb
        return
        movlw    0x31        ;0xc    1100
        movwf    sa
        movwf    sb
        return
        call     fill1s      ;0xd    1101    fill with 1,s
        movlw    0x30
        movwf    sc
        return
        call     fill1s      ;0xe    1110    fill with 1,s
        movlw    0x30
        movwf    sd
        return
        goto     fill1s      ;0xf    1111    fill with 1,s
        return
```

Fill With 1's Subroutine

```
fill1s  movlw    0x31
        movwf    sa
        movwf    sb
        movwf    sc
        movwf    sd
        return
```

Program Listing

The complete program listing follows. Notice that "table" and "makbits" (also a table) are at the beginning of the listing so that the assembler will put them in the first 256 locations of program memory. This can be verified by looking at the file DISPLHEX.LST after the assembler does it's thing.

```
;======DISPLHEX.ASM===============================5/9/97==
        list    p=16c84
        radix   hex
;------------------------------------------------------------
;       cpu equates (memory map)
indf    equ     0x00
pc      equ     0x02
status  equ     0x03
fsr     equ     0x04
hexbyte equ     0x0c
ms_dig  equ     0x0d
ls_dig  equ     0x0e
hold    equ     0x0f
sa      equ     0x10
sb      equ     0x11
sc      equ     0x12
sd      equ     0x13
count1  equ     0x14
;------------------------------------------------------------
;       bit equates
c       equ     0
;------------------------------------------------------------
;note: this works in MPSIM, not in chip
        org     0x000
;
start   movlw   0x01            ;load w with 0x__, test byte
        call    disphex         ;call display hex byte sub
;                               returns with display RAM filled
circle  goto    circle          ;done
;------------------------------------------------------------
table   addwf   pc,f            ;add offset to program counter
        retlw   0x00            ;0
        retlw   0x01            ;1
        retlw   0x04            ;2
        retlw   0x07            ;3
        retlw   0x0b            ;4
        retlw   0x0e            ;5
        retlw   0x12            ;6
        retlw   0x16            ;7
        retlw   0x1a            ;8
        retlw   0x1d            ;9
        retlw   0x21            ;a
        retlw   0x25            ;b
        retlw   0x29            ;c
        retlw   0x2d            ;d
```

```
        retlw   0x31            ;e
        retlw   0x35            ;f
;-----------------------------------------------------------
makbits addwf   pc,f            ;add offset to program counter
        return                  ;0x0    0000    leave as is
        movlw   0x31            ;0x1    0001
        movwf   sd
        return
        movlw   0x31            ;0x2    0010
        movwf   sc
        return
        movlw   0x31            ;0x3    0011
        movwf   sc
        movwf   sd
        return
        movlw   0x31            ;0x4    0100
        movwf   sb
        return
        movlw   0x31            ;0x5    0101
        movwf   sb
        movwf   sd
        return
        movlw   0x31            ;0x6    0110
        movwf   sb
        movwf   sc
        return
        call    fill1s          ;0x7    0111    fill with 1,s
        movlw   0x30
        movwf   sa
        return
        movlw   0x31            ;0x8    1000
        movwf   sa
        return
        movlw   0x31            ;0x9    1001
        movwf   sa
        movwf   sd
        return
        movlw   0x31            ;0xa    1010
        movwf   sa
        movwf   sc
        return
        call    fill1s          ;0xb    1011    fill with 1,s
        movlw   0x30
        movwf   sb
        return
        movlw   0x31            ;0xc    1100
        movwf   sa
        movwf   sb
        return
        call    fill1s          ;0xd    1101    fill with 1,s
        movlw   0x30
        movwf   sc
        return
        call    fill1s          ;0xe    1110    fill with 1,s
```

```
        movlw   0x30
        movwf   sd
        return
        goto    fill1s      ;0xf     1111    fill with 1,s
        return
;-------------------------------------------------------------
fill1s  movlw   0x31
        movwf   sa
        movwf   sb
        movwf   sc
        movwf   sd
        return
;-------------------------------------------------------------
disphex movwf   hexbyte     ;store copy of hex byte
        call    blanks      ;fill display RAM with blanks
        call    sephex      ;separate hex byte into 2 ASCII digits
        movf    ms_dig,w    ;get MS digit
        movwf   0x20        ;to display RAM
        movf    ls_dig,w    ;get LS digit
        movwf   0x21        ;to display RAM
        swapf   hexbyte,w   ;get copy of hex byte, swap MS/LS
        andlw   0x0f        ;mask HI nibble
        call    hexbits     ;call hex to bits
        movf    sa,w        ;get first bit
        movwf   0x23        ;to display RAM
        movf    sb,w        ;get second bit
        movwf   0x24        ;to display RAM
        movf    sc,w        ;etc.
        movwf   0x25
        movf    sd,w
        movwf   0x26
        movf    hexbyte,w   ;get copy of hex byte
        andlw   0x0f        ;mask HI nibble
        call    hexbits     ;call hex to bits
        movf    sa,w        ;get first bit
        movwf   0x28        ;to display RAM
        movf    sb,w        ;get second bit
        movwf   0x29        ;to display RAM
        movf    sc,w        ;etc.
        movwf   0x2a
        movf    sd,w
        movwf   0x2b
        return
;-------------------------------------------------------------
sephex  movf    hexbyte,w   ;get copy of hex byte
        andlw   0x0f        ;mask hi nibble
        call    hex2asc     ;hex to ASCII conversion
        movwf   ls_dig      ;store
        swapf   hexbyte,w   ;get copy of hex byte, swap MS/LS
        andlw   0x0f        ;mask hi nibble
        call    hex2asc     ;hex to ASCII conversion
        movwf   ms_dig      ;store
        return
;-------------------------------------------------------------
```

82

```
hex2asc  movwf   hold         ;store copy of hex digit
         sublw   0x09         ;subtract w from 1 less than 0x0a
         btfss   status,c     ;carry flag set if w < 0x0a
         goto    add37
         goto    add30
add37    movf    hold,w       ;get hex digit
         addlw   0x37
         return               ;return with ascii in w
add30    movf    hold,w       ;get hex digit
         addlw   0x30
         return               ;return with ascii in w
;----------------------------------------------------------------
hexbits  movwf   hold         ;save copy of hex digit
         movlw   0x30         ;fill with ascii 0's
         movwf   sa
         movwf   sb
         movwf   sc
         movwf   sd
         movf    hold,w       ;get hex digit, use as offset
         call    table        ;get 2nd offset for subroutine table
         call    makbits      ;to appropriate create bits sub
         return
;----------------------------------------------------------------
blanks   movlw   0x10         ;count=16
         movwf   count1
         movlw   0x20         ;first display RAM address
         movwf   fsr          ;indexed addressing
         movlw   0x20         ;ascii blank
store    movwf   indf         ;store in display RAM location
;                                 pointed to by file select register
         decfsz  count1,f     ;16?
         goto    incfsr       ;no
         return               ;yes, done
incfsr   incf    fsr,f        ;increment file select register
         goto    store
;----------------------------------------------------------------
         end
;----------------------------------------------------------------
;at blast time, select:
;       memory unprotected
;       watchdog timer disabled (default is enabled)
;       standard crystal (using 4 MHz osc for test)
;       power-up timer on
;================================================================
```

To Use/Test Display Hex Byte:

To put the display hex byte subroutine to work, we need the program which follows. It (TESTHEX.ASM) includes a new short main program (similar to LCD8.ASM) and DISPLHEX.ASM. The subroutines "table" and "makbits" are located at the beginning of the program so as to be in the first 256 bytes of program memory.

```
;======TESTHEX.ASM================================5/14/97==
        list    p=16c84
        radix   hex
;------------------------------------------------------------
;       cpu equates (memory map)
indf     equ    0x00
pc       equ    0x02
status   equ    0x03
fsr      equ    0x04
porta    equ    0x05
portb    equ    0x06
hexbyte  equ    0x0c
ms_dig   equ    0x0d
ls_dig   equ    0x0e
hold     equ    0x0f
sa       equ    0x10
sb       equ    0x11
sc       equ    0x12
sd       equ    0x13
count1   equ    0x14
count2   equ    0x15
trisa    equ    0x85
trisb    equ    0x86
;------------------------------------------------------------
;       bit equates
c        equ    0
z        equ    2
rp0      equ    5
;------------------------------------------------------------
        org     0x000
;
start   goto    main            ;leap over tables
;------------------------------------------------------------
table   addwf   pc,f            ;add offset to program counter
        retlw   0x00            ;0
        retlw   0x01            ;1
        retlw   0x04            ;2
        retlw   0x07            ;3
        retlw   0x0b            ;4
        retlw   0x0e            ;5
        retlw   0x12            ;6
        retlw   0x16            ;7
        retlw   0x1a            ;8
        retlw   0x1d            ;9
        retlw   0x21            ;a
        retlw   0x25            ;b
        retlw   0x29            ;c
        retlw   0x2d            ;d
        retlw   0x31            ;e
        retlw   0x35            ;f
;------------------------------------------------------------
makbits addwf   pc,f            ;add offset to program counter
        return                  ;0x0    0000    leave as is
```

```
movlw    0x31        ;0x1    0001
movwf    sd
return
movlw    0x31        ;0x2    0010
movwf    sc
return
movlw    0x31        ;0x3    0011
movwf    sc
movwf    sd
return
movlw    0x31        ;0x4    0100
movwf    sb
return
movlw    0x31        ;0x5    0101
movwf    sb
movwf    sd
return
movlw    0x31        ;0x6    0110
movwf    sb
movwf    sc
return
call     fill1s      ;0x7    0111    fill with 1,s
movlw    0x30
movwf    sa
return
movlw    0x31        ;0x8    1000
movwf    sa
return
movlw    0x31        ;0x9    1001
movwf    sa
movwf    sd
return
movlw    0x31        ;0xa    1010
movwf    sa
movwf    sc
return
call     fill1s      ;0xb    1011    fill with 1,s
movlw    0x30
movwf    sb
return
movlw    0x31        ;0xc    1100
movwf    sa
movwf    sb
return
call     fill1s      ;0xd    1101    fill with 1,s
movlw    0x30
movwf    sc
return
call     fill1s      ;0xe    1110    fill with 1,s
movlw    0x30
movwf    sd
return
goto     fill1s      ;0xf    1111    fill with 1,s
return
```

```
;-----------------------------------------------------------
main     bsf      status,rp0   ;switch to bank 1
         movlw    b'00000000'  ;outputs
         movwf    trisa
         movwf    trisb
         bcf      status,rp0   ;switch back to bank 0
         movlw    b'00000000'  ;all outputs low
         movwf    porta
         movwf    portb
         call     del_5        ;allow lcd time to initialize itself
         call     initlcd      ;initialize display
         movlw    0x01         ;load w with 0x__, test byte
         call     disphex      ;call display hex byte sub
;                                 returns with display RAM filled
         call     disp16       ;send 16 characters to display
circle   goto     circle       ;done
;-----------------------------------------------------------
fill1s   movlw    0x31
         movwf    sa
         movwf    sb
         movwf    sc
         movwf    sd
         return
;-----------------------------------------------------------
disphex  movwf    hexbyte      ;store copy of hex byte
         call     blanks       ;fill display RAM with blanks
         call     sephex       ;separate hex byte into 2 ASCII digits
         movf     ms_dig,w     ;get MS digit
         movwf    0x20         ;to display RAM
         movf     ls_dig,w     ;get LS digit
         movwf    0x21         ;to display RAM
         swapf    hexbyte,w    ;get copy of hex byte, swap MS/LS
         andlw    0x0f         ;mask HI nibble
         call     hexbits      ;call hex to bits
         movf     sa,w         ;get first bit
         movwf    0x23         ;to display RAM
         movf     sb,w         ;get second bit
         movwf    0x24         ;to display RAM
         movf     sc,w         ;etc.
         movwf    0x25
         movf     sd,w
         movwf    0x26
         movf     hexbyte,w    ;get copy of hex byte
         andlw    0x0f         ;mask HI nibble
         call     hexbits      ;call hex to bits
         movf     sa,w         ;get first bit
         movwf    0x28         ;to display RAM
         movf     sb,w         ;get second bit
         movwf    0x29         ;to display RAM
         movf     sc,w         ;etc.
         movwf    0x2a
         movf     sd,w
         movwf    0x2b
         return
```

86

```
;----------------------------------------------------------------
sephex  movf    hexbyte,w       ;get copy of hex byte
        andlw   0x0f            ;mask hi nibble
        call    hex2asc         ;hex to ASCII conversion
        movwf   ls_dig          ;store
        swapf   hexbyte,w       ;get copy of hex byte, swap MS/LS
        andlw   0x0f            ;mask hi nibble
        call    hex2asc         ;hex to ASCII conversion
        movwf   ms_dig          ;store
        return
;----------------------------------------------------------------
hex2asc movwf   hold            ;store copy of hex digit
        sublw   0x09            ;subtract w from 1 less than 0x0a
        btfss   status,c        ;carry flag set if w < 0x0a
        goto    add37
        goto    add30
add37   movf    hold,w          ;get hex digit
        addlw   0x37
        return                  ;return with ascii in w
add30   movf    hold,w          ;get hex digit
        addlw   0x30
        return                  ;return with ascii in w
;----------------------------------------------------------------
hexbits movwf   hold            ;save copy of hex digit
        movlw   0x30            ;fill with ascii 0's
        movwf   sa
        movwf   sb
        movwf   sc
        movwf   sd
        movf    hold,w          ;get hex digit, use as offset
        call    table           ;get 2nd offset for subroutine table
        call    makbits         ;to appropriate create bits sub
        return
;----------------------------------------------------------------
blanks  movlw   0x10            ;count=16
        movwf   count1
        movlw   0x20            ;first display RAM address
        movwf   fsr             ;indexed addressing
        movlw   0x20            ;ascii blank
store   movwf   indf            ;store in display RAM location
;                                   pointed to by file select register
        decfsz  count1,f        ;16?
        goto    incfsr          ;no
        return                  ;yes, done
incfsr  incf    fsr,f           ;increment file select register
        goto    store
;----------------------------------------------------------------
initlcd bcf     porta,1         ;E line low
        bcf     porta,2         ;RS line low, set up for control
        call    del_125         ;delay 125 microseconds
        movlw   0x38            ;8-bit, 5X7
        movwf   portb           ;0011 1000
        call    pulse           ;pulse and delay
        movlw   0x0c            ;display on, cursor off
```

```
        movwf   portb       ;0000 1100
        call    pulse
        movlw   0x06        ;increment mode, no display shift
        movwf   portb       ;0000 0110
        call    pulse
        call    del_5       ;delay 5 milliseconds - required
;                               before sending data
        return
;-------------------------------------------------------------
disp16  bcf     porta,1     ;E line low
        bcf     porta,2     ;RS line low, set up for control
        call    del_125     ;delay 125 microseconds
        movlw   0x80        ;control word = address first half
        movwf   portb
        call    pulse       ;pulse and delay
        bsf     porta,2     ;RS=1, set up for data
        call    del_125     ;delay 125 microseconds
        movlw   0x20        ;initialize file select register
        movwf   fsr
getchar movf    0x00,w      ;get character from display RAM
;                               location pointed to by file select
;                               register
        movwf   portb
        call    pulse       ;send data to display
        movlw   0x27        ;8th character sent?
        subwf   fsr,w       ;subtract w from fsr
        btfsc   status,z    ;test z flag
        goto    half        ;set up for last 8 characters
        movlw   2f          ;test number
        subwf   fsr,w
        btfsc   status,z    ;test z flag
        return              ;16 characters sent to lcd
        incf    fsr,f       ;move to next character location
        goto    getchar
half    bcf     porta,2     ;RS=0, set up for control
        call    del_125     ;delay 125 microseconds
        movlw   0xc0        ;control word = address second half
        movwf   portb
        call    pulse       ;pulse and delay
        bsf     porta,2     ;RS=1, set up for data
        incf    fsr,f       ;increment file select register to
;                               select next character
        call    del_125     ;delay 125 microseconds
        goto    getchar
;-------------------------------------------------------------
del_125 movlw   0x2a        ;approx 42x3 cycles (decimal)
        movwf   count1      ;load counter
repeat  decfsz  count1,f    ;decrement counter
        goto    repeat      ;not 0
        return              ;counter 0, ends delay
;-------------------------------------------------------------
del_5   movlw   0x29        ;decimal 40
        movwf   count2      ;to counter
delay   call    del_125     ;delay 125 microseconds
```

```
        decfsz  count2,f    ;do it 40 times = 5 milliseconds
        goto    delay
        return              ;counter 0, ends delay
;----------------------------------------------------------------
pulse   bsf     porta,1     ;pulse E line
        nop                 ;delay
        bcf     porta,1
        call    del_125     ;delay 125 microseconds
        return
;----------------------------------------------------------------
        end
;----------------------------------------------------------------
;at blast time, select:
;       memory unprotected
;       watchdog timer disabled (default is enabled)
;       standard crystal (using 4 MHz osc for test)
;       power-up timer on
;================================================================
```

4-BIT MODE

We started out operating the LCD in the 8-bit mode, meaning instructions and data are transmitted to the LCD over 8 wires. This is the simplest in terms of understanding their operation and writing code. PIC16 devices don't have lots of pins, so minimizing the number devoted to communicating with the LCD may be essential. These displays will also run in the 4-bit mode using the higher order 4 data lines (D7, 6, 5,4).

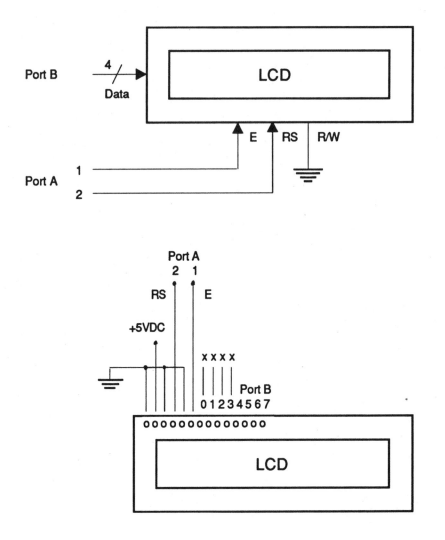

In the 8-bit mode, a byte is presented to the LCD followed by pulsing the E line and then a 125 microsecond delay. In the 4-bit mode, the byte must be cracked into two nibbles by a subroutine. The MS nibble is presented to the LCD first followed by pulsing the E line. Then the LS nibble is presented to the LCD followed by pulsing the E line. A 125 microsecond delay follows pulsing the second nibble.

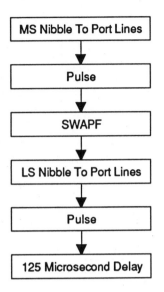

The initialization process is a little confusing. The LCD is first told that the mode will be 8-bit. Then it is told the mode will really be 4-bit. Then it is told to be in the 4-bit mode again followed by the lower nibble of the function set instruction byte.

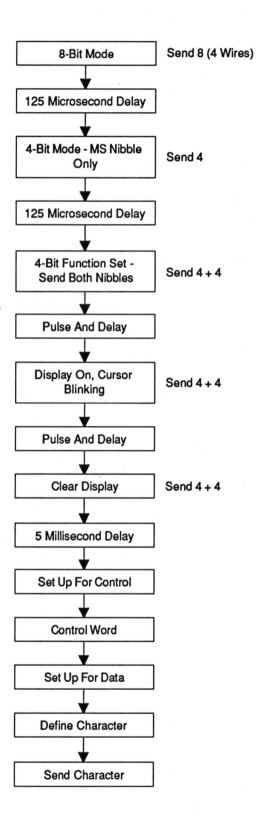

8-Bit Mode	Send 8 (4 Wires)
125 Microsecond Delay	
4-Bit Mode - MS Nibble Only	Send 4
125 Microsecond Delay	
4-Bit Function Set - Send Both Nibbles	Send 4 + 4
Pulse And Delay	
Display On, Cursor Blinking	Send 4 + 4
Pulse And Delay	
Clear Display	Send 4 + 4
5 Millisecond Delay	
Set Up For Control	
Control Word	
Set Up For Data	
Define Character	
Send Character	

The 4-bit demo program initializes the LCD with the cursor blinking at the MS bit position and then sends one ASCII character ("A"). The display will show "A" followed by a blinking cursor.

```
;=======LCDTST4.ASM===============================5/26/97==
        list    p=16c84
        radix   hex
;-----------------------------------------------------------
;       cpu equates (memory map)
status  equ     0x03
porta   equ     0x05
portb   equ     0x06
count1  equ     0x0c
count2  equ     0x0d
bits    equ     0x0e
trisa   equ     0x85
trisb   equ     0x86
;-----------------------------------------------------------
;       bit equates
rp0     equ     5
;-----------------------------------------------------------
        org     0x000
;
start   bsf     status,rp0  ;switch to bank 1
        movlw   b'00000000' ;outputs
        movwf   trisa
        movwf   trisb
        bcf     status,rp0  ;switch back to bank 0
        movlw   b'00000000' ;all outputs low
        movwf   porta
        movwf   portb
        call    del_5       ;allow lcd time to initialize itself
        call    initlcd     ;initialize display
        call    display     ;send 'A' character
circle  goto    circle      ;done
;-----------------------------------------------------------
display bcf     porta,1     ;E line low
        bcf     porta,2     ;RS line low, set up for control
        call    del_125     ;delay 125 microseconds
        movlw   0x80        ;control word = address first half
        call    send
        bsf     porta,2     ;RS=1, set up for data
        call    del_125     ;delay 125 microseconds
        movlw   'A'         ;define character
        call    send
        return
;-----------------------------------------------------------
initlcd bcf     porta,1     ;E line low
        bcf     porta,2     ;RS line low, set up for control
        call    del_125     ;delay 125 microseconds
        movlw   0x38        ;8-bit, 5X7 mode
        movwf   bits        ;0011 1000
        call    flipbit     ;output 4 MS bits (LS not used)
```

```
        call    pulse           ;send bits
        call    del_125         ;delay
        movlw   0x28            ;4-bit, 5x7 mode
        movwf   bits            ;0010 1000
        call    flipbit         ;output 4 MS bits (LS not used)
        call    pulse           ;get into 4-bit mode
        call    del_125
        movlw   0x28            ;4-bit, 5x7 mode
        call    send            ;send both nibbles
        movlw   0x0f            ;display on, cursor blinking
        call    send
        movlw   0x01            ;clear display
        call    send
        call    del_5           ;delay 5 milliseconds
        return
;-------------------------------------------------------------
send    movwf   bits
        call    flipbit
        call    pulse
        swapf   bits,f          ;swap MS and LS nibbles
        call    flipbit         ;output what was LS nibble
        call    pulse
        call    del_125
        return
;-------------------------------------------------------------
flipbit bcf     portb,4         ;default
        btfsc   bits,4          ;test bit in "bits"
        bsf     portb,4         ;bit in "bits" set
        bcf     portb,5
        btfsc   bits,5
        bsf     portb,5
        bcf     portb,6
        btfsc   bits,6
        bsf     portb,6
        bcf     portb,7
        btfsc   bits,7
        bsf     portb,7
        return
;-------------------------------------------------------------
del_125 movlw   0x2a            ;approx 42x3 cycles (decimal)
        movwf   count1          ;load counter
repeat  decfsz  count1,f        ;decrement counter
        goto    repeat          ;not 0
        return                  ;counter 0, ends delay
;-------------------------------------------------------------
del_5   movlw   0x29            ;decimal 40
        movwf   count2          ;to counter
delay   call    del_125         ;delay 125 microseconds
        decfsz  count2,f        ;do it 40 times = 5 milliseconds
        goto    delay
        return                  ;counter 0, ends delay
;-------------------------------------------------------------
pulse   bsf     porta,1         ;pulse E line
```

94

```
        nop                   ;delay
        bcf      porta,1
        return
;------------------------------------------------------------------
        end
;------------------------------------------------------------------
;at blast time, select:
;       memory unprotected
;       watchdog timer disabled (default is enabled)
;       standard crystal (using 4 MHz osc for test) XT
;       power-up timer on
;==================================================================
```

LCD MODULE SERIAL INTERFACE

It would be very useful or convenient to use the LCD module as a piece of test equipment or as part of a more complex system if it could be connected to another PIC16 via a 1-wire serial interface. We can do that! We can do it by combining techniques and boards we already have. The '84 on a board will be the "master" and the LCD/PIC16 unit will be the slave.

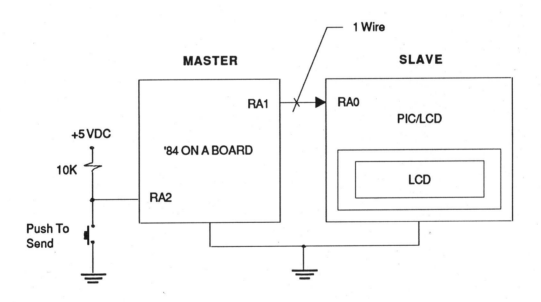

My list of functions the slave should perform under direction of the master is:

- Display "HELLO" at power-on
- Display "TEST" on command
- Blank display
- Place a single ASCII character in any one of 16 display RAM locations
- Send the contents of display RAM to the display
- Display a hex byte as 2 hex digits and as 8 bits

There are lots of ways to do this. My solution follows. You may want to modify mine for your own use or to do it a different way altogether.

Any time something is sent to the display, the instruction must be included to tell the slave what to do. Sometimes there will be an ASCII character or hex byte to be sent. Sometimes an address (RAM location) must be specified. I decided the easiest way to do this is always send 3 bytes at a time even if only 1 or 2 are needed. This makes the software simpler at the flow chart level.

Packets - 3 bytes (2nd and 3rd may be garbage).

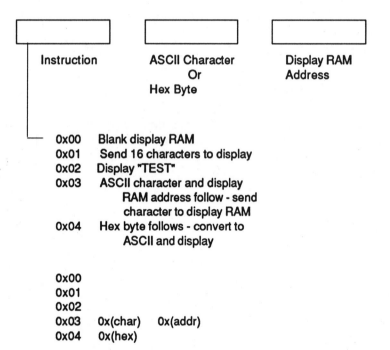

Instruction   ASCII Character   Display RAM
                          Or   Address
                       Hex Byte

0x00   Blank display RAM
0x01   Send 16 characters to display
0x02   Display "TEST"
0x03   ASCII character and display
            RAM address follow - send
            character to display RAM
0x04   Hex byte follows - convert to
            ASCII and display

0x00
0x01
0x02
0x03   0x(char)   0x(addr)
0x04   0x(hex)

Master

The main program depends on the task, but always sends the 3 bytes (instr, char, addr).

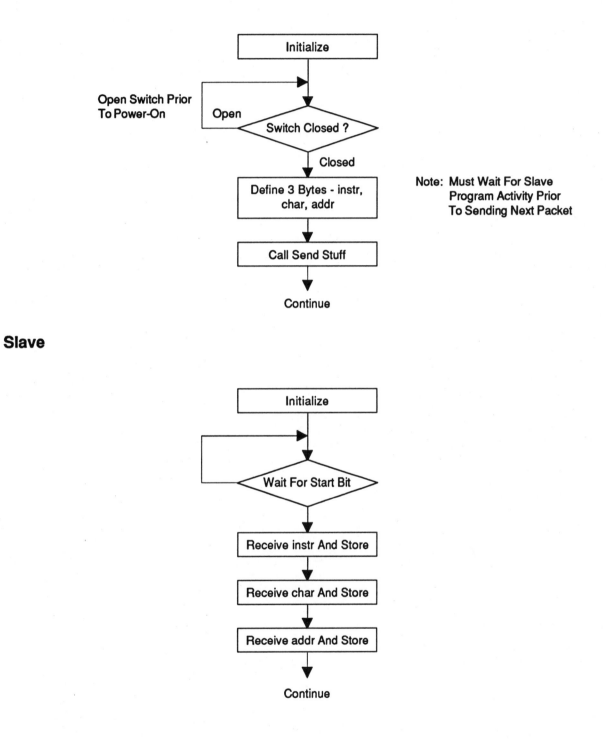

Note: Must Wait For Slave
Program Activity Prior
To Sending Next Packet

Slave

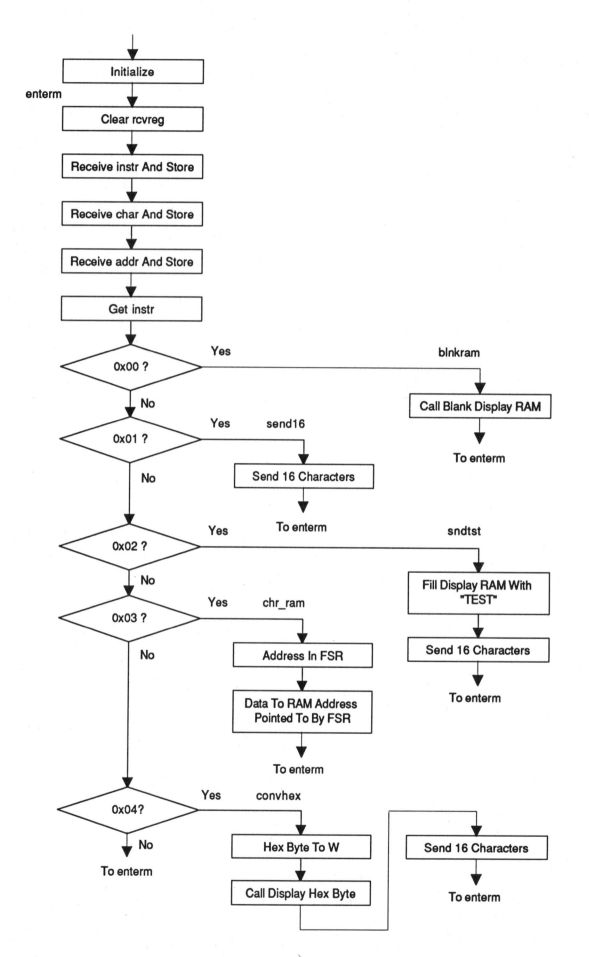

Initialize

enterm

Clear rcvreg

Receive instr And Store

Receive char And Store

Receive addr And Store

Get instr

0x00 ? —Yes— blnkram → Call Blank Display RAM → To enterm

No

0x01 ? —Yes— send16 → Send 16 Characters → To enterm

No

0x02 ? —Yes— sndtst → Fill Display RAM With "TEST" → Send 16 Characters → To enterm

No

0x03 ? —Yes— chr_ram → Address In FSR → Data To RAM Address Pointed To By FSR → To enterm

No

0x04? —Yes— convhex → Hex Byte To W → Call Display Hex Byte → Send 16 Characters → To enterm

No

To enterm

98

The slave program looks at the instruction byte by comparing it with legal instruction bytes until a match is found. If the comparison results in setting the Z flag, the bytes (instructions) are equal (same) and program execution is directed to the appropriate code.

Sometimes a delay will be required in the master program to allow the slave time to execute the instruction (fill display RAM with blanks or send 16 characters to the display for example).

The program listing LCDMSTR.ASM has three blocks of main program code "hidden" from the assembler at the end. The actual main code and three blocks should be examined. Each instructs the slave to perform different functions. You can substitute them for the display "test" portion of the main program if you wish.

You have seen much of the code in previous examples.

The master board has a "send" switch. This assures that the slave is running and the LCD has been initialized prior to sending serial information to it.

```
;======LCDMSTR.ASM===============================5/19/97==
        list    p=16c84
        radix   hex
;----------------------------------------------------------
;       cpu equates (memory map)
tmr0    equ     0x01
status  equ     0x03
porta   equ     0x05
intcon  equ     0x0b
sendreg equ     0x0c
count   equ     0x0d
instr   equ     0x0e
char    equ     0x0f
addr    equ     0x10
count1  equ     0x11
optreg  equ     0x81
trisa   equ     0x85
;----------------------------------------------------------
;       bit equates
c       equ     0
rp0     equ     5
;----------------------------------------------------------
;note: power-on with switch off
;----------------------------------------------------------
        org     0x000
;
start   bsf     status,rp0    ;switch to bank 1
        movlw   b'00000100'   ;port A inputs/outputs
        movwf   trisa
        bcf     status,rp0    ;switch back to bank 0
        bsf     porta,1       ;output mark, bit 1
switch  btfsc   porta,2       ;start send?
        goto    switch        ;not yet
;display "TEST"
        movlw   0x02          ;display "test"
        movwf   instr
```

```
        call      sndstf        ;call send stuff
;long delay required here if other tasks follow
circle  goto      circle  ;done
;-----------------------------------------------------------
sndstf  movf      instr,w        ;get instruction
        movwf     sendreg        ;to be sent
        call      ser_out        ;to serial out subroutine
        movf      char,w         ;get character or hex byte
        movwf     sendreg        ;to be sent
        call      ser_out        ;to serial out subroutine
        movf      addr,w         ;get address
        movwf     sendreg        ;to be sent
        call      ser_out        ;to serial out subroutine
        return
;-----------------------------------------------------------
ser_out bcf       intcon,5       ;disable tmr0 interrupts
        bcf       intcon,7       ;disable global interrupts
        clrf      tmr0           ;clear timer/counter
        clrwdt                   ;clear wdt prep prescaler assign
        bsf       status,rp0  ;to page 1
        movlw     b'11011000'  ;set up timer/counter
        movwf     optreg
        bcf       status,rp0     ;back to page 0
        movlw     0x08           ;init shift counter
        movwf     count
        bcf       porta,1        ;start bit
        clrf      tmr0           ;start timer/counter
        bcf       intcon,2       ;clear tmr0 overflow flag
time1   btfss     intcon,2       ;timer overflow?
        goto      time1          ;no
        bcf       intcon,2       ;yes, clear overflow flag
nxtbit  rlf       sendreg,f      ;rotate msb into carry flag
        bcf       porta,1        ;clear port A, bit 1
        btfsc     status,c       ;test carry flag
        bsf       porta,1        ;bit is set
time2   btfss     intcon,2       ;timer overflow?
        goto      time2          ;no
        bcf       intcon,2       ;clear overflow flag
        decfsz    count,f        ;shifted 8?
        goto      nxtbit         ;no
        bsf       porta,1        ;yes, output mark
time3   btfss     intcon,2       ;timer overflow?
        goto      time3          ;no
        return                   ;done
;-----------------------------------------------------------
del_125 movlw     0x2a           ;approx 42x3 cycles (decimal)
        movwf     count1         ;load counter
repeat  decfsz    count1,f       ;decrement counter
        goto      repeat         ;not 0
        return                   ;counter 0, ends delay
;-----------------------------------------------------------
        end
;-----------------------------------------------------------
;at blast time, select:
```

```
;           memory unprotected
;           watchdog timer disabled (default is enabled)
;           standard crystal (using 4 MHz osc for test) XT
;           power-up timer on
;==============================================================

;send blanks to display RAM
            movlw    0x00            ;blanks to display RAM
            movwf    instr
            call     sndstf          ;call send stuff
            call     del_125         ;wait for slave to fill w/blanks
            movlw    0x01            ;send 16 characters to display
            movwf    instr
            call     sndstf          ;call send stuff

;display "A" followed by blanks
            movlw    0x00            ;blanks to display RAM
            movwf    instr
            call     sndstf          ;call send stuff
            call     del_125         ;wait for slave to do it's thing
            movlw    0x03            ;ascii character follows
            movwf    instr
            movlw    "A"             ;define ascii "A"
            movwf    char
            movlw    0x20            ;first display RAM address
            movwf    addr
            call     sndstf          ;call send stuff
            movlw    0x01            ;send 16 characters to display
            movwf    instr
            call     sndstf          ;call send stuff

;display hex byte
            movlw    0x04            ;hex byte follows
            movwf    instr
            movlw    0x01            ;define hex byte 0x__
            movwf    char
            call     sndstf          ;call send stuff
```

```
;=======LCDSLV.ASM==================================5/19/97==
        list    p=16c84
        radix   hex
;----------------------------------------------------------------
;       cpu equates (memory map)
indf    equ     0x00
tmr0    equ     0x01
pc      equ     0x02
status  equ     0x03
fsr     equ     0x04
porta   equ     0x05
portb   equ     0x06
intcon  equ     0x0b
hexbyte equ     0x0c
ms_dig  equ     0x0d
ls_dig  equ     0x0e
hold    equ     0x0f
sa      equ     0x10
sb      equ     0x11
sc      equ     0x12
sd      equ     0x13
count1  equ     0x14
count2  equ     0x15
rcvreg  equ     0x16
count   equ     0x17
temp    equ     0x18
instr   equ     0x19
char    equ     0x1a
addr    equ     0x1b
optreg  equ     0x81
trisa   equ     0x85
trisb   equ     0x86
;----------------------------------------------------------------
;       bit equates
c       equ     0
z       equ     2
rp0     equ     5
;----------------------------------------------------------------
        org     0x000
;
start   goto    main            ;leap over tables
;----------------------------------------------------------------
table   addwf   pc,f            ;add offset to program counter
        retlw   0x00            ;0
        retlw   0x01            ;1
        retlw   0x04            ;2
        retlw   0x07            ;3
        retlw   0x0b            ;4
        retlw   0x0e            ;5
        retlw   0x12            ;6
        retlw   0x16            ;7
        retlw   0x1a            ;8
        retlw   0x1d            ;9
        retlw   0x21            ;a
```

```
        retlw    0x25          ;b
        retlw    0x29          ;c
        retlw    0x2d          ;d
        retlw    0x31          ;e
        retlw    0x35          ;f
;--------------------------------------------------------------
makbits addwf    pc,f          ;add offset to program counter
        return                 ;0x0    0000    leave as is
        movlw    0x31          ;0x1    0001
        movwf    sd
        return
        movlw    0x31          ;0x2    0010
        movwf    sc
        return
        movlw    0x31          ;0x3    0011
        movwf    sc
        movwf    sd
        return
        movlw    0x31          ;0x4    0100
        movwf    sb
        return
        movlw    0x31          ;0x5    0101
        movwf    sb
        movwf    sd
        return
        movlw    0x31          ;0x6    0110
        movwf    sb
        movwf    sc
        return
        call     fill1s        ;0x7    0111    fill with 1,s
        movlw    0x30
        movwf    sa
        return
        movlw    0x31          ;0x8    1000
        movwf    sa
        return
        movlw    0x31          ;0x9    1001
        movwf    sa
        movwf    sd
        return
        movlw    0x31          ;0xa    1010
        movwf    sa
        movwf    sc
        return
        call     fill1s        ;0xb    1011    fill with 1,s
        movlw    0x30
        movwf    sb
        return
        movlw    0x31          ;0xc    1100
        movwf    sa
        movwf    sb
        return
        call     fill1s        ;0xd    1101    fill with 1,s
        movlw    0x30
```

```
        movwf   sc
        return
        call    fill1s      ;0xe    1110    fill with 1,s
        movlw   0x30
        movwf   sd
        return
        goto    fill1s      ;0xf    1111    fill with 1,s
        return
;------------------------------------------------------------
main    bsf     status,rp0  ;switch to bank 1
        movlw   b'00000001' ;port A inputs/outputs
        movwf   trisa
        movlw   b'00000000' ;port B outputs
        movwf   trisb
        bcf     status,rp0  ;back to bank 0
        movlw   b'00000000' ;all outputs low
        movwf   portb
        bcf     porta,1     ;all outputs low
        bcf     porta,2
        bcf     porta,3
        bcf     porta,4
        call    blanks      ;fill display RAM with blanks
        call    hello       ;create message in display RAM
        call    del_5       ;allow lcd time to initialize itself
        call    initlcd     ;initialize display
        call    disp16      ;send 16 characters to display
enterm  clrf    rcvreg      ;yes
        call    ser_in      ;to serial in subroutine
        movf    rcvreg,w    ;get byte received
        movwf   instr       ;store instruction
        clrf    rcvreg
        call    ser_in      ;to serial in subroutine
        movf    rcvreg,w    ;get byte received
        movwf   char        ;store character or byte
        clrf    rcvreg
        call    ser_in      ;to serial in subroutine
        movf    rcvreg,w    ;get byte received
        movwf   addr        ;store address
        movf    instr,w     ;get copy of instruction
        sublw   0x00        ;compare with 0x00
        btfsc   status,z    ;z flag set if bytes are equal
        goto    blnkram     ;bytes equal
        movf    instr,w     ;get copy of instruction
        sublw   0x01        ;compare with 0x01
        btfsc   status,z    ;z flag set if bytes are equal
        goto    send16      ;bytes equal
        movf    instr,w     ;get copy of instruction
        sublw   0x02        ;compare with 0x02
        btfsc   status,z    ;z flag set if bytes are equal
        goto    sndtst      ;bytes equal
        movf    instr,w     ;get copy of instruction
        sublw   0x03        ;compare with 0x03
        btfsc   status,z    ;z flag set if bytes are equal
        goto    chr_ram     ;bytes equal
```

```
        movf    instr,w     ;get copy of instruction
        sublw   0x04        ;compare with 0x04
        btfsc   status,z    ;z flag set if bytes are equal
        goto    convhex     ;bytes equal
        goto    enterm      ;wait for next transmission
;-----------------------------------------------------------
blnkram call    blanks      ;fill display ram with blanks
        goto    enterm      ;back to main
;-----------------------------------------------------------
send16  call    disp16      ;send display RAM contents to LCD
        goto    enterm      ;back to main
;-----------------------------------------------------------
sndtst  call    test        ;load display RAM with msg "TEST"
        call    disp16      ;send display RAM contents to LCD
        goto    enterm      ;back to main
;-----------------------------------------------------------
chr_ram movf    addr,w      ;get copy of display RAM address
        movwf   fsr         ;store in file select register
        movf    char,w      ;get copy of character to be display
        movwf   indf        ;to RAM address pointed to by FSR
        goto    enterm      ;back to main
;-----------------------------------------------------------
convhex movf    char,w      ;get copy of hex byte to be converted
        call    disphex     ;convert hex byte for display
        call    disp16      ;send display RAM contents to LCD
        goto    enterm      ;back to main
;-----------------------------------------------------------
fill1s  movlw   0x31
        movwf   sa
        movwf   sb
        movwf   sc
        movwf   sd
        return
;-----------------------------------------------------------
disphex movwf   hexbyte     ;store copy of hex byte
        call    blanks      ;fill display RAM with blanks
        call    sephex      ;separate hex byte into 2 ASCII digits
        movf    ms_dig,w    ;get MS digit
        movwf   0x20        ;to display RAM
        movf    ls_dig,w    ;get LS digit
        movwf   0x21        ;to display RAM
        swapf   hexbyte,w   ;get copy of hex byte, swap MS/LS
        andlw   0x0f        ;mask HI nibble
        call    hexbits     ;call hex to bits
        movf    sa,w        ;get first bit
        movwf   0x23        ;to display RAM
        movf    sb,w        ;get second bit
        movwf   0x24        ;to display RAM
        movf    sc,w        ;etc.
        movwf   0x25
        movf    sd,w
        movwf   0x26
        movf    hexbyte,w   ;get copy of hex byte
        andlw   0x0f        ;mask HI nibble
```

```
        call    hexbits         ;call hex to bits
        movf    sa,w            ;get first bit
        movwf   0x28            ;to display RAM
        movf    sb,w            ;get second bit
        movwf   0x29            ;to display RAM
        movf    sc,w            ;etc.
        movwf   0x2a
        movf    sd,w
        movwf   0x2b
        return
;------------------------------------------------------------
sephex  movf    hexbyte,w       ;get copy of hex byte
        andlw   0x0f            ;mask hi nibble
        call    hex2asc         ;hex to ASCII conversion
        movwf   ls_dig          ;store
        swapf   hexbyte,w       ;get copy of hex byte, swap MS/LS
        andlw   0x0f            ;mask hi nibble
        call    hex2asc         ;hex to ASCII conversion
        movwf   ms_dig          ;store
        return
;------------------------------------------------------------
hex2asc movwf   hold            ;store copy of hex digit
        sublw   0x09            ;subtract w from 1 less than 0x0a
        btfss   status,c        ;carry flag set if w < 0x0a
        goto    add37
        goto    add30
add37   movf    hold,w          ;get hex digit
        addlw   0x37
        return                  ;return with ascii in w
add30   movf    hold,w          ;get hex digit
        addlw   0x30
        return                  ;return with ascii in w
;------------------------------------------------------------
hexbits movwf   hold            ;save copy of hex digit
        movlw   0x30            ;fill with ascii 0's
        movwf   sa
        movwf   sb
        movwf   sc
        movwf   sd
        movf    hold,w          ;get hex digit, use as offset
        call    table           ;get 2nd offset for subroutine table
        call    makbits         ;to appropriate create bits sub
        return
;------------------------------------------------------------
blanks  movlw   0x10            ;count=16
        movwf   count1
        movlw   0x20            ;first display RAM address
        movwf   fsr             ;indexed addressing
        movlw   0x20            ;ascii blank
store   movwf   indf            ;store in display RAM location
;                                   pointed to by file select register
        decfsz  count1,f        ;16?
        goto    incfsr          ;no
        return                  ;yes, done
```

```
incfsr  incf     fsr,f          ;increment file select register
        goto     store
;----------------------------------------------------------------
hello   movlw    'H'
        movwf    0x20
        movlw    'E'
        movwf    0x21
        movlw    'L'
        movwf    0x22
        movwf    0x23
        movlw    'O'
        movwf    0x24
        return
;----------------------------------------------------------------
test    movlw    'T'
        movwf    0x20
        movwf    0x23
        movlw    'E'
        movwf    0x21
        movlw    'S'
        movwf    0x22
        movlw    ' '
        movwf    0x24
        return
;----------------------------------------------------------------
initlcd bcf      porta,1        ;E line low
        bcf      porta,2        ;RS line low, set up for control
        call     del_125        ;delay 125 microseconds
        movlw    0x38           ;8-bit, 5X7
        movwf    portb          ;0011 1000
        call     pulse          ;pulse and delay
        movlw    0x0c           ;display on, cursor off
        movwf    portb          ;0000 1100
        call     pulse
        movlw    0x06           ;increment mode, no display shift
        movwf    portb          ;0000 0110
        call     pulse
        call     del_5          ;delay 5 milliseconds - required
;                                    before sending data
        return
;----------------------------------------------------------------
disp16  bcf      porta,1        ;E line low
        bcf      porta,2        ;RS line low, set up for control
        call     del_125        ;delay 125 microseconds
        movlw    0x80           ;control word = address first half
        movwf    portb
        call     pulse          ;pulse and delay
        bsf      porta,2        ;RS=1, set up for data
        call     del_125        ;delay 125 microseconds
        movlw    0x20           ;initialize file select register
        movwf    fsr
getchar movf     0x00,w         ;get character from display RAM
;                                    location pointed to by file select
;                                    register
```

```
        movwf    portb
        call     pulse        ;send data to display
        movlw    0x27         ;8th character sent?
        subwf    fsr,w        ;subtract w from fsr
        btfsc    status,z      ;test z flag
        goto     half         ;set up for last 8 characters
        movlw    2f           ;test number
        subwf    fsr,w
        btfsc    status,z      ;test z flag
        return                ;16 characters sent to lcd
        incf     fsr,f        ;move to next character location
        goto     getchar
half    bcf      porta,2      ;RS=0, set up for control
        call     del_125      ;delay 125 microseconds
        movlw    0xc0         ;control word = address second half
        movwf    portb
        call     pulse        ;pulse and delay
        bsf      porta,2      ;RS=1, set up for data
        incf     fsr,f        ;increment file select register to
;                                  select next character
        call     del_125      ;delay 125 microseconds
        goto     getchar
;-------------------------------------------------------------
del_125 movlw    0x2a         ;approx 42x3 cycles (decimal)
        movwf    count1       ;load counter
repeat  decfsz   count1,f     ;decrement counter
        goto     repeat       ;not 0
        return                ;counter 0, ends delay
;-------------------------------------------------------------
del_5   movlw    0x29         ;decimal 40
        movwf    count2       ;to counter
delay   call     del_125      ;delay 125 microseconds
        decfsz   count2,f     ;do it 40 times = 5 milliseconds
        goto     delay
        return                ;counter 0, ends delay
;-------------------------------------------------------------
pulse   bsf      porta,1      ;pulse E line
        nop                   ;delay
        bcf      porta,1
        call     del_125      ;delay 125 microseconds
        return
;-------------------------------------------------------------
ser_in  bcf      intcon,5     ;disable tmr0 interrupts
        bcf      intcon,7     ;disable global interrupts
        clrf     tmr0         ;clear timer/counter
        clrwdt                ;clear wdt prep prescaler assign
        bsf      status,rp0   ;to page 1
        movlw    b'11011000'  ;set up timer/counter
        movwf    optreg
        bcf      status,rp0   ;back to page 0
        movlw    0x08         ;init shift counter
        movwf    count
sbit    btfsc    porta,0      ;look for start bit
        goto     sbit         ;mark
```

```
        movlw   0x80            ;start bit received, half bit time
        movwf   tmr0            ;load and start timer/counter
        bcf     intcon,2        ;clear tmr0 overflow flag
time1   btfss   intcon,2        ;timer overflow?
        goto    time1           ;no
        btfsc   porta,0         ;start bit still low?
        goto    sbit            ;false start, go back
        clrf    tmr0            ;yes, half bit time - start timer/ctr
        bcf     intcon,2        ;clear tmr0 overflow flag
time2   btfss   intcon,2        ;timer overflow?
        goto    time2           ;no
        bcf     intcon,2        ;yes, clear tmr0 overflow flag
        movf    porta,w         ;read port A
        movwf   temp            ;store
        rrf     temp,f          ;rotate bit 0 into carry flag
        rlf     rcvreg,f        ;rotate carry into rcvreg bit 0
        decfsz  count,f         ;shifted 8?
        goto    time2           ;no
time3   btfss   intcon,2        ;timer overflow?
        goto    time3           ;no
        return                  ;yes, byte received
;-------------------------------------------------------------
        end
;-------------------------------------------------------------
;at blast time, select:
;       memory unprotected
;       watchdog timer disabled (default is enabled)
;       standard crystal (using 4 MHz osc for test)
;       power-up timer on
;=============================================================
```

LCD EXPERIMENTS

You may want to experiment with the operation of the display module.

Try Your Own Variations:

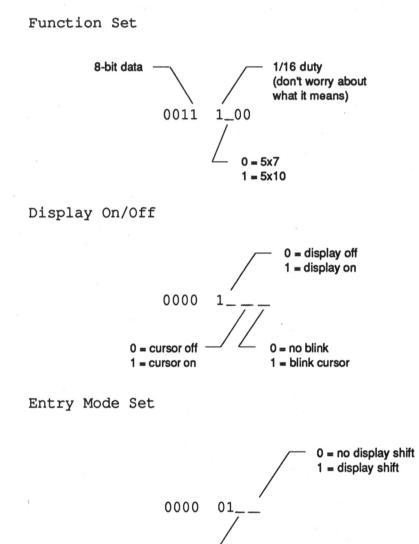

Function Set

8-bit data — 1/16 duty (don't worry about what it means)

0011 1_00

0 = 5x7
1 = 5x10

Display On/Off

0 = display off
1 = display on

0000 1_ _ _

0 = cursor off   0 = no blink
1 = cursor on   1 = blink cursor

Entry Mode Set

0 = no display shift
1 = display shift

0000 01_ _

0 = decrement
1 = increment

MORE ABOUT ASCII

Many ASCII characters can be defined directly using MPASM as seen previously. For your reference, a table of ASCII characters follows. You will note that there is quite a variety available for your use. Just look up the HI and LO nibbles and away you go!

LCD FONT TABLE

```
                        ------------------
                        UPPER NIBBLE
  LOWER NIBBLE    0x2   3   4   5   6   7
  ------------          ------------------
        0x0                 0       P       p
         1          !       1   A   Q   a   q
         2          "       2   B   R   b   r
         3          #       3   C   S   c   s
         4          $       4   D   T   d   t
         5          %       5   E   U   e   u
         6          &       6   F   V   f   v
         7          '       7   G   W   g   w
         8          (       8   H   X   h   x
         9          )       9   I   Y   i   y
         A          *       :   J   Z   j   z
         B          +       ;   K       k
         C          ,       <   L       l
         D          -       =   M       m
         E          .       >   N   ^   n
         F          /       ?   O   _   o
```

Example: 0x41 = A

Note: 0x20 = Blank

The LCD has more fonts available. Refer to the manufacturer's data book for details.

SCANNING KEYPADS

Keypads are available wired in various ways. If the switches are arranged in a matrix, they can be scanned by a microcontroller to see if one of the switches is closed (ie, a key is pressed).

For 5 switches/keys or less, it is best to use one port line per switch/key. For 6 keys or more, a matrix arrangement is most efficient (minimize number of port lines).

The keypad shown below has 12 switches arranged in a 4 row by 3 column matrix. Pressing a key closes a switch which electrically connects one row to one column.

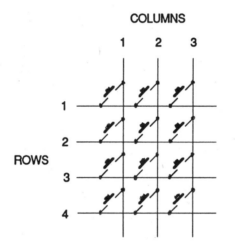

Each keypad switch in the matrix is connected to the microcontroller as shown:

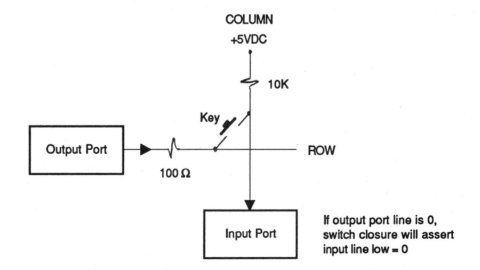

At the time the input port line is read, its logic level depends, first, on whether the switch is open or closed. If the switch is closed, the logic level at the input port line will be the same as the output port line logic level.

	SWITCH OPEN	SWITCH CLOSED	
		Output = 0	Output = 1
INPUT	1	0	1

From the table, we can see that the output line must be low at the time the input line is read to see if the switch is closed.

It is easy to scan a keypad matrix by doing the following:

1. Set the first row LO and make the other rows HI.

2. Read the column lines individually looking for a LO.

3. If a LO is detected, the switch connecting the LO row and the LO column is closed.

The columns are pulled up to 5 volts with 10K resistors and are connected to 3 input port lines. The rows are connected to output port lines. The matrix is scanned under software control.

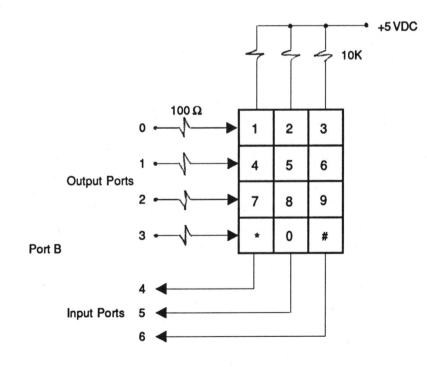

We will use a standard telephone keypad format as our example. The switches are wired in a matrix. How this is done physically varies. The keypad I pirated from an old telephone has most of the "wiring" on a flat very thin flexible sheet of plastic. Visualize it as being a thin single-sided printed circuit board. The rest of the "wiring" is on the main telephone board. You can scavenge a phone keypad, make your own matrix using individual SPST push-button momentary contact switches, or buy a nice commercial unit.

For our example, the 10 decimal digit keys will be used for that purpose. The * and # keys will be used as function keys.

The 10 decimal keys are used together, so software will scan the 3 x 3 matrix covering the 1 through 9 keys to determine which (if any) number key is pressed. Software will scan the "0" key separately.

The 2 function keys are used one at a time at predictable times, so software will look for specific function key presses at the appropriate times.

It is apparent that the software must "know" which row is LO when a column LO is detected. See the software description for more details on how this may be accomplished.

The meaning of having a specific key pressed is totally up to the designer who will determine what label is placed on the key (to tell the user what that key's function is) and what the software does when that key is pressed. Next time you use a microwave oven, run a copy, or use an automated teller machine (ATM), think about what each key does, what the software is looking for when you press each key and what occurs immediately after you press each key.

SOFTWARE DESIGN

It occurred to me that for programming purposes it would be most convenient to think of the keypad as a group of decimal number keys and two function keys. The function keys are used at some times and the number keys at others. The two are not mixed. Going further, it made sense to me to try to develop a loop or series of loops to scan the number portion of the keypad by itself and to increment a counter in the process of scanning each key. If a key is pressed, the counter will contain the same decimal digit as the key position.

The function keys are used at semi-predictable times (depends on your application).

Next, I made a flow chart for the program. Then I wrote code.

SCAN DECIMAL SUBROUTINE

The scan decimal subroutine uses 5 file register (RAM) locations:

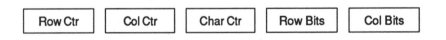

| Row Ctr | Col Ctr | Char Ctr | Row Bits | Col Bits |

The scan decimal subroutine scans the 10 decimal key portion of the pad looking for a pressed key (switch closure). As the subroutine steps through the rows and columns, a counter is incremented. When a key press is detected, the character counter will contain the decimal digit corresponding to the key. It is available for use by the main program which called the scan decimal subroutine.

The "0" key location is out of sequence (physically), so it is treated as a special case. After that, the keys are scanned in numerical order.

Starting with "1", the scan sequence is the same as the sequence of the keys.

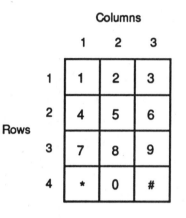

```
------------------------------
ROW    COL    CHARACTER COUNTER
------------------------------
 1      1            1
 1      2            2              Steps across row 1,
 1      3            3              then row 2, etc.
 2      1            4
 2      2            5
 .
 .
 .
 3      3            9
```

Two other counters are used in addition to the character counter. One counter keeps track of the row number and another counter keeps track of the column number.

The row bit register contains the bit pattern which is output to the keypad rows. The column bit register contains the bit pattern which is compared with the pattern read from the column input port lines when the port B is read.

The RLF (rotate one bit left) instruction is used to shift the 1 one position to the left in the bit pattern obtained from either bit register. The RLF instruction fills in the least significant bit with the contents of the carry flag. Since the carry flag contains garbage, bit 0 is cleared right after the RLF instruction is executed.

```
0000 0001  Before RLF
0000 001X  After RLF
0000 0010  After BCF
```

CMOS works best if an input is normally held high (+5V) by a pullup resistor and asserted low when a change is required. To check for a switch closure, the row is asserted low (0) and the columns are tested for 0 which indicates a switch is closed at the intersection of the two lines.

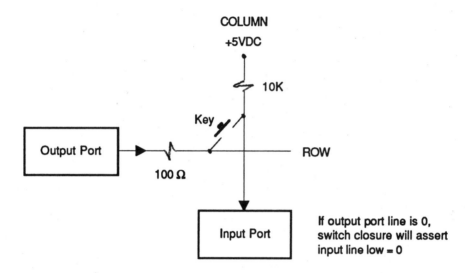

Because of the hardware considerations and because a shift left instruction which fills in behind with 1's is not available, the row and column bits must be changed to their complements using the XORLW (exclusive OR) instruction prior to use.

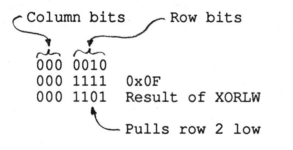

```
000 0010
000 1111  0x0F
000 1101  Result of XORLW
          Pulls row 2 low
```

To continue:

```
010 0000  Column bits from register
100 000X  Shift one bit left (RLF)
111 0000  0xFF
011 0000  Result of XORLW

          Pulls column 3 low
```

116

To visualize how all this works (for digits 1 through 9), you may want to mentally follow through the flow chart and fill in the following table as you go:

TEST COLUMN TRIP THROUGH	CHAR COUNT	ROW COUNT	COL COUNT
1st	1	1	1
2nd	2	1	2
3rd	3	1	3
4th	4	2	1
.			
.			
9th	9	3	3

Note that:

1. Character counter must start at 0, look at 0, then increment to 1.
2. Column counter starts at 1. Test for done = 3.
3. Column bits starts at 001 0000.
4. Row counter starts at 1. Test for done = 3.
5. Row bits starts at 000 0001.

USING KEYPAD AND LCD WITH PIC16

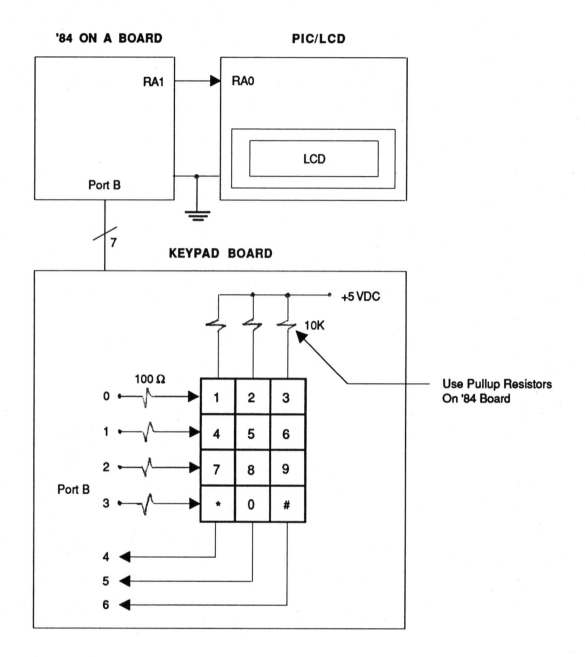

```
RA1 = serial out to LCD module
Port B

    Bits   7 6 5 4 3 2 1 0
           X 3 2 1 4 3 2 1
           ‿‿‿‿  ‿‿‿‿
            Col      Row

Need "debounce" time delay = 400 milliseconds
```

DEBOUNCE

The time delay subroutine called "pause" in **Easy** PIC'n is used. Two file register (RAM) locations are used as the M counter and the N counter. Switch contacts tend to bounce and may be sensed as several key presses unless there is a time delay between samples. 400 milliseconds works well as determined by experiment.

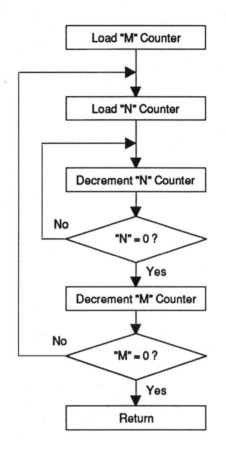

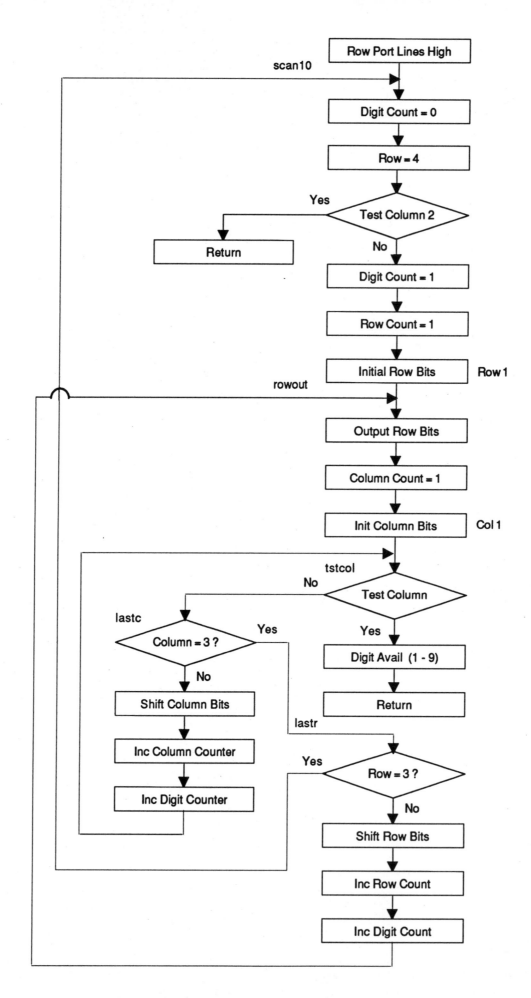

120

On reset, the LCD module will display "HELLO". Press any digit key and the corresponding number will be displayed. Press either function key (* or #) and nothing will happen. Why?

```
;======SCANPAD.ASM==============================5/20/97==
        list    p=16c84
        radix   hex
;--------------------------------------------------------
;       cpu equates (memory map)
tmr0    equ     0x01
status  equ     0x03
porta   equ     0x05
portb   equ     0x06
intcon  equ     0x0b
sendreg equ     0x0c
count   equ     0x0d
instr   equ     0x0e
char    equ     0x0f
addr    equ     0x10
count1  equ     0x11
digctr  equ     0x12
rowctr  equ     0x13
colctr  equ     0x14
rowbits equ     0x15
colbits equ     0x16
temp    equ     0x17
ncount  equ     0x18
mcount  equ     0x19
optreg  equ     0x81
trisa   equ     0x85
trisb   equ     0x86
;--------------------------------------------------------
;       bit equates
c       equ     0
z       equ     2
rp0     equ     5
;--------------------------------------------------------
        org     0x000
;
start   bsf     status,rp0   ;switch to bank 1
        movlw   b'00000000'  ;port A outputs
        movwf   trisa
        movlw   b'01110000'  ;port B inputs/outputs
        movwf   trisb
        bcf     status,rp0   ;switch back to bank 0
        bsf     porta,1      ;output mark, bit 1 (serial - LCD)
        bsf     portb,0      ;rows high
        bsf     portb,1
        bsf     portb,2
        bsf     portb,3
        bcf     portb,7      ;unused line low
ckpad   call    scan10
        movlw   0x04         ;hex byte follows
        movwf   instr
```

```
        movf    digctr,w        ;get digit
        movwf   char
        call    sndstf          ;call send stuff
        call    debounce        ;time delay - debounce switches
        goto    ckpad           ;repeat
;------------------------------------------------------------
scan10  bsf     portb,0         ;rows high
        bsf     portb,1
        bsf     portb,2
        bsf     portb,3
        clrf    digctr          ;digit counter=0
        bcf     portb,3         ;row=4
        btfss   portb,5         ;test column 2
        return                  ;"0" key press
        bsf     portb,3         ;deselect row 4
        movlw   0x01
        movwf   digctr          ;digit counter=1
        movwf   rowctr          ;row counter=1
        movwf   rowbits         ;row bits = 0000 0001
rowout  movf    rowbits,w       ;get row bits
        xorlw   0x0f            ;complement row bits
        movwf   portb           ;output row bits
        movlw   0x01
        movwf   colctr          ;column counter=1
        movlw   0x10            ;0001 0000
        movwf   colbits         ;col=1
tstcol  movf    portb,w         ;read port B
        andlw   0x70            ;mask off rows and bit 7
        movwf   temp            ;columns
        movf    colbits,w       ;get column bits
        xorlw   0x70            ;complement column bits
        subwf   temp,w          ;compare with contents of temp
        btfsc   status,z
        return                  ;digit available
lastc   movf    colctr,w        ;get column count
        sublw   0x03
        btfsc   status,z        ;=3 ?
        goto    lastr
        rlf     colbits,f       ;shift column bits
        bcf     colbits,0       ;fix carry flag garbage
        incf    colctr,f
        incf    digctr,f
        goto    tstcol
lastr   movf    rowctr,w        ;get row count
        sublw   0x03
        btfsc   status,z        ;=3 ?
        goto    scan10          ;scan 10 digit keys again
        rlf     rowbits,f       ;shift row bits
        bcf     rowbits,0       ;fix carry flag garbage
        incf    rowctr,f
        incf    digctr,f
        goto    rowout
;------------------------------------------------------------
debounce movlw  0xff            ;M
```

```
        movwf   mcount      ;to M counter
loadn   movlw   0xff        ;N
        movwf   ncount      ;to N counter
decn    decfsz  ncount,f    ;decrement N
        goto    decn        ;again
        decfsz  mcount,f    ;decrement M
        goto    loadn       ;again
        return              ;done
;----------------------------------------------------------
sndstf  movf    instr,w     ;get instruction
        movwf   sendreg     ;to be sent
        call    ser_out     ;to serial out subroutine
        movf    char,w      ;get character or hex byte
        movwf   sendreg     ;to be sent
        call    ser_out     ;to serial out subroutine
        movf    addr,w      ;get address
        movwf   sendreg     ;to be sent
        call    ser_out     ;to serial out subroutine
        return
;----------------------------------------------------------
ser_out bcf     intcon,5    ;disable tmr0 interrupts
        bcf     intcon,7    ;disable global interrupts
        clrf    tmr0        ;clear timer/counter
        clrwdt              ;clear wdt prep prescaler assign
        bsf     status,rp0  ;to page 1
        movlw   b'11011000' ;set up timer/counter
        movwf   optreg
        bcf     status,rp0  ;back to page 0
        movlw   0x08        ;init shift counter
        movwf   count
        bcf     porta,1     ;start bit
        clrf    tmr0        ;start timer/counter
        bcf     intcon,2    ;clear tmr0 overflow flag
time1   btfss   intcon,2    ;timer overflow?
        goto    time1       ;no
        bcf     intcon,2    ;yes, clear overflow flag
nxtbit  rlf     sendreg,f   ;rotate msb into carry flag
        bcf     porta,1     ;clear port A, bit 1
        btfsc   status,c    ;test carry flag
        bsf     porta,1     ;bit is set
time2   btfss   intcon,2    ;timer overflow?
        goto    time2       ;no
        bcf     intcon,2    ;clear overflow flag
        decfsz  count,f     ;shifted 8?
        goto    nxtbit      ;no
        bsf     porta,1     ;yes, output mark
time3   btfss   intcon,2    ;timer overflow?
        goto    time3       ;no
        return              ;done
;----------------------------------------------------------
        end
;----------------------------------------------------------
;at blast time, select:
;       memory unprotected
```

```
;                 watchdog timer disabled (default is enabled)
;                 standard crystal (using 4 MHz osc for test) XT
;                 power-up timer on
;================================================================
```

FUNCTION KEYS

The function keys * and # are scanned separately. In a typical control application, the program is looking either for a command or for a number entry (not both at the same time). Individual subroutines handle each task as needed.

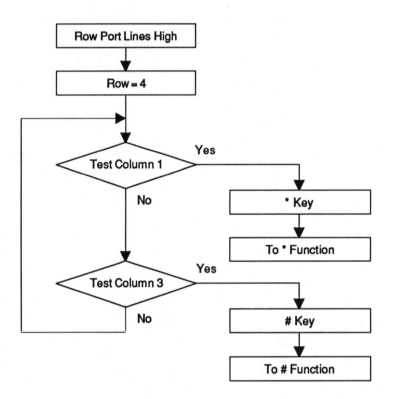

An "escape" has not been provided here. You can use reset or perhaps add that capability by using the "0" key and scanning it along with the two function keys. It then acts as a third function key when the scan function subroutine is running.

```
;=======SCANFCT.ASM===============================5/21/97==
        list    p=16c84
        radix   hex
;-------------------------------------------------------------
;       cpu equates (memory map)
tmr0    equ     0x01
status  equ     0x03
porta   equ     0x05
portb   equ     0x06
intcon  equ     0x0b
```

124

```
sendreg equ      0x0c
count   equ      0x0d
instr   equ      0x0e
char    equ      0x0f
addr    equ      0x10
count1  equ      0x11
ncount  equ      0x12
mcount  equ      0x13
funct   equ      0x14
optreg  equ      0x81
trisa   equ      0x85
trisb   equ      0x86
;---------------------------------------------------------------
;        bit equates
c       equ      0
rp0     equ      5
;---------------------------------------------------------------
        org      0x000
;
start   bsf      status,rp0  ;switch to bank 1
        movlw    b'00000000' ;port A outputs
        movwf    trisa
        movlw    b'01110000' ;port B inputs/outputs
        movwf    trisb
        bcf      status,rp0  ;switch back to bank 0
        bsf      porta,1     ;output mark, bit 1 (serial - LCD)
        bsf      portb,0     ;rows high
        bsf      portb,1
        bsf      portb,2
        bsf      portb,3
        bcf      portb,7     ;unused line low
ckpad   call     scanfct
        movlw    0x04        ;hex byte follows
        movwf    instr
        movf     funct,w     ;get character
        movwf    char
        call     sndstf      ;call send stuff
        call     debounce    ;time delay - debounce switches
        goto     ckpad       ;repeat
;---------------------------------------------------------------
scanfct bsf      portb,0     ;rows high
        bsf      portb,1
        bsf      portb,2
        bsf      portb,3
        clrf     funct
        bcf      portb,3     ;row=4
testk   btfss    portb,4     ;test column 1
        goto     star        ;"*" key pressed
        btfss    portb,6     ;test column 3
        goto     pound       ;# key pressed
        goto     testk       ;no key pressed
star    movlw    0xaa        ;*
        movwf    funct
        return
```

125

```
pound     movlw    0x88            ;#
          movwf    funct
          return
;------------------------------------------------------------
debounce  movlw    0xff            ;M
          movwf    mcount          ;to M counter
loadn     movlw    0xff            ;N
          movwf    ncount          ;to N counter
decn      decfsz   ncount,f        ;decrement N
          goto     decn            ;again
          decfsz   mcount,f        ;decrement M
          goto     loadn           ;again
          return                   ;done
;------------------------------------------------------------
sndstf    movf     instr,w         ;get instruction
          movwf    sendreg         ;to be sent
          call     ser_out         ;to serial out subroutine
          movf     char,w          ;get character or hex byte
          movwf    sendreg         ;to be sent
          call     ser_out         ;to serial out subroutine
          movf     addr,w          ;get address
          movwf    sendreg         ;to be sent
          call     ser_out         ;to serial out subroutine
          return
;------------------------------------------------------------
ser_out   bcf      intcon,5        ;disable tmr0 interrupts
          bcf      intcon,7        ;disable global interrupts
          clrf     tmr0            ;clear timer/counter
          clrwdt                   ;clear wdt prep prescaler assign
          bsf      status,rp0      ;to page 1
          movlw    b'11011000'     ;set up timer/counter
          movwf    optreg
          bcf      status,rp0      ;back to page 0
          movlw    0x08            ;init shift counter
          movwf    count
          bcf      porta,1         ;start bit
          clrf     tmr0            ;start timer/counter
          bcf      intcon,2        ;clear tmr0 overflow flag
time1     btfss    intcon,2        ;timer overflow?
          goto     time1           ;no
          bcf      intcon,2        ;yes, clear overflow flag
nxtbit    rlf      sendreg,f       ;rotate msb into carry flag
          bcf      porta,1         ;clear port A, bit 1
          btfsc    status,c        ;test carry flag
          bsf      porta,1         ;bit is set
time2     btfss    intcon,2        ;timer overflow?
          goto     time2           ;no
          bcf      intcon,2        ;clear overflow flag
          decfsz   count,f         ;shifted 8?
          goto     nxtbit          ;no
          bsf      porta,1         ;yes, output mark
time3     btfss    intcon,2        ;timer overflow?
          goto     time3           ;no
          return                   ;done
```

```
;-----------------------------------------------------------
          end
;-----------------------------------------------------------
;at blast time, select:
;         memory unprotected
;         watchdog timer disabled (default is enabled)
;         standard crystal (using 4 MHz osc for test) XT
;         power-up timer on
;===========================================================
```

On reset, "HELLO" is displayed. Pressing the * key causes "AA" to be displayed. Pressing the # key results in "88" being displayed. I am certain you will come up with more imaginative things to do.

DIGITAL TO ANALOG CONVERSION

DO IT YOURSELF D/A USING A RESISTOR NETWORK

For control purposes, you may wish to output an analog voltage. To do so requires the conversion of a binary number to an analog voltage level. This may be done using a precision reference voltage, a resistor network and an op-amp.

Here is a 4-bit version which can be interfaced with four PIC16 port lines. You can easily write the code to exercise it on your own. Once a binary code is presented to the four output lines, the voltage at the op-amp output remains fixed. This is in contrast to the pulse width modulation (PWM) method which follows where, for simple methods of implementing PWM, the PIC16 is kept busy doing PWM and may have little or no time (depending on the method used) for anything else.

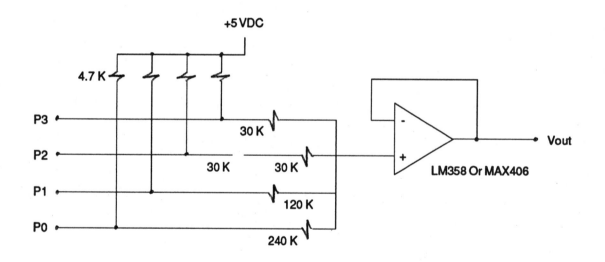

Example:

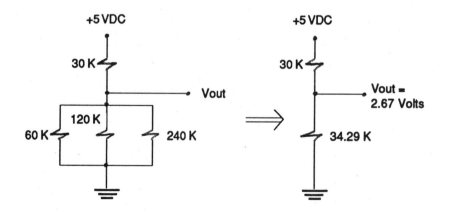

```
-------------
Bits
3210        Vout
-------------
0000        0.00
0001        0.33
0010        0.67
0011        1.00
0100        1.33
0101        1.67
0110        2.00
0111        2.33
1000        2.67
1001        3.00
1010        3.33
1011        3.67
1100        4.00
1110        4.67
1111        5.00
```

8-BIT PARALLEL D/A CONVERTER

A single package 8-bit D/A converter is available from Analog Devices as P/N AD558 which has the resistor network and summing amplifier built in. It operates directly from the microprocessor system 5 volt supply. It produces 0 to 2.55 volts out corresponding directly to the binary numbers written to it.

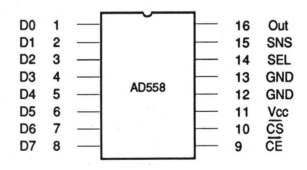

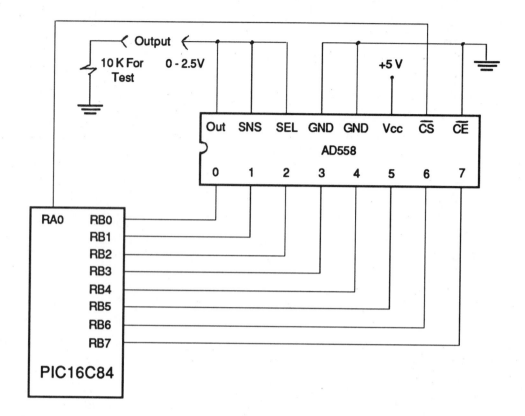

The functions of $\overline{CS}$ and $\overline{CE}$ are the same. Wire one of them ($\overline{CE}$) to ground. $\overline{CS}$ latches data with a low-to-high transition, so don't let the fact that $\overline{CE}$ has a veniculum over it mislead you as it did me.

To test the circuit, write a binary number to the converter and measure the output voltage with a voltmeter or scope.

```
;=======DA558.ASM=================================6/3/97==
        list    p=16c84
        radix   hex
;------------------------------------------------------------
;       cpu equates (memory map)
status  equ     0x03
porta   equ     0x05
portb   equ     0x06
trisa   equ     0x85
trisb   equ     0x86
;------------------------------------------------------------
```

```
;       bit equates
rp0     equ     5
;---------------------------------------------------------------
        org     0x000
;
start   bsf     status,rp0   ;switch to bank 1
        movlw   b'00000000'  ;outputs
        movwf   trisa
        movwf   trisb
        bcf     status,rp0   ;switch back to bank 0
        movlw   b'00000000'
        movwf   porta        ;initialize, cs low
        movlw   b'10000000'  ;volts - range 0 to 255 decimal
        movwf   portb        ;data to D/A
        bsf     porta,0      ;pulse D/A to latch data
        bcf     porta,0
circle  goto    circle
;---------------------------------------------------------------
        end
;---------------------------------------------------------------
;at blast time, select:
;       memory unprotected
;       watchdog timer disabled (default is enabled)
;       standard crystal (using 4 MHz osc for test) XT
;       power-up timer on
;===============================================================
```

Hex Number	Output Voltage
$FF	2.55
00	0.00
0F	0.15
80	1.27

A D/A converter may be used to generate a variety of analog output voltage waveforms such as ramp, sawtooth, sine wave, etc. Binary numbers representing narrow segments of the waveform are sent sequentially to the D/A converter. An 8-bit D/A allows 256 possible voltage levels which is enough for many applications. 10, 12, 14 and 16-bit converters are available if better resolution or accuracy is required.

Code for producing a ramp output voltage waveform follows. The period is about 1.75 milliseconds, frequency about 570 Hz. Adding a time delay at the end of each cycle will reduce the frequency but the output will be "jagged".

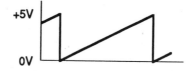

```
;=======558RAMP.ASM================================6/3/97==
        list    p=16c84
        radix   hex
;------------------------------------------------------------
;       cpu equates (memory map)
status  equ     0x03
porta   equ     0x05
portb   equ     0x06
volts   equ     0x0c
count1  equ     0x0d
trisa   equ     0x85
trisb   equ     0x86
;------------------------------------------------------------
;       bit equates
rp0     equ     5
;------------------------------------------------------------
        org     0x000
;
start   bsf     status,rp0  ;switch to bank 1
        movlw   b'00000000' ;outputs
        movwf   trisa
        movwf   trisb
        bcf     status,rp0  ;switch back to bank 0
        movlw   b'00000000'
        movwf   porta       ;initialize, cs low
        clrf    volts       ;zero
loop    movf    volts,w     ;get volts
        movwf   portb       ;data to D/A
        bsf     porta,0     ;pulse D/A to latch data
        bcf     porta,0
        incf    volts,f
        goto    loop
;------------------------------------------------------------
        end
;------------------------------------------------------------
;at blast time, select:
;       memory unprotected
;       watchdog timer disabled (default is enabled)
;       standard crystal (using 4 MHz osc for test) XT
;       power-up timer on
;============================================================
```

Binary numbers representing voltage levels can be stored sequentially in a table in program memory and accessed using relative addressing. A sine wave example follows. This example only has 19 voltage levels in the table (sine values at 10 degree intervals), so the output is jagged. You can add more values to the table. The frequency will be lower as it takes more time to output the additional values. Also, a time delay is included. You may want to experiment with changing the delay time and with adding an RC filter to the output (see D/A conversion chapter).

```
N = 1
T = 0.86 milliseconds
f = 1163 Hz
```

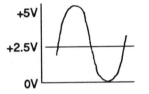

```
;=======558SINE.ASM===============================6/3/97==
        list    p=16c84
        radix   hex
;-----------------------------------------------------------
;       cpu equates (memory map)
pc      equ     0x02
status  equ     0x03
porta   equ     0x05
portb   equ     0x06
count1  equ     0x0c
offctr  equ     0x0d
trisa   equ     0x85
trisb   equ     0x86
;-----------------------------------------------------------
;       bit equates
c       equ     0
z       equ     2
rp0     equ     5
;-----------------------------------------------------------
        org     0x000
;
start   goto    do_it           ;jump over table
;-----------------------------------------------------------
table   addwf   pc,f            ;add offset to program counter
        retlw   0x80            ;1.28 volts
        retlw   0x95            ;1.50
        retlw   0xad            ;1.72
        retlw   0xc1            ;1.92
        retlw   0xd3            ;2.10
        retlw   0xe2            ;2.26
        retlw   0xef            ;2.39
        retlw   0xf8            ;2.48
        retlw   0xfd            ;2.54
        retlw   0xff            ;2.55
        retlw   0xfd            ;2.54
```

```
        retlw    0xf8          ;2.48
        retlw    0xef          ;2.39
        retlw    0xe2          ;2.26
        retlw    0xd3          ;2.10
        retlw    0xc1          ;1.92
        retlw    0xad          ;1.72
        retlw    0x95          ;1.50
        retlw    0x80          ;1.28
        retlw    0x6a          ;1.06
        retlw    0x54          ;0.84
        retlw    0x40          ;0.64
        retlw    0x2e          ;0.46
        retlw    0x1e          ;0.30
        retlw    0x11          ;0.17
        retlw    0x08          ;0.08
        retlw    0x02          ;0.02
        retlw    0x00          ;0.00
        retlw    0x02          ;0.02
        retlw    0x08          ;0.08
        retlw    0x11          ;0.17
        retlw    0x1e          ;0.30
        retlw    0x2e          ;0.46
        retlw    0x40          ;0.64
        retlw    0x54          ;0.84
        retlw    0x6a          ;1.06
;---------------------------------------------------------------
do_it   bsf      status,rp0    ;switch to bank 1
        movlw    b'00000000'   ;outputs
        movwf    trisa
        movwf    trisb
        bcf      status,rp0    ;switch back to bank 0
        movlw    0x00          ;00000000
        movwf    porta         ;initialize, cs low
cycle   clrf     offctr        ;clear table offset counter
step    movf     offctr,w      ;get offset count
        call     table         ;get volts from table
        movwf    portb         ;output data to D/A
        bsf      porta,0       ;pulse D/A to latch data
        bcf      porta,0
        call     delay         ;delay
        movf     offctr,w      ;get offset count
        sublw    0x23          ;compare - cycle complete?
        btfsc    status,z
        goto     cycle
        incf     offctr        ;increment offset counter
        goto     step
;---------------------------------------------------------------
delay   movlw    0x01          ;3N+3 cycles (decimal), N=1 shown
        movwf    count1        ;load counter
repeat  decfsz   count1,f      ;decrement counter
        goto     repeat        ;not 0
        return                 ;counter 0, ends delay
;---------------------------------------------------------------
        end
```

```
;----------------------------------------------------------------
;at blast time, select:
;       memory unprotected
;       watchdog timer disabled (default is enabled)
;       standard crystal (using 4 MHz osc for test) XT
;       power-up timer on
;================================================================
```

DO IT YOURSELF D/A USING PULSE WIDTH MODULATION

Digital-to-analog conversion may be done using pulse width modulation (PWM) and a single PIC16 pin.

PWM Basics

PWM involves outputting a train of pulses at a fixed frequency. The duty cycle (logic HI time, usually expressed as a percentage of the PWM period) is varied to change the average output voltage.

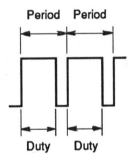

At the end of the duty cycle, the output goes low and at the end of the period, the output goes high (except for the special cases where the duty cycle is 100 percent or 0 percent).

As examples:

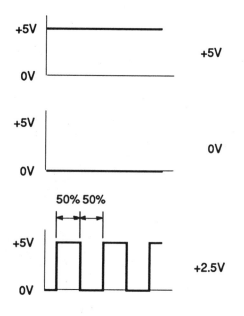

Let's assume we want to generate a 0-5VDC analog voltage level on pin RB0 of a PIC16C84 with a 4.0 clock oscillator. We will use a pulse train period of 256 times 3 internal clock cycles which equates to a frequency of about 300 Hz. Using 256 makes the binary math easy. The time delay requires 3 instruction cycles so the total PWM period is 768 microseconds.

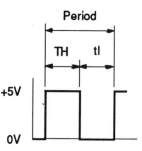

We will use a software time delay subroutine. To make the duty cycle 50 percent, we will use the hexadecimal value 0x7F for duty and 0x80 for low time.

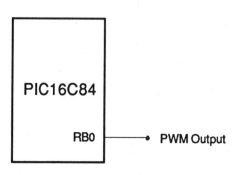

136

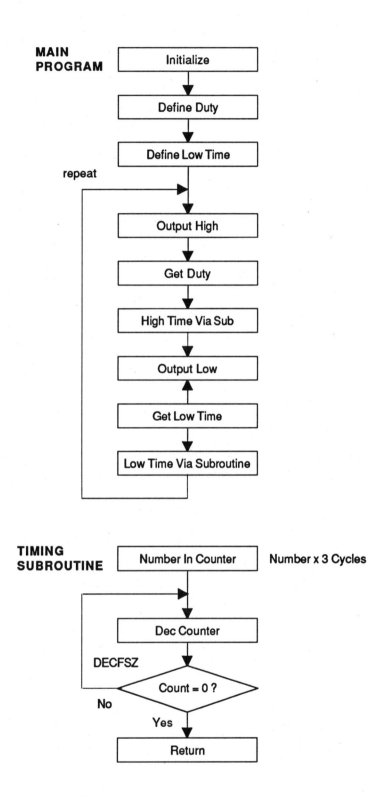

MAIN PROGRAM

Initialize

Define Duty

Define Low Time

repeat

Output High

Get Duty

High Time Via Sub

Output Low

Get Low Time

Low Time Via Subroutine

TIMING SUBROUTINE

Number In Counter

Number x 3 Cycles

Dec Counter

DECFSZ

Count = 0 ?

No

Yes

Return

137

```
;======PWMDEMO.ASM==================================6/4/97==
          list    p=16c84
          radix   hex
;----------------------------------------------------------
;         cpu equates (memory map)
status    equ     0x03
porta     equ     0x05
portb     equ     0x06
duty      equ     0x0c
low_t     equ     0x0d
count     equ     0x0e
trisa     equ     0x85
trisb     equ     0x86
;----------------------------------------------------------
;         bit equates
rp0       equ     5
;----------------------------------------------------------
          org     0x000
;
start     bsf     status,rp0   ;switch to bank 1
          movlw   b'00000000'  ;outputs
          movwf   trisb
          bcf     status,rp0   ;switch back to bank 0
          movlw   b'00000000'  ;all outputs low
          movwf   portb
          movlw   0x7f         ;initial duty cycle 50 percent
          movwf   duty
          movlw   0x80         ;initial low time 50 percent
          movwf   low_t
repeat    bsf     portb,0      ;output high, start duty
          movf    duty,w       ;get duty
          call    time
          bcf     portb,0      ;output low, start low time
          movf    low_t,w      ;get low time
          call    time
          goto    repeat
;----------------------------------------------------------
time      movwf   count        ;time
loop      decfsz  count,f
          goto    loop
          return
;----------------------------------------------------------
          end
;----------------------------------------------------------
;at blast time, select:
;         memory unprotected
;         watchdog timer disabled (default is enabled)
;         standard crystal (using 4 MHz osc for test) XT
;         power-up timer on
;==========================================================
```

Connect a DVM to RB0 and measure the average voltage with the PWM routine running. The result should be about 2.5V.

Next, calculate the hex numbers to use in the program to get output voltages of 1.25 and 3.75 volts. Then test them.

LOW-PASS FILTERS

A filter is a frequency-selective circuit which passes a certain range of frequencies and attenuates others. A simple RC low-pass filter is shown below:

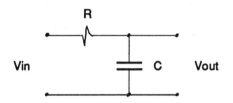

This is called a first order (single RC section) low-pass filter. Its frequency response falls off at higher frequencies. The voltage out is 0.71 times the voltage in at a special point called the 3db point which is the half-power point. This is also known as the cutoff frequency. For the RC low-pass filter, the cutoff frequency is:

$$f_c = f_{3db} = \frac{1}{2\pi RC} = \frac{1}{6.28RC}$$

```
Where f_c is in KHz
      R is in K ohms
      C is in microfarads
```

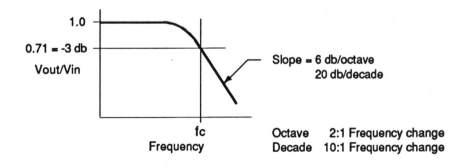

If the input signal is a square wave with period T and frequency f:

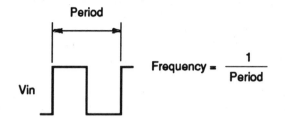

Frequency = $\dfrac{1}{\text{Period}}$

The filter will be effective if the cutoff frequency f_c is 1/10f.

Using our 0.3KHz PWM example, we can easily add a filter to smooth the output and observe the results.

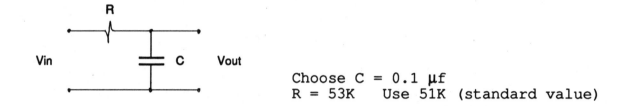

```
Choose C = 0.1 μf
R = 53K    Use 51K (standard value)
```

Try this with the 50% duty cycle code example (PWMDEMO.ASM).

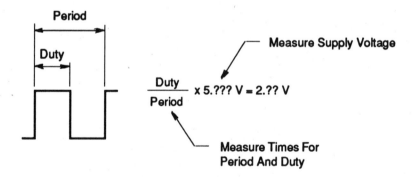

$\dfrac{\text{Duty}}{\text{Period}}$ x 5.??? V = 2.?? V

140

PWM USING FILTER WITH UNITY GAIN FOLLOWER

Adding an op-amp unity gain follower to the RC low-pass filter prevents loading of the RC circuit (including loading by a DVM while measuring the output). The result is called an ideal low pass filter.

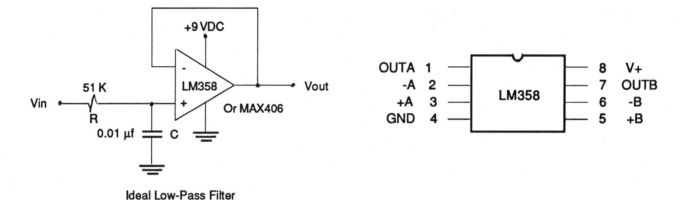

Ideal Low-Pass Filter

MORE PWM PHILOSOPHY

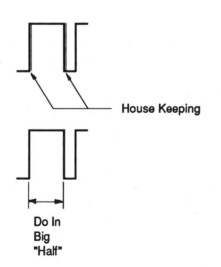

Notice that 100% and 0% duty cycles are special cases that must be handled separately. Also, their existence means that a simple program which simply goes HI/lo/HI/lo.won't work. A short high time will occur for 0% duty cycle and a short low time will occur for 100% duty cycle. So a simple Up/Down program doesn't solve the problem.

ANALOG OUTPUT - INCREASE/DECREASE BUTTONS

The next example shows how an adjustable analog output on a single PIC16 pin can be created using PWM. The circuit is controlled by an increase (voltage) button and a decrease button. Increase/decrease is proportional to the time the button is pressed (to a maximum of 5 volts at the output or a minimum of 0 volts). The rate of increase/decrease is proportional to the time between checks of the associated button which is determined by the number of trips through a program loop between checks. When you test this circuit and program, you can change the number and observe the results. The number is 0x30 (key response) in the listing AOUTPWM.ASM.

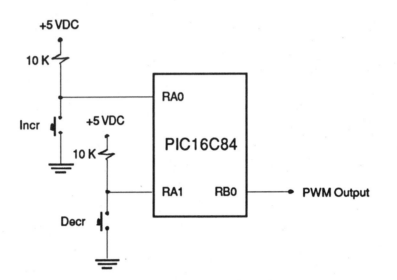

OVERVIEW

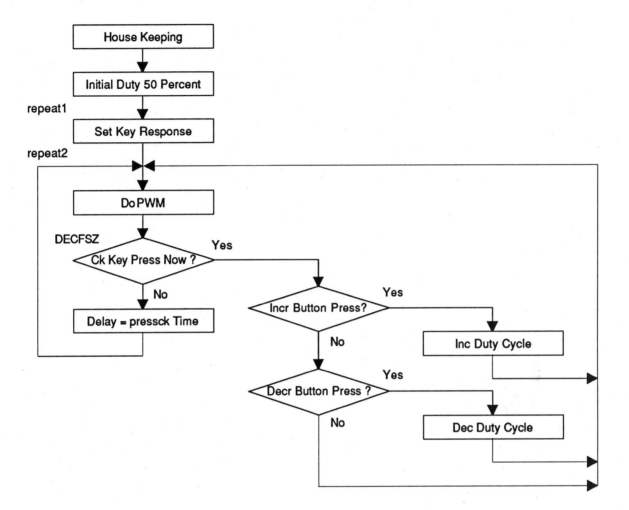

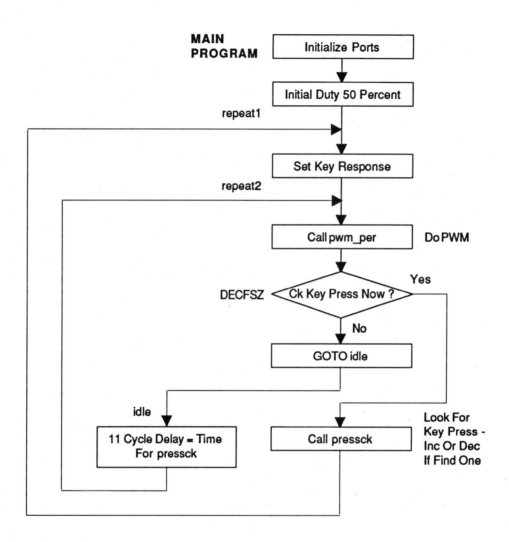

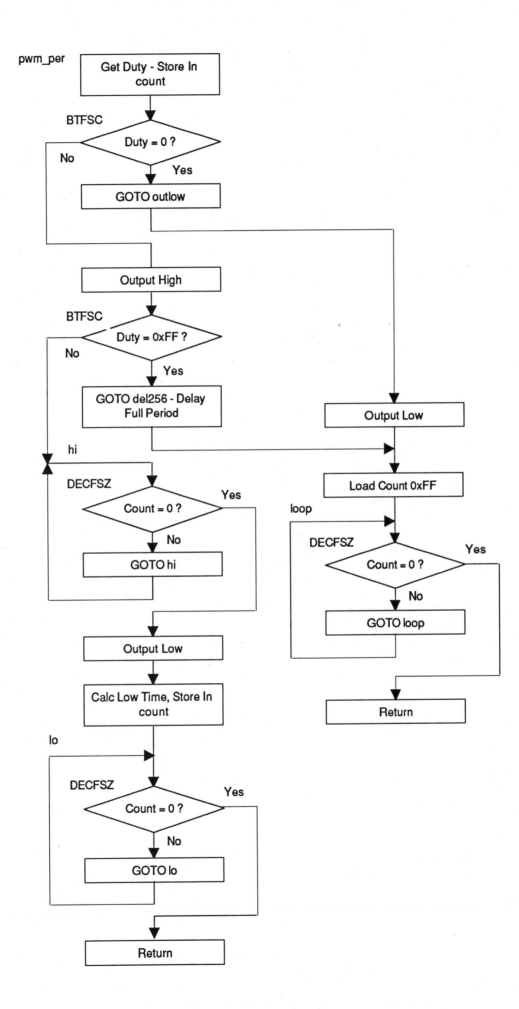

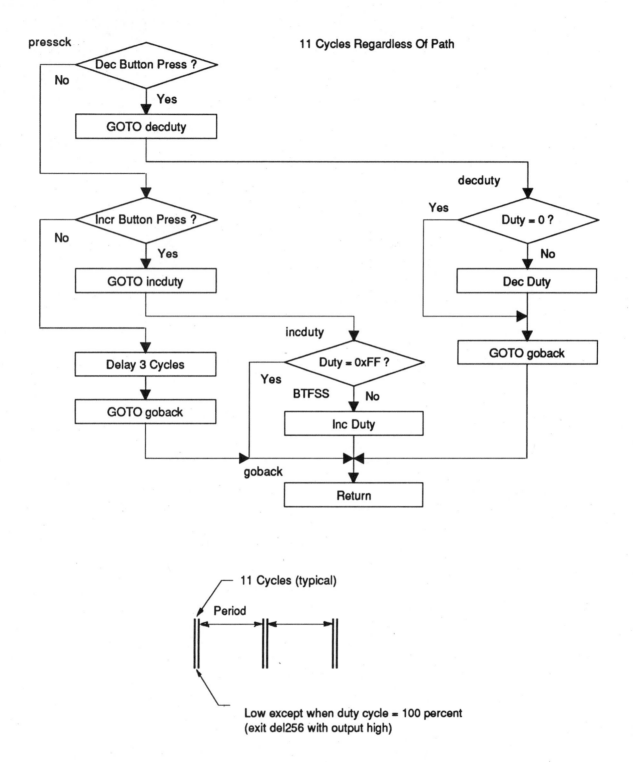

The program handles 0 percent and 100 percent duty cycles. The pressck subroutine takes 11 instruction cycles regardless of the path taken through it. The period of the output is the same whether or not a check for a button press is made.

Change the button (key) response number to see the effect.

146

```
;=======AOUTPWM.ASM===============================5/29/97==
        list    p=16c84
        radix   hex
;-------------------------------------------------------------
;       cpu equates (memory map)
status  equ     0x03
porta   equ     0x05
portb   equ     0x06
duty    equ     0x0c
response equ    0x0d
count   equ     0x0e
trisa   equ     0x85
trisb   equ     0x86
;-------------------------------------------------------------
;       bit equates
z       equ     2
rp0     equ     5
;-------------------------------------------------------------
        org     0x000
;
start   bsf     status,rp0  ;switch to bank 1
        movlw   b'00000011' ;inputs/outputs
        movwf   trisa
        movlw   b'00000000' ;outputs
        movwf   trisb
        bcf     status,rp0  ;switch back to bank 0
        movlw   b'00000000' ;all outputs low
        movwf   portb
        movlw   0x7f        ;initial duty cycle 50 percent
        movwf   duty
repeat1 movlw   0x30        ;initial key response
        movwf   response
repeat2 call    pwm_per     ;call PWM period subroutine
        decfsz  response    ;decrement/test button response
        goto    idle        ;delay to make things even
        call    pressck     ;look for incr/decr button press
        goto    repeat1
;-------------------------------------------------------------
pressck btfss   porta,1     ;decrease button pressed?
        goto    decduty     ;yes, decrement duty cycle
        btfss   porta,0     ;increase button pressed?
        goto    incduty     ;yes, increment duty cycle
        nop
        nop
        nop
        goto    goback
incduty movf    duty,w      ;get duty cycle into W
        sublw   0xff        ;duty cycle=0xff?
        btfss   status,z
        incf    duty        ;increment duty cycle
goback  return              ;press check done
decduty movf    duty,w      ;get duty cycle into W
        sublw   0x00        ;duty cycle=0?
```

```
         btfss   status,z
         decf    duty            ;decrement duty cycle
         goto    goback
;------------------------------------------------------------
idle     nop
         nop
         nop
         nop
         nop
         nop
         nop
         nop
         nop
         goto    repeat2
;------------------------------------------------------------
pwm_per  movf    duty,w          ;get duty cycle
         movwf   count
         sublw   0x00            ;compare w/0
         btfsc   status,z
         goto    outlow
         bsf     portb,0         ;output high
         movf    duty,w          ;get duty cycle
         sublw   0xff            ;compare w/0xff
         btfsc   status,z
         goto    del256
hi       decfsz  count,f         ;high time
         goto    hi
         bcf     portb,0         ;output low
         movf    duty,w          ;get duty cycle
         sublw   0xff
         movwf   count           ;low time
lo       decfsz  count,f
         goto    lo
         return
;------------------------------------------------------------
outlow   bcf     portb,0         ;output low
del256   movlw   0xff            ;delay full period
         movwf   count
loop     decfsz  count,f
         goto    loop
         return
;------------------------------------------------------------
         end
;------------------------------------------------------------
;at blast time, select:
;       memory unprotected
;       watchdog timer disabled (default is enabled)
;       standard crystal (using 4 MHz osc for test) XT
;       power-up timer on
;============================================================
```

Run the program with an oscilloscope monitoring the output. Press the increase or decrease button and observe the result.

PWM USING SOFTWARE, TMR0 AND INTERRUPTS - PHILOSOPHY

PWM may not be a full-time job for the microcontroller (depending on the application), but the PWM functions that are performed must be done when needed on a periodic basis as long as the PWM output is required.

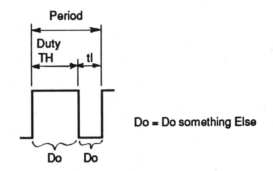

Do = Do something Else

If the TH or tl is short (could be 0), there may not be time to do anything else during that time interval. Code can be written to determine which is longer, TH or tl. The other tasks can then be performed in the longer of the two time intervals. The PWM routine runs as the main program and lets the other tasks be performed during TH or tl, whichever is longer. One of the other tasks is to monitor inputs and determine duty cycle. The updated duty cycle value is stored in the TH (duty) register.

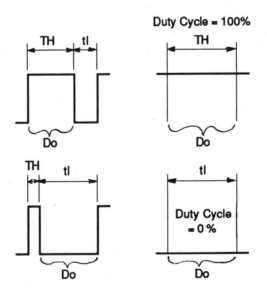

Using this technique requires that the non-PWM task be accomplished in something less than half the PWM period. If the period = 256 instruction (OSC/4) cycles, then the non-PWM task would have to be accomplished in 128 cycles less the time required to service the TMR0 interrupts, etc. An example of this concept follows.

We will use a period counter value of 256 and divide the internal clock by 4 using the prescaler.

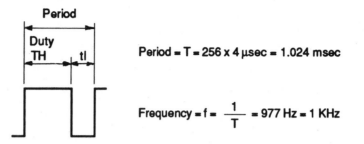

Period = T = 256 x 4 μsec = 1.024 msec

Frequency = f = $\dfrac{1}{T}$ = 977 Hz = 1 KHz

The test circuit is shown below. The switches on port B are used to input the duty cycle as an 8-bit number. The switch settings may be changed as the program runs. Again, the output may be monitored using an oscilloscope.

User options include using the prescaler to slow down TMR0.

- More time to do useful stuff.
- Software overhead will cause smaller percentage error.

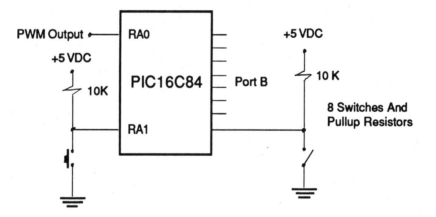

MAIN PROGRAM

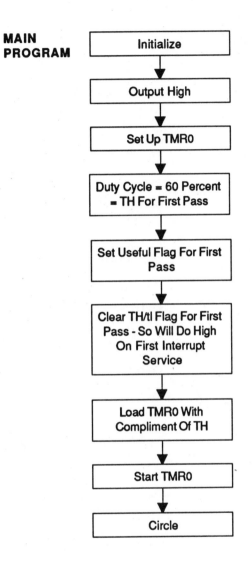

Initialize

Output High

Set Up TMR0

Duty Cycle = 60 Percent = TH For First Pass

Set Useful Flag For First Pass

Clear TH/tl Flag For First Pass - So Will Do High On First Interrupt Service

Load TMR0 With Compliment Of TH

Start TMR0

Circle

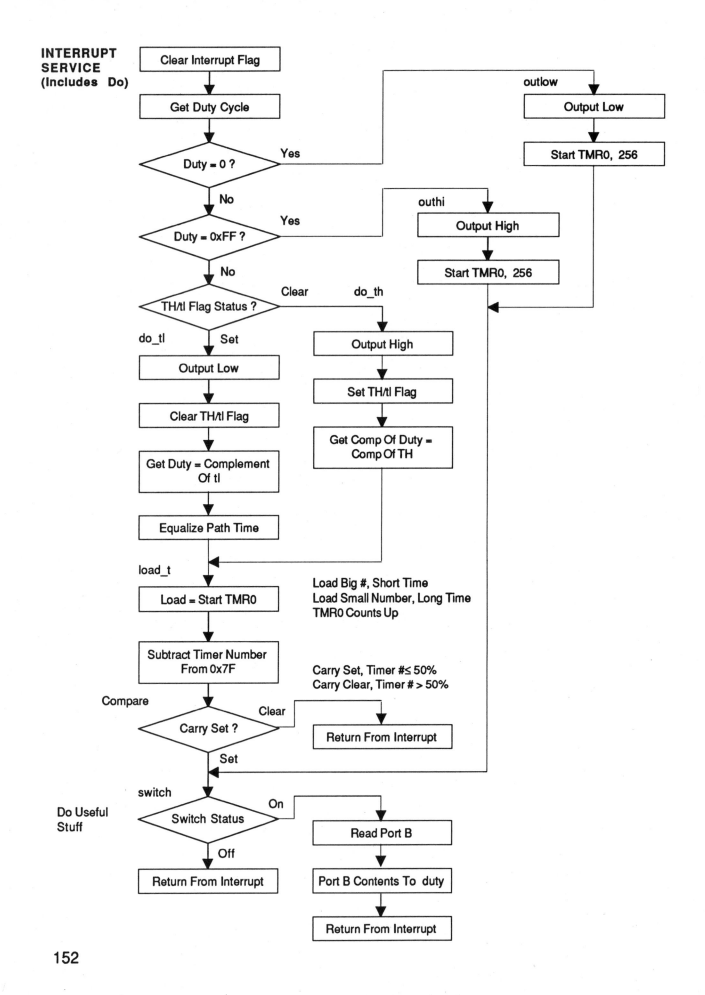

INTERRUPT SERVICE (Includes Do)

Clear Interrupt Flag

Get Duty Cycle

Duty = 0 ?
— Yes → **outlow**: Output Low → Start TMR0, 256

No

Duty = 0xFF ?
— Yes → **outhi**: Output High → Start TMR0, 256

No

TH/tl Flag Status ?
— Clear → **do_th**: Output High → Set TH/tl Flag → Get Comp Of Duty = Comp Of TH

do_tl / Set

Output Low

Clear TH/tl Flag

Get Duty = Complement Of tl

Equalize Path Time

load_t

Load = Start TMR0

Load Big #, Short Time
Load Small Number, Long Time
TMR0 Counts Up

Subtract Timer Number From 0x7F

Carry Set, Timer # ≤ 50%
Carry Clear, Timer # > 50%

Compare

Carry Set ?
— Clear → Return From Interrupt

Set

switch

Do Useful Stuff

Switch Status
— On → Read Port B → Port B Contents To duty → Return From Interrupt

Off

Return From Interrupt

152

```
;======THtlPWM.ASM===================================6/5/97==
          list    p=16c84
          radix   hex
;-------------------------------------------------------------
;         cpu equates (memory map)
tmr0    equ     0x01
status  equ     0x03
porta   equ     0x05
portb   equ     0x06
intcon  equ     0x0b
duty    equ     0x0c
flags   equ     0x0d
opt     equ     0x81
trisa   equ     0x85
trisb   equ     0x86
;-------------------------------------------------------------
;         bit equates
c       equ     0
z       equ     2
rp0     equ     5
t       equ     0
;-------------------------------------------------------------
          org     0x000
          goto    start           ;skip over location pointed to by
                                  ;   interrupt vector
          org     0x004
          goto    iserv
;-------------------------------------------------------------
start   bsf     status,rp0      ;switch to bank 1
          movlw   b'00000010'     ;inputs/outputs
          movwf   trisa
          movlw   b'11111111'     ;inputs
          movwf   trisb
          bcf     status,rp0      ;switch back to bank 0
          bsf     porta,0         ;output high
          bcf     intcon,2        ;clear TMR0 interrupt flag
          bsf     intcon,7        ;enable global interrupts
          bsf     intcon,5        ;enable TMR0 interrupts
          clrwdt                  ;clear WDT prep prescale assign
          bsf     status,rp0      ;switch to bank 1
          movlw   b'11010001'     ;select TMR0, internal
;                                      clock source, prescale 4
          movwf   opt
          bcf     status,rp0      ;return to bank 0
          clrf    tmr0            ;start timer known state
          movlw   0x99            ;initial duty cycle 60 percent
          movwf   duty
          movf    duty,w          ;get duty cycle
          sublw   0xff            ;complement
          movwf   tmr0            ;start TMR0
circle  goto    circle          ;wait for interrupt
;-------------------------------------------------------------
iserv   bcf     intcon,2        ;clear TMR0 interrupt flag
```

```
        movf    duty,w          ;get duty cycle
        sublw   0x00            ;compare w/0x00
        btfsc   status,z
        goto    outlow
        movf    duty,w          ;get duty cycle
        sublw   0xff            ;compare w/0xff
        btfsc   status,z
        goto    outhi
        btfss   flags,t         ;test TH/tl flag
        goto    do_th           ;flag is clear
do_tl   bcf     porta,0         ;output low
        bcf     flags,t         ;flag is set, clear it
        movf    duty,w          ;get duty = comp of tl
        nop                     ;equalize time for paths
        nop
        nop
load_t  movwf   tmr0            ;start TMR0
        sublw   0x7f            ;compare with 50 percent
        btfss   status,c
        retfie
switch  btfsc   porta,1         ;check data ready switch
        retfie
        movf    portb,w         ;switch pressed, read data
        movwf   duty            ;store in duty cycle register
        retfie
;-------------------------------------------------------------
do_th   bsf     porta,0         ;output high
        bsf     flags,t         ;TH/tl flag is clear, set it
        movf    duty,w          ;get duty cycle
        sublw   0xff            ;complement
        goto    load_t
;-------------------------------------------------------------
outlow  bcf     porta,0         ;output low
        clrf    tmr0            ;start TMR0, 256
        goto    switch
;-------------------------------------------------------------
outhi   bsf     porta,0         ;output high
        clrf    tmr0            ;start TMR0, 256
        goto    switch
;-------------------------------------------------------------
        end
;-------------------------------------------------------------
;at blast time, select:
;       memory unprotected
;       watchdog timer disabled (default is enabled)
;       standard crystal (using 4 MHz osc for test) XT
;       power-up timer on
;=============================================================
```

Note that doing other stuff besides PWM includes changing the TH value (tl calculated) to change the PWM duty cycle.

Changing the output voltage may be done in response to program instructions or to sensing something in the outside world such as a pushbutton switch closure or a varying analog signal.

HARDWARE PWM

Another possibility is to use a PIC16/17 with a capture/compare/PWM (CCP) module such as the PIC16C62. The CCP module is designed to do PWM unattended, meaning once the CCP module is programmed to do PWM and the frequency and duty cycle are loaded, PWM occurs with no further intervention from the PIC16/17 except to change duty cycle when needed.

Much shorter periods (higher frequencies) are possible using hardware PWM.

8-BIT SERIAL D/A CONVERTER

The MAX522 from Maxim Integrated Products is a dual 8-bit serial D/A converter in an 8-pin DIP.

The MAX522 has 3 control lines:

- Data in
- Clock
- Chip select ($\overline{CS}$)

Bringing $\overline{CS}$ low starts the serial communication process. Raising $\overline{CS}$ high ends the process. While $\overline{CS}$ is low, 16 bits are clocked in. The first 8 bits are an instruction word (only 4 of the 8 bits are used). The second 8 bits are the data or may not be used. We will see how this works by example.

The table shows the commands for the MAX522.

Function	Control									Data	
					SB	SA				MS	LS
Load Data To DAC B	0	0	1	•	•	0	1	0		8-Bit DAC Data	
Load Data To DAC A	0	0	1	•	•	0	0	1		8-Bit DAC Data	
Load Both DAC Registers With Same Data	0	0	1	•	•	0	1	1		8-Bit DAC Data	
DAC A And DAC B Active	0	0	1	0	0	0	0	0		0 0 0 0 0 0 0 0	
Shut Down DAC B	0	0	1	1	0	0	0	0		0 0 0 0 0 0 0 0	
Shut Down DAC A	0	0	1	0	1	0	0	0		0 0 0 0 0 0 0 0	
Shut Down DAC A And DAC B	0	0	1	1	1	0	0	0		0 0 0 0 0 0 0 0	

Note: "•" means put in a "0" or "1" according to following rules.
       When using a load data command, an active vs. shut down
       bit is included for each DAC (SA and SB bits).

```
-----------------
SA and SB bits
-----------------
SA controls DAC A
SB controls DAC B

1 shuts down
0 activates
```

The tables in the MAXIM data book show uncommitted bits and don't care bits (X's). I made them all "0's". I also blew out all the unassigned commands. Much less intimidating!

Notice that the MSB of the control word must be shifted out of the PIC16 to the MAX522 first.

The LA and LB bits in the control word determine which DAC register (A, B or both) the data goes to. The number "1" loads, "0" does not. The SA and SB bits are used to turn on or shut down the DAC(s) (A, B or both). A "0" activates the selected DAC, "1" shuts it down.

Turning DACs on or off and loading data may be combined into one control word.

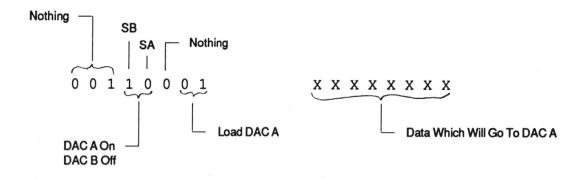

The circuit looks like this:

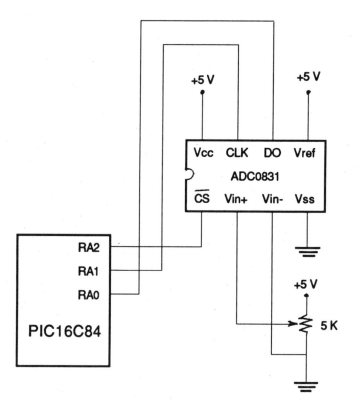

The reference voltage input (Vref) is tied to 5V for this example.

The data codes vs. voltage out goes as follows:

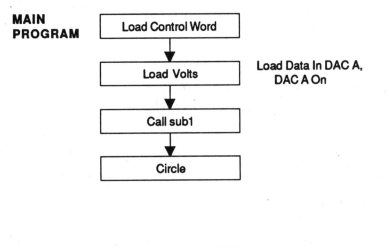

```
------------------------
  Code Input     Volts Out
Bit 7        0
------------------------
    1111 1111      4.98      Ref x (255/256)
    1000 0000      2.50      Ref x (128/256) = Ref/2
    0000 0001      0.02      Ref x (1/256)
    0000 0000      0.00
```

approx. 20mV steps

Output A Voltage Level

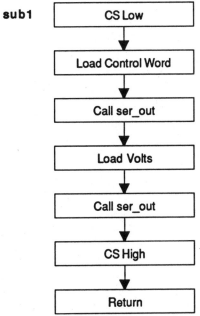

MAIN PROGRAM

| Load Control Word |
| Load Volts | → Load Data In DAC A, DAC A On
| Call sub1 |
| Circle |

sub1

| CS Low |
| Load Control Word |
| Call ser_out |
| Load Volts |
| Call ser_out |
| CS High |
| Return |

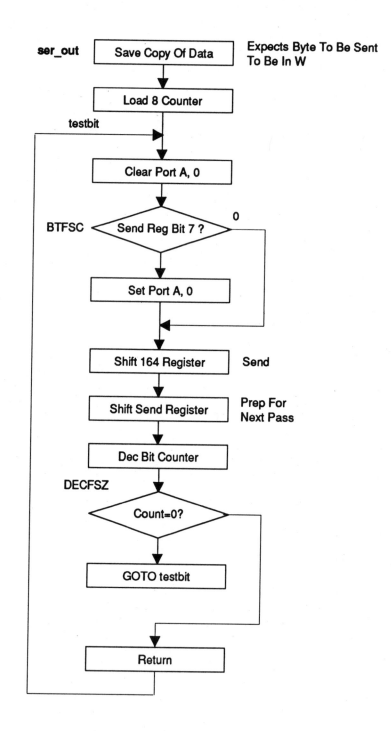

ser_out — Save Copy Of Data — Expects Byte To Be Sent To Be In W

Load 8 Counter

testbit

Clear Port A, 0

BTFSC — Send Reg Bit 7 ? — 0

Set Port A, 0

Shift 164 Register — Send

Shift Send Register — Prep For Next Pass

Dec Bit Counter

DECFSZ — Count=0?

GOTO testbit

Return

```
;======MAX522.ASM=================================5/22/97==
        list    p=16c84
        radix   hex
;----------------------------------------------------------
;       cpu equates (memory map)
status  equ     0x03
porta   equ     0x05
sendreg equ     0x0c
count   equ     0x0d
control equ     0x0e
volts   equ     0x0f
trisa   equ     0x85
;----------------------------------------------------------
;       bit equates
rp0     equ     5
;----------------------------------------------------------
        org     0x000
;
start   bsf     status,rp0   ;switch to bank 1
        movlw   b'00000000'  ;outputs
        movwf   trisa
        bcf     status,rp0   ;switch back to bank 0
        movlw   0x04         ;0000 0100
        movwf   porta        ;initialize port
        movlw   b'00110001'  ;define control word
        movwf   control      ;store - ready for sub
        movlw   b'10000000'  ;2.50 volts out
        movwf   volts        ;store - ready for sub
        call    sub1
circle  goto    circle       ;done
;----------------------------------------------------------
sub1    bcf     porta,2      ;CS low - start serial comm process
        movf    control,w    ;get control word
        call    ser_out      ;to serial out subroutine
        movf    volts,w      ;get data
        call    ser_out      ;to serial out subroutine
        bsf     porta,2      ;CS high - end serial comm process
        return
;----------------------------------------------------------
ser_out movwf   sendreg      ;save copy of byte
        movlw   0x08         ;init 8 counter
        movwf   count
testbit bcf     porta,0      ;default
        btfsc   sendreg,7    ;test byte bit 7
        bsf     porta,0      ;bit is set
shift   bsf     porta,1      ;shift register
        bcf     porta,1
rotlft  rlf     sendreg,f    ;shift byte left
        decfsz  count,f      ;decrement bit counter
        goto    testbit      ;next bit
        return               ;done
;----------------------------------------------------------
        end
;----------------------------------------------------------
```

```
;at blast time, select:
;        memory unprotected
;        watchdog timer disabled (default is enabled)
;        standard crystal (using 4 MHz osc for test) XT
;        power-up timer on
;================================================================
```

Output A Ramp Voltage

A ramp voltage output is created using a loop and by incrementing a counter. The output signal
has a long period due to the overhead involved in communicating serially with the D/A. A
parallel output D/A is lots faster.

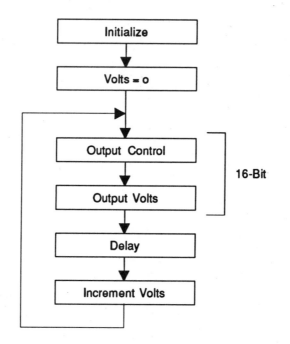

```
;=======RAMP.ASM====================================6/3/97==
        list    p=16c84
        radix   hex
;----------------------------------------------------------------
;       cpu equates (memory map)
status  equ     0x03
porta   equ     0x05
sendreg equ     0x0c
count   equ     0x0d
control equ     0x0e
volts   equ     0x0f
count1  equ     0x10
trisa   equ     0x85
;----------------------------------------------------------------
;       bit equates
rp0     equ     5
;----------------------------------------------------------------
```

```
        org     0x000
;
start   bsf     status,rp0   ;switch to bank 1
        movlw   b'00000000'  ;outputs
        movwf   trisa
        bcf     status,rp0   ;switch back to bank 0
        movlw   0x04         ;0000 0100
        movwf   porta        ;initialize port
        movlw   b'00110001'  ;define control word
        movwf   control      ;store - ready for sub
        movlw   b'00000000'  ;0 volts out to start
        movwf   volts        ;store - ready for sub
loop    call    sub1
        call    del_10       ;delay
        incf    volts        ;increment voltage
        goto    loop
;--------------------------------------------------------------
sub1    bcf     porta,2      ;CS low - start serial comm process
        movf    control,w    ;get control word
        call    ser_out      ;to serial out subroutine
        movf    volts,w      ;get data
        call    ser_out      ;to serial out subroutine
        bsf     porta,2      ;CS high - end serial comm process
        return
;--------------------------------------------------------------
ser_out movwf   sendreg      ;save copy of byte
        movlw   0x08         ;init 8 counter
        movwf   count
testbit bcf     porta,0      ;default
        btfsc   sendreg,7    ;test byte bit 7
        bsf     porta,0      ;bit is set
shift   bsf     porta,1      ;shift register
        bcf     porta,1
rotlft  rlf     sendreg,f    ;shift byte left
        decfsz  count,f      ;decrement bit counter
        goto    testbit      ;next bit
        return               ;done
;--------------------------------------------------------------
del_10  movlw   0x03         ;approx 9 cycles (decimal)
        movwf   count1       ;load counter
repeat  decfsz  count1,f     ;decrement counter
        goto    repeat       ;not 0
        return               ;counter 0, ends delay
;--------------------------------------------------------------
        end
;--------------------------------------------------------------
;at blast time, select:
;       memory unprotected
;       watchdog timer disabled (default is enabled)
;       standard crystal (using 4 MHz osc for test) XT
;       power-up timer on
;==============================================================
```

Notice that it is possible to make V_{min} and V_{max} any level between 0 and 5 volts and to adjust the frequency via time delays between output level changes.

Output A Sine Wave

A sine wave voltage output may be generated by using a lookup table to store the voltage values for each point in time.

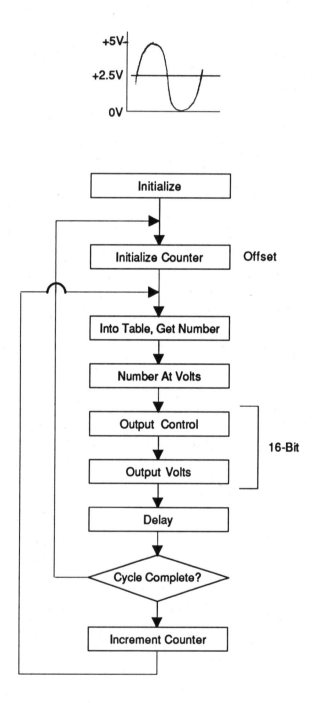

```
;=======SINE.ASM====================================6/3/97==
        list    p=16c84
        radix   hex
;----------------------------------------------------------------
;       cpu equates (memory map)
pc      equ     0x02
status  equ     0x03
porta   equ     0x05
sendreg equ     0x0c
count   equ     0x0d
control equ     0x0e
volts   equ     0x0f
count1  equ     0x10
offctr  equ     0x11
trisa   equ     0x85
;----------------------------------------------------------------
;       bit equates
z       equ     2
rp0     equ     5
;----------------------------------------------------------------
        org     0x000
;
start   goto    do_it           ;jump over table
;----------------------------------------------------------------
table   addwf   pc,f            ;add offset to program counter
        retlw   0x80            ;2.50 volts
        retlw   0x95            ;2.94
        retlw   0xad            ;3.36
        retlw   0xc1            ;3.75
        retlw   0xd3            ;4.11
        retlw   0xe2            ;4.41
        retlw   0xef            ;4.67
        retlw   0xf8            ;4.85
        retlw   0xfd            ;4.96
        retlw   0xff            ;4.98
        retlw   0xfd            ;4.96
        retlw   0xf8            ;4.85
        retlw   0xef            ;4.67
        retlw   0xe2            ;4.41
        retlw   0xd3            ;4.11
        retlw   0xc1            ;3.75
        retlw   0xad            ;3.36
        retlw   0x95            ;2.94
        retlw   0x80            ;2.50
        retlw   0x6a            ;2.06
        retlw   0x54            ;1.64
        retlw   0x40            ;1.25
        retlw   0x2e            ;0.90
        retlw   0x1e            ;0.59
        retlw   0x11            ;0.33
        retlw   0x08            ;0.15
        retlw   0x02            ;0.04
        retlw   0x00            ;0.00
        retlw   0x02            ;0.04
```

```
        retlw     0x08          ;0.15
        retlw     0x11          ;0.33
        retlw     0x1e          ;0.59
        retlw     0x2e          ;0.90
        retlw     0x40          ;1.25
        retlw     0x54          ;1.64
        retlw     0x6a          ;2.06
;----------------------------------------------------------------
do_it   bsf       status,rp0    ;switch to bank 1
        movlw     b'00000000'   ;outputs
        movwf     trisa
        bcf       status,rp0    ;switch back to bank 0
        movlw     0x04          ;0000 0100
        movwf     porta         ;initialize port
        movlw     b'00110001'   ;define control word
        movwf     control       ;store - ready for sub
cycle   clrf      offctr        ;clear table offset counter
step    movf      offctr,w      ;get offset count
        call      table         ;get volts from table
        movwf     volts         ;store in "volts"
        call      sub1          ;send volts to a/d
        call      del_10        ;delay
        movf      offctr,w      ;get offset count
        sublw     0x23          ;compare - cycle complete?
        btfsc     status,z
        goto      cycle
        incf      offctr        ;increment offset counter
        goto      step
;----------------------------------------------------------------
sub1    bcf       porta,2       ;CS low - start serial comm process
        movf      control,w     ;get control word
        call      ser_out       ;to serial out subroutine
        movf      volts,w       ;get data
        call      ser_out       ;to serial out subroutine
        bsf       porta,2       ;CS high - end serial comm process
        return
;----------------------------------------------------------------
ser_out movwf     sendreg       ;save copy of byte
        movlw     0x08          ;init 8 counter
        movwf     count
testbit bcf       porta,0       ;default
        btfsc     sendreg,7     ;test byte bit 7
        bsf       porta,0       ;bit is set
shift   bsf       porta,1       ;shift register
        bcf       porta,1
rotlft  rlf       sendreg,f     ;shift byte left
        decfsz    count,f       ;decrement bit counter
        goto      testbit       ;next bit
        return                  ;done
;----------------------------------------------------------------
del_10  movlw     0x03          ;approx 9 cycles (decimal)
        movwf     count1        ;load counter
repeat  decfsz    count1,f      ;decrement counter
        goto      repeat        ;not 0
```

```
        return                  ;counter 0, ends delay
;--------------------------------------------------------------
        end
;--------------------------------------------------------------
;at blast time, select:
;       memory unprotected
;       watchdog timer disabled (default is enabled)
;       standard crystal (using 4 MHz osc for test) XT
;       power-up timer on
;==============================================================
```

SENSORS - ANALOG VOLTAGE OUTPUT

Many sensors such as photocells and thermistors have a voltage output. A light level or temperature is represented by or corresponds to a voltage. Our objective is to interface sensors of this type with a PIC16. This may require some analog signal conditioning.

In most cases, we will simply use a potentiometer to generate a voltage for test purposes.

LM335 TEMPERATURE SENSOR

For a little more fun and experience, we will use a LM335 temperature sensor from National Semiconductor for a couple of experiments. It is simple, inexpensive and readily available. It will provide a vehicle for learning how to deal with sensors.

The LM335 acts like a zener diode with a breakdown voltage directly proportional to absolute temperature. The output voltage of the basic LM335 circuit is 2.73 volts at 0 °C. The sensor has a theoretical output of 0V at 0°K = -273° C. Its output is 10mV/°K, hence the 2.73V output at 273°K= 0°C.

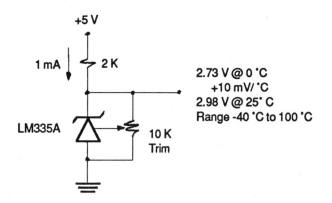

2.73 V @ 0 °C
+10 mV/ °C
2.98 V @ 25° C
Range -40 °C to 100 °C

Accuracy without trimming is +/– 1°C
Accuracy with trimming
     Single point calibration
     Better than+/- 1°C over –40°C to + 100°C operating range
Will operate at current range of 400 μA to 5mA

TO - 92

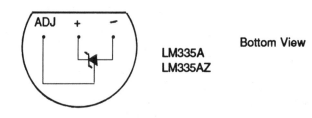

LM335A
LM335AZ

Bottom View

As an experiment, let's lay the ground work for designing a PIC16-based thermometer with a temperature range of 0°C to 50°C (32°F to 122°F).

```
                        LM335
      °C    °F      Voltage Out
      ---   ---     -----------
       0    32         2.73
      50    122        3.23
```

To obtain the voltage output for the LM335 at a given temperature in °C:

$$+ \, °C \, \frac{273}{}$$

$$T \times 10^{-2} = LM335 \; Vout$$

Example:

$$54 \; F = 12.2 \; °C$$

```
      273
     +12.2
     285.2  ──►  2.85 volts
```

You may have noticed that for our temperature range, the output voltage swing is only 0.5 volt. Since the A/D converters we will be looking at accept a wider range at their input and also because it would be convenient to have 0V represent 0°C, we need to look at some signal conditioning methods.

OFFSET AND SCALE

DC offset of a transducer's output signal is required if the output is not zero volts when the physical variable (temperature, etc.) is at the bottom of its range (or the range you are interested in). DC offset is also required if part of a transducer's range is to be magnified to improve resolution.

Scaling transforms a transducer's output range to the input voltage of the A/D converter (typically 0 to 5V DC).

Life is simpler if the offset or level shifting operation is done first and scaling (span adjustment) is done second.

THREE AMPLIFIER DESIGN

Following is a circuit for providing offset and scale.

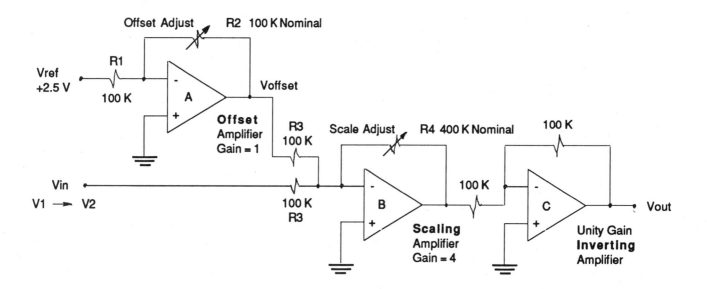

This is not the simplest possible circuit, as you will soon see, but it is "intuitive". It has three main functions in three separate blocks laid out so you can readily understand it.

The offset amplifier inverts the reference voltage (V_{ref}) and applies it to the inverting input of the scaling amplifier where it is added to the transducer voltage. The gain of the offset amplifier is adjusted so that its output is equal in magnitude to the minimum transducer voltage (V_1) and opposite in polarity. Adding them together results in a zero volt input to the scaling amplifier. The two R_3 resistors provide a summing junction at the inverting input of the scaling amplifier.

170

The reference voltage must be stable. A resistor voltage divider will work if the application is non critical and the power supply is stable. An LM336 voltage reference is better. It has a 2.5V output and is stable.

The scaling amplifier sums V_{in} from the transducer and V_{offset}. The gain of the scaling amplifier expands the transducer output voltage range to the input range of the A/D converter.

```
output = (input - offset)gain

input voltage range    V₁ ⟶ V₂
output voltage range   0V ⟶ 5V = range of A/D
```

$$V_{out} = \left[V_{in} + \left(-\frac{R_2}{R_1} \times V_{ref} \right) \right] \times \left(-\frac{R_4}{R_3} \right)$$

```
gain of A is  - R₂   inverting
                R₁
```

```
gain of B is  - R₄   inverting
                R₃
```

```
Adjust Vref first
To adjust offset, apply V₁ volts to Vin and adjust gain of
     offset amplifier (vary R₂) until Vout = 0V.
```

$$V_{offset} = -\frac{R_2}{R_1} V_{ref}$$

```
Vref is usually = 1 to 5 volts

To adjust scaling (span), apply V₂ volts to Vin and adjust
     gain of scaling amplifier (vary R₄) until Vout = Vmax of
     the A/D (usually 5V).

     With Vin = V₂:
```

$$V_{out} = V_{max\ A/D} = (V_2 - V_1) \times \left(-\frac{R_4}{R_3} \right)$$

```
Gains of less than unity are possible in "B" amplifier

Zin for A = R₁
Zin for B = R₃
```

The output voltage of the scaling amplifier is inverted with respect to the input, so a third amplifier is added to turn this voltage right-side-up. The gain of the third stage amplifier is unity.

To try all this out, let's assume a transducer output voltage range of 2.5 to 3.75 volts. We will use a reference voltage = 2.5V.

The ever-popular 741C op-amp is shown. The 1458 is two 741C's in a single 8-pin mini-DIP and may be used instead. Other dual-supply op-amps will work.

A 5K pot is used as an adjustable voltage reference and another 5K pot is used to generate the "transducer" output voltage.

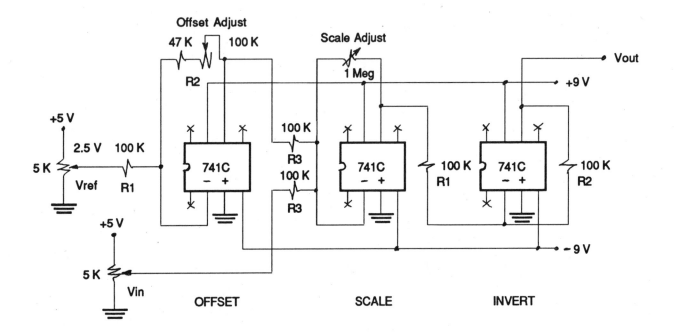

First adjust V_{ref} = 2.5V

To adjust offset:
        Apply $V_{in\ min}$
        Adjust gain of offset amplifier until V_{out} = 0V

To adjust scaling = span:
        Apply $V_{in\ max}$
        Adjust gain of scaling amplifier until V_{out} = V_{max} of
                the A/D = 5V

Three op-amp offset and scale:

```
Adjust V_ref        = 2.5 volts
Adjust offset       V_in = 2.5 V,  V_out = 0V
Adjust scale        V_in = 3.75V,  V_out = 5V
```

V_{in} (volts)	V_{out} (volts)
2.5	0.0
2.7	0.8
3.0	2.0
3.3	3.15
3.5	3.95
3.75	5.0

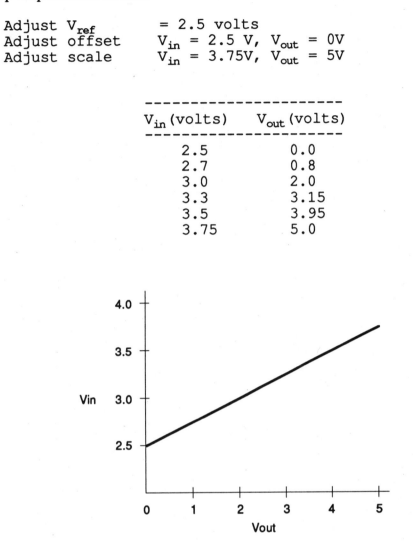

The result is a straight line relationship between V_{in} and V_{out}. The 1.25 volt input range is expanded to 0 to 5 volts offset to 0 volts when $V_{in} = 2.5$V.

SINGLE AMPLIFIER DESIGN

Offset and scaling may be accomplished using a single op-amp with a 5V supply. The output is scaled, but inverted. This can be turned right-side-up in software by subtracting the binary output from 256 (assuming 0 to 5V A/D input and 8-bits).

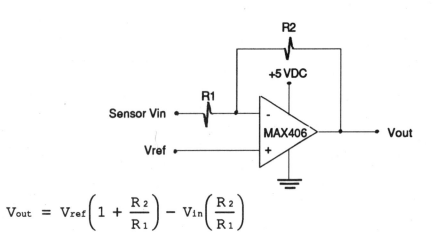

$$V_{out} = V_{ref}\left(1 + \frac{R_2}{R_1}\right) - V_{in}\left(\frac{R_2}{R_1}\right)$$

V1 will be in the range of the transducer output.

At $V_{in\ max}$, want V_{out} to be = 0V

So $$V_{ref}\left(1 + \frac{R_2}{R_1}\right) = V_{in\ max}\left(\frac{R_2}{R_1}\right)$$

At $V_{in\ min}$, want V_{out} to be = 5V

So $$5 = V_{ref}\left(1 + \frac{R_2}{R_1}\right) - V_{in\ min}\left(\frac{R_2}{R_1}\right)$$

Let $\dfrac{R_2}{R_1} = R$

$V_{ref}(1 + R) = V_{in\ max}\ R$

$5 = V_{ref}(1 + R) - V_{in\ min}\ R$

$V_{ref}(1 + R) = V_{in\ min}\ R - 5$

$V_{in\ max}\ R = V_{in\ min}\ R - 5$

$R(V_{in\ max} - V_{in\ min}) = -5$

$$R = -\frac{5}{V_{in\ max} - V_{in\ min}}$$

Assuming a transducer output range of 2.5 to 3.75 volts as in the previous example:

$$R = -\frac{5}{3.75 - 2.5} = -4$$

Let $R_1 = 100$ K (much larger than sensor)
Let $R_2 = 400$ K

$$V_{ref}\left(1 + \frac{R_2}{R_1}\right) = V_{in\ max}\left(\frac{R_2}{R_1}\right)$$

$$V_{ref}(1 + 4) = 3.75(4)$$

$$V_{ref} = 3\,volts$$

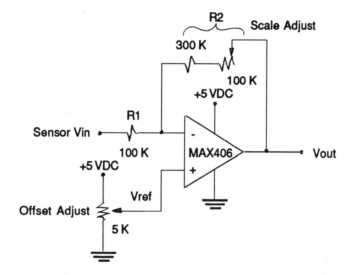

$$V_{in\ max} \longrightarrow V_{out} = 0V$$
$$V_{in} = \text{range of sensor output}$$

Design for range
      Sample   2.5 $\longrightarrow$ 3.75 volts
               $V_1 \longrightarrow V_2$
    $R_1 = 100K$
    $R_2 = 400K$
    $V_{ref} = 3$ volts nominal

To set scaling = span:
    V_{in} max applied to V_{in} (3.75V)   Adjust gain so $V_{out} = 0V$
To set offset = zero
    V_{in} min applied to V_{in} (2.5V)   Adjust V_2 so $V_{out} = 5V$

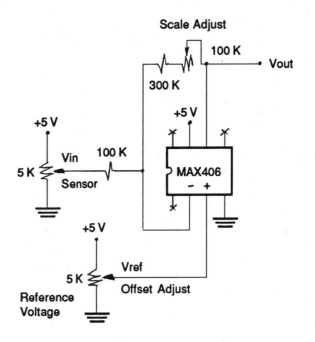

Single op-amp offset and scale:

```
Adjust scale = span first (3 volts at V_ref).
Adjust offset = zero second (approx 470K).
```

V_{in} (volts)	V_{out} (volts)
2.5	4.9
2.7	4.2
3.0	3.05
3.2	2.25
3.5	1.05
3.75	0.05

Input range
2.5 $\longrightarrow$ 3.75V

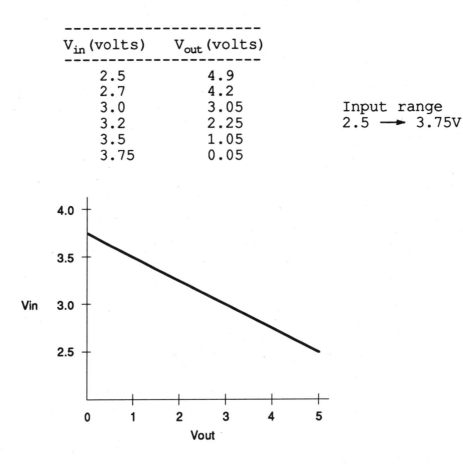

Again the result is a straight line relationship between V_{in} and V_{out}. The 1.25 volt input range is expanded to 0 to 5 volts offset to 0 volts when $V_{in} = 2.5V$.

WHY 1 OP-AMP vs 3 OP-AMPS?

The single op-amp design has far fewer components and one power supply which is the 5 volt logic supply but it is less intuitive (for learning purposes) and has an inverted binary output. Inverting the output in software is simple--just complement it (0's to 1's, 1's to 0's). This assumes an 8-bit A/D.

ANALOG TO DIGITAL CONVERSION

Analog to digital (A/D) conversion is essential to PIC'n because PIC16's can only process digital information. Analog signals, usually voltages from sensors, must be converted to binary numbers digestible by the PIC16. As usual, this may be done by one of several methods with the usual cost/accuracy/resolution/PCB in^2/etc. tradeoffs to be made.

PIC16's can measure resistance in a crude way using one digital I/O pin. The PIC16C7X series parts have A/D converters built in. A variety of serial A/D converters are available. We will look at examples of these three possibilities.

PIC16 PIN AND RC TIME CONSTANT

An interesting characteristic of a PIC16 digital I/O pin is that there is a threshold voltage below which an input is recognized as low and above which it is recognized as high. You can measure it easily using a potentiometer, an LED with series resistor and a DVM. I used 8 LED's here to avoid rewiring for experiments which appear later in this chapter.

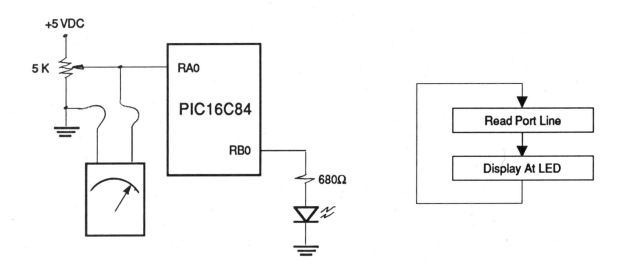

Initially adjust the voltage at the pin to a little less than 1 volt. The voltage input will be interpreted as low. Then slowly increase the voltage until the LED's turn on. I call that voltage V_{flip}. V_{flip} will vary with power supply voltage and slightly from device to device. By my measurement, V_{flip} is around 1.23 volts for Vdd = 5 V

```
;======VFLIP.ASM===================================6/6/97==
        list    p=16c84
        radix   hex
;------------------------------------------------------------
;       cpu equates (memory map)
status  equ     0x03
porta   equ     0x05
portb   equ     0x06
trisa   equ     0x85
trisb   equ     0x86
;------------------------------------------------------------
;       bit equates
rp0     equ     5
;------------------------------------------------------------
        org     0x000
;
start   bsf     status,rp0  ;switch to bank 1
        movlw   b'00000000' ;outputs
        movwf   trisb
        movlw   b'00000001' ;input/outputs
        movwf   trisa
        bcf     status,rp0  ;switch back to bank 0
        clrf    portb       ;initialize, LED's off
loop    btfss   porta,0     ;look at input
        goto    outlo       ;display input status
        bsf     portb,0     ;   at port b, bit 0
        goto    loop
outlo   bcf     portb,0
        goto    loop
;------------------------------------------------------------
        end
;------------------------------------------------------------
;at blast time, select:
;       memory unprotected
;       watchdog timer disabled (default is enabled)
;       standard crystal (using 4 MHz osc for test) XT
;       power-up timer on
;============================================================
```

Measuring Resistance Via PIC16 Pin And RC Time Constant

Armed with this information, we can now measure resistance using one PIC16 pin! We can do this by charging a capacitor through a resistor of unknown value and measuring the time it takes for the voltage across the capacitor to reach V_{flip}. In advance, we will need to run a bunch of experiments using resistors (or pot) of known value. We will use TMR0 to measure time.

The first step in the measurement process is to discharge the capacitor. This is accomplished by making the pin an output followed by outputting a "0". Then, after a suitable time for discharging the capacitor has elapsed, the pin is made an input and TMR0 is started. The program watches the pin. When the voltage on the pin reaches V_{flip}, the timer is read. The time interval is proportional to resistance.

Following are a program listing and test data for:

- PIC16C84
- C = 0.1 µf
- Prescaler = 4
- 4.00 MHz clock oscillator

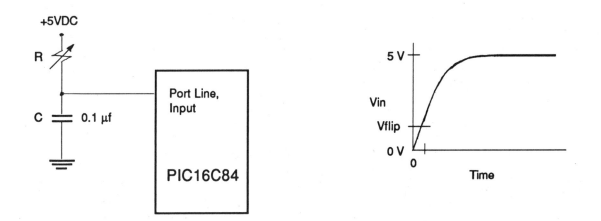

```
;=======RCTIME.ASM================================6/6/97==
        list    p=16c84
        radix   hex
;-----------------------------------------------------------
;       cpu equates (memory map)
tmr0    equ     0x01
status  equ     0x03
porta   equ     0x05
portb   equ     0x06
intcon  equ     0x0b
opt     equ     0x81
trisa   equ     0x85
trisb   equ     0x86
;-----------------------------------------------------------
;       bit equates
rp0     equ     5
```

```
;--------------------------------------------------------------
        org     0x000
        goto    start           ;skip over location pointed to by
                                ;   interrupt vector
        org     0x004
        goto    iserv
;--------------------------------------------------------------
start   bsf     status,rp0      ;switch to bank 1
        movlw   b'00000000'     ;outputs
        movwf   trisa
        movwf   trisb
        bcf     status,rp0      ;switch back to bank 0
        clrf    portb           ;LED's off
        bcf     intcon,2        ;clear TMR0 interrupt flag
        bsf     intcon,7        ;enable global interrupts
        bsf     intcon,5        ;enable TMR0 interrupts
        clrwdt                  ;clear WDT prep prescale assign
        bsf     status,rp0      ;switch to bank 1
        movlw   b'11010001'     ;select TMR0, internal
;                                       clock source, prescale 4
        movwf   opt
        bcf     status,rp0      ;return to bank 0
        bcf     porta,0         ;discharge cap
        clrf    tmr0            ;start timer, known state
dischg  btfss   tmr0,7          ;time for cap discharge
        goto    dischg
        bsf     status,rp0      ;switch to bank 1
        bsf     trisa,0         ;porta, bit 0 input
        bcf     status,rp0      ;switch back to bank 0
        clrf    tmr0            ;start TMR0
flip    btfss   porta,0         ;look at input
        goto    flip            ;input low
        movf    tmr0,w          ;input flipped,read timer
        movwf   portb           ;display time at port B
        bcf     intcon,5        ;disable TMR0 interrupts
circle  goto    circle          ;done
;--------------------------------------------------------------
iserv   bcf     intcon,5        ;disable further TMR0 interrupts
        movlw   0xaa
        movwf   portb           ;display timer overflow condition
idle    goto    idle


;--------------------------------------------------------------
        end
;--------------------------------------------------------------
;at blast time, select:
;       memory unprotected
;       watchdog timer disabled (default is enabled)
;       standard crystal (using 4 MHz osc for test) XT
;       power-up timer on
;==============================================================
```

The following graph shows resistance vs. counts from TMR0. The "resistance" in an application could be a potentiometer, thermistor, or photo cell. The counts could be proportional to position, temperature, or light level.

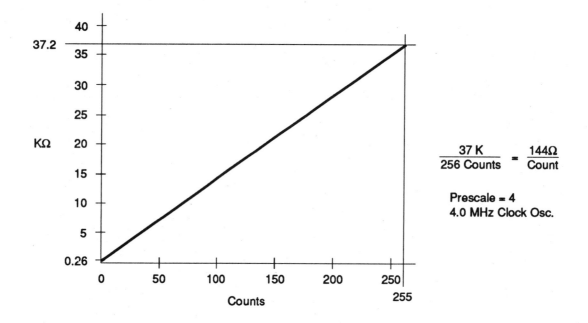

$$\frac{37\,K}{256\ \text{Counts}} = \frac{144\Omega}{\text{Count}}$$

Prescale = 4
4.0 MHz Clock Osc.

A/D Via PIC16 Digital I/O Pin And RC Time Constant

Voltage can be measured in a similar way. R and C are fixed and the time to charge the capacitor to V_{flip} is proportional to the voltage applied to the resistor.

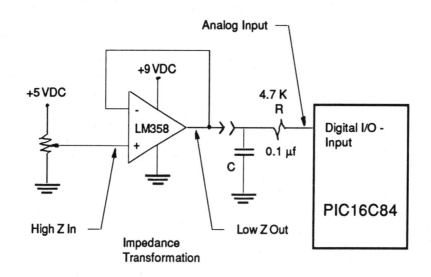

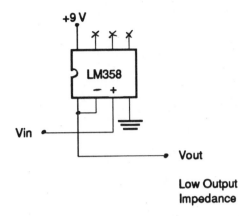

Low Output
Impedance

The output impedance of the source must be small compared to R. I used a pot to derive the voltage and an op-amp for impedance transformation.

The program is the same as for the resistance measurement example. A plot of counts vs. voltage is shown. Notice that it is very nonlinear (as you might expect).

There is nothing magic about the values I chose for R, C and prescaler division ratio (except that they work I suppose). This is merely an example to illustrate the concept. There is not much resolution high on the curve. Measuring voltages in the range of 1.5 to 2.5 V would work well. Resolution could be improved by reducing the prescaler division ratio or by increasing the clock oscillator frequency to 5.00 MHz or both. TMR0 could be allowed to roll over with the number of times being counted.

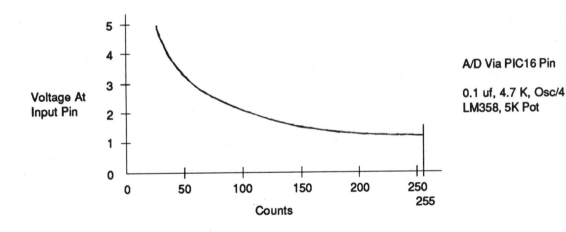

A/D Via PIC16 Pin

0.1 uf, 4.7 K, Osc/4
LM358, 5K Pot

SERIAL 8-BIT A/D CONVERTER - ADC0831

The ADC0831 from National Semiconductor is an 8-bit serial single channel successive approx-imation A/D converter in an 8-pin DIP.

It has built-in zero and span capability, but we won't use it right away. It has a 0-5V input range operating with a single 5V supply. The A/D may be located right next to the sensor where it will transmit noise-immune digital data to the PIC16.

The ADC0831 has 3 control lines:

- Data out
- Clock
- Chip select $\overline{CS}$

Data is shifted out MSB first

Referring to the timing diagram, pulling $\overline{CS}$ low starts initializing the chip for an A/D conversion. The chips goes through its setup process which is completed when the clock line goes high (minimum T_{setup} 250 ns). When the clock line goes low, the conversion process starts. A leading "0" appears on the data out (D_0) line. The clock line is used to shift out 8 data bits.

The clock rate or frequency (f_{clk}) must be between 10 KHz and 400 KHz. We will flow chart the program and get a rough estimate of frequency from that.

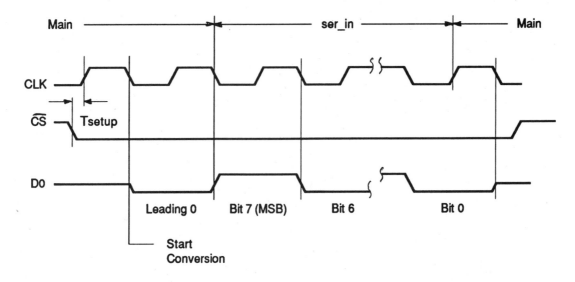

For our initial experiment, we will use the following circuit:

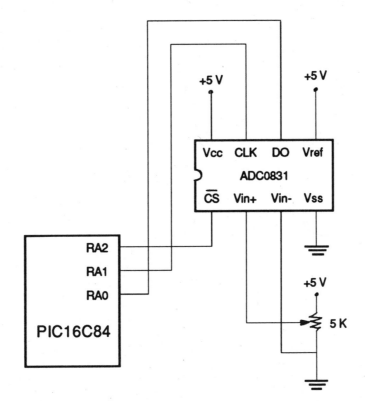

$\overline{CS}$ is for selecting the chip and for starting the conversion. CLK is for shifting data.

MAIN PROGRAM

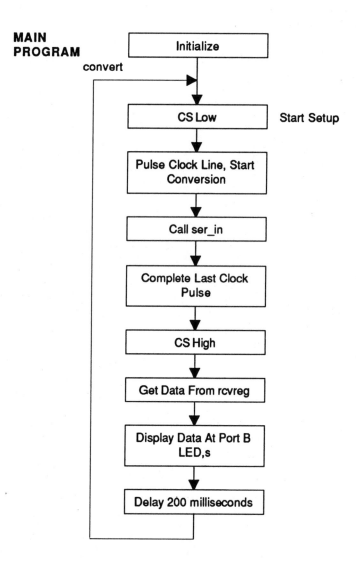

convert

Initialize

CS Low — Start Setup

Pulse Clock Line, Start Conversion

Call ser_in

Complete Last Clock Pulse

CS High

Get Data From rcvreg

Display Data At Port B LED,s

Delay 200 milliseconds

```
Adjust Pot
Monitor Vin via DVM
Watch LED's
Dial in 0x80 (10000000) using pot
Voltage Vin should be 1/2 Vref
```

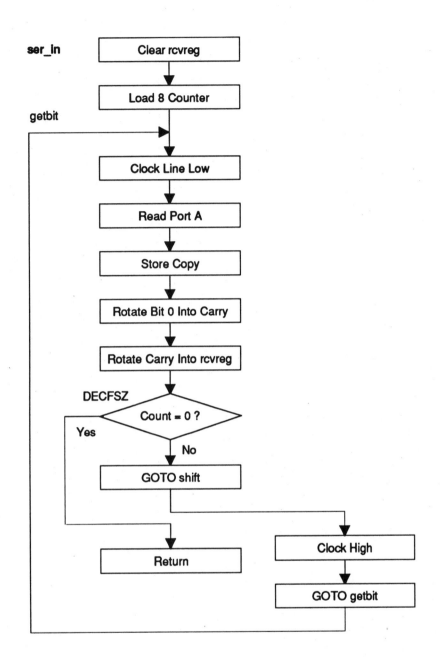

The clock frequency is not symmetrical as shown in previous timing diagrams. It is roughly 77 KHz.

$$T = 13\mu \text{ sec}$$

$$\text{frequency} = \frac{1}{T} = \frac{1}{13 \times 10^{-6}} = 77\,\text{KHz}$$

```
;=======ADC0831.ASM===============================5/27/97==
          list    p=16c84
          radix   hex
;----------------------------------------------------------
;         cpu equates (memory map)
porta     equ     0x05
portb     equ     0x06
status    equ     0x03
rcvreg    equ     0x0c
count     equ     0x0d
temp      equ     0x0e
ncount    equ     0x10
mcount    equ     0x11
trisa     equ     0x85
trisb     equ     0x86
;----------------------------------------------------------
;         bit equates
c         equ     0
z         equ     2
rp0       equ     5
;----------------------------------------------------------
          org     0x000
;
start     bsf     status,rp0   ;switch to bank 1
          movlw   b'00000001'  ;bit 0 = input
          movwf   trisa
          movlw   b'00000000'  ;outputs
          movwf   trisb
          bcf     status,rp0   ;switch back to bank 0
          movlw   0x04         ;0000 0100
          movwf   porta        ;initialize
          nop                  ;delay
convert   bcf     porta,2      ;T setup, CS low
          nop
          bsf     porta,1      ;clock high
          nop                  ;delay
          bcf     porta,1      ;clock low - start conversion
          nop                  ;delay
          bsf     porta,1      ;clock high
          call    ser_in       ;to serial input subroutine
          bsf     porta,1      ;last clock pulse
          nop
          bcf     porta,1      ;clock low
          nop
          bsf     porta,2      ;CS high
          movf    rcvreg,w     ;get data
          movwf   portb        ;display data via LED'S
          call    debounce     ;wait a while (200 milliseconds)
          goto    convert      ;look at voltage again
;----------------------------------------------------------
ser_in    clrf    rcvreg       ;clear receive register
          movlw   0x08         ;init 8 counter
          movwf   count
```

```
getbit  bcf      porta,1      ;clock low
        nop                   ;delay 1 instr cycle
        movf     porta,w      ;read port A
        movwf    temp         ;store copy
        rrf      temp,f       ;rotate bit into carry flag
        rlf      rcvreg,f     ;rotate carry flag into rcvreg
        decfsz   count,f      ;decrement counter
        goto     shift
        return                ;done
shift   bsf      porta,1      ;clock high
        goto     getbit       ;again
;----------------------------------------------------------------
debounce movlw   0xff         ;M
        movwf    mcount       ;to M counter
loadn   movlw    0xff         ;N
        movwf    ncount       ;to N counter
decn    decfsz   ncount,f     ;decrement N
        goto     decn         ;again
        decfsz   mcount,f     ;decrement M
        goto     loadn        ;again
        return                ;done
;----------------------------------------------------------------
        end
;----------------------------------------------------------------
;at blast time, select:
;      memory unprotected
;      watchdog timer disabled (default is enabled)
;      standard crystal (using 4 MHz osc for test) XT
;      power-up timer on
;================================================================
```

ADC0831 Built-In Offset And Scale

The ADC0831 has built-in offset and scale capability. The differential analog voltage input allows offsetting the analog zero input voltage value. Also, the voltage reference input can be adjusted to allow encoding any smaller analog voltage span to the full 8 bits of resolution.

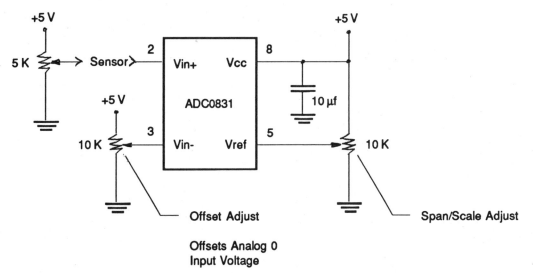

Try an input range of 2.5 to 3.75 volts as an example.

```
With the example code running and observing the port B LED's:

2.5 volts at V_in+

    Adjust offset to just get 00000000 to 00000001
            transition

3.75 volts at V_in+

    Adjust scale to get 11111110 to 11111111 transition
```

TEMPERATURE MEASUREMENT USING LM335 TEMPERATURE SENSOR

Three Op-Amp Offset And Scale

If you wish, you can try out your three op-amp offset and scale circuit in conjunction with the serial A/D converter.

```
0 to 50 °C thermometer (32 to 122 °F)
```

°F	°K	°C	LM335 V_{out}	Amp V_{out}
32	273	0	2.73	0
122	323	50	3.23	5

```
To get LM335 V_out, add °C to 273.  Multiply result x10⁻² to
    get LM335 V_out.
```

To get LM335 V_{out}, add °C to 273. Multiply result $\times 10^{-2}$ to get LM335 V_{out}.

```
Example:

    54 F = 12.2 °C

    273
  + 12.2
    285.2  ───▶  2.85 volts  ───▶  1.2 volts at amplifier V_out
```

ADC0831/LM335 TEMPERATURE MEASUREMENT

The LM335 may be interfaced directly with a LM335 temperature sensor making use of the built-in offest and scale capabilities of the ADC0831.

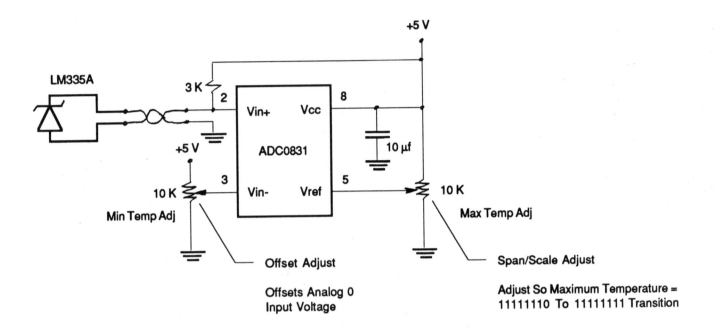

The A/D may be located right next to the LM335 sensor which will transmit noise immune digital data to the microcontroller. See the National Semiconductor "Data Acquisition Linear Devices" data book for more information.

PIC16C71 ON-BOARD A/D

The PIC16C71 has 4 pins which may (or may not) be used as A/D channels. These are port A, bits 3,2,1,0. The four analog inputs are multiplexed into one sample and hold circuit. The output of the sample and hold is the input to a successive approximation converter. The reference voltage may be the 5 volt supply to the PIC16C71 (range 0-5V) or an external reference (range 3.0 to Vcc +0.3 volts) via pin RA3. If an external reference is used, only 3 A/D channels are available.

Important electrical specs are:

```
V_ain    V_ss-0.3v to V_ref      (0 to 5V if V_ref = logic supply)
V_ref    3.0V to V_dd+0.3V
Maximum source impedance 10K
```

We will make a simplifying assumption about timing by assuming it is not critical to get the A/D conversion done in the shortest time possible. We will use a 4 mHz clock oscillator. The clock frequency is divided to obtain the clock source for the converter function. The data book talks about clock period (clock period - T_{OSC}), so it may be better to think of the clock period being multiplied rather than clock oscillator frequently being divided. We will use the largest clock period multiplier which is 32. If you develop an application where time is of the essence, you will need to refer to the data book for timing considerations/options/calculations. Our objective here is to simplify matters and to get something working.

Two registers are used to control the A/D converters and one is used to hold the result of the conversion.

ADCON1

Controls the port pin functions.

7	6	5	4	3	2	1	0	
						PCFG1	PCFG0	0x88

Bits7-2 are unimplemented, read as "0"
Bits 0 and 1 are "0's" after power-on reset

```
------------------------------------------------
PCFG1 & PCFG0   RA3   RA2   RA1   RA0   Vref
------------------------------------------------
       00        A     A     A     A    Vdd
       01       Vref   A     A     A    RA3
       10        D     D     A     A    Vdd
       11        D     D     D     D
```

A = analog input
D = digital I/O

ADCON0

Controls the A/D module.

R/W	R/W	U	R/W	R/W	R/W	R/W	R/W	
ADCS1	ADCS0	__(1)	CHS1	CHS0	GO/$\overline{\text{DONE}}$	ADIF	ADON	0x08

7   0

R = Readable bit
W = Writeable bit
U = Unimplemented bit, read as "0"
Power on reset 00000000

Bits 7,6   **ADCS1:ADCS0:** A/D conversion clock select bits
00 = Fosc/2
01 = Fosc/8
10 = Fosc/32
11 = Frc (clock derived from RC oscillator)

Bit 5   Unimplemented, read as "0"

Bits 4,3   **CHS2:CHS0:** Analog channel select bits
00 = channel 0 (RA0/AN0)
01 = channel 1 (RA1/AN1)
10 = channel 2 (RA2/AN2)
11 = channel 3 (RA3/AN3)

Bit 2   **GO/$\overline{\text{DONE}}$:** A/D conversion status bit
If ADON bit = 1
     1 = A/D conversion in progress (setting this
        bit starts the A/D conversion)
     0 = A/D conversion not in progress (this bit
        is automatically cleared by hardware when
        the A/D conversion is complete)

Bit 1   **ADIF:** A/D conversion complete interrupt flag bit
1 = conversion complete (must be cleared in
     software)
0 = conversion is not complete

Bit 0   **ADON:** A/D on bit
1 = A/D converter module is operating
0 = A/D module is shut off and consumes no
     operating current

Note 1:   Bit 5 of ADCON0 is a general purpose R/W bit for
the PIC16C71 only. For the PIC16C710/711,
this bit is unimplemented and reads as "0".

ADRES

The A/D result register contains the result (data) on completion of the conversion process. The address is 0x09.

The procedure for performing an A/D conversion is:

- Configure the port A pins - done once during the setup portion of the main program
- Select = enable an A/D channel
- Wait for the A/D to acquire the data (20 μsec)
- Start the conversion - set go/$\overline{done}$ bit in ADCON0 register
- Use interrupt or polling go/$\overline{done}$ bit in ADCON0 register to detect conversion completion
- Read data in A/D result register
- If you want to do another conversion, wait 16 μsec

How will we known when the conversion process is complete? There are two bits in the ADCON0 register which can be used. The go/$\overline{done}$ bit (bit 2) may be polled. It is set to start the conversion process and is cleared when the conversion is complete. The ADIF bit (bit 1) is the conversion complete interrupt flag. It is set on conversion completion. Note that it must be cleared in software as part of the interrupt service routine. Of course, the interrupt must be enabled prior to starting the conversion if this method is used. Bit 6 of the INTCON register is the A/D interrupt enable (ADIE) flag.

Conversion complete:

- Result in ADRES register
- Go/$\overline{done}$ bit in ADCON0 (bit 2) is cleared
- A/D interrupt flag bit (ADIF) in ADCON0 (bit 1) is set

EXAMPLE

This example shows how to use channel 0 on pin RA0/AN0. We can't use channel 0 as the only analog input (see table for ADCON1), so we will make port A, pins 1 and 0 analog inputs with pin 1 tied to ground and make port A, pins 3 and 2 digital outputs.

PIC16C71
4 MHz clock, $T_{osc} = 0.25$ μsec
A/D clock source = $T_{ad} = T_{osc} \times 32 = 8$ μsec
$V_{ref} = 5V$

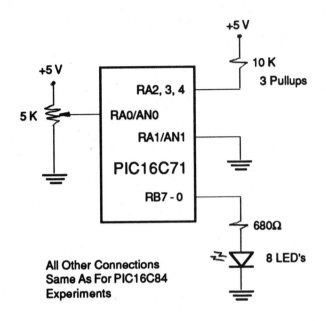

All Other Connections
Same As For PIC16C84
Experiments

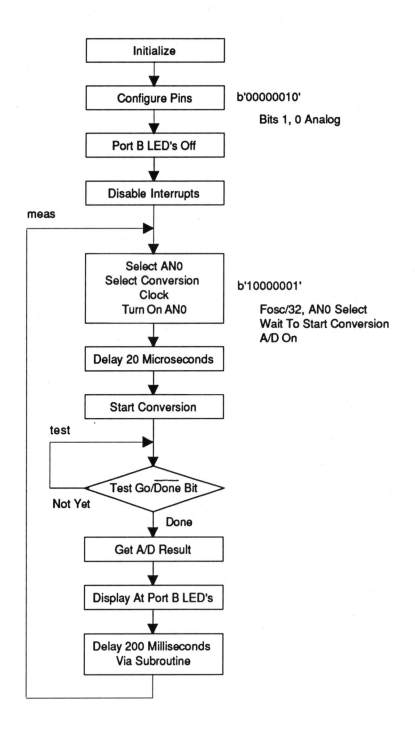

```
;======AD16C71.ASM================================6/12/97==
        list    p=16c71
        radix   hex
;-------------------------------------------------------------
;       cpu equates (memory map)
porta   equ     0x05
portb   equ     0x06
status  equ     0x03
adcon0  equ     0x08
adres   equ     0x09
intcon  equ     0x0b
count   equ     0x0d
ncount  equ     0x10
mcount  equ     0x11
trisa   equ     0x85
trisb   equ     0x86
adcon1  equ     0x88
;-------------------------------------------------------------
;       bit equates
rp0     equ     5
;-------------------------------------------------------------
        org     0x000
;
start   bsf     status,rp0      ;switch to bank 1
        movlw   b'00000011'     ;inputs/outputs
        movwf   trisa
        movlw   b'00000000'     ;outputs
        movwf   trisb
        movlw   b'00000010'     ;port A, bits 1,0 analog input
        movwf   adcon1          ;      bits 3,2 digital I/O
        bcf     status,rp0      ;switch back to bank 0
        clrf    portb           ;LEDs off
        bcf     intcon,7        ;global interrupt disable
meas    movlw   b'10000001'     ;configure A/D - select AN0
        movwf   adcon0          ;      select conv clock, AN0 on
        call    del_20          ;delay 20 microseconds
        bsf     adcon0,2        ;start conversion
test    btfsc   adcon0,2        ;test go/done bit
        goto    test
        movf    adres,w         ;conv complete, get A/D result
        movwf   portb           ;display data via LED's
        call    debounce        ;wait a while (200 milliseconds)
        goto    meas            ;look at voltage again
;-------------------------------------------------------------
del_20  movlw   0x07            ;delay 20 microseconds
        movwf   count
repeat  decfsz  count
        goto    repeat
        return
;-------------------------------------------------------------
debounce movlw  0xff            ;M
        movwf   mcount          ;to M counter
loadn   movlw   0xff            ;N
```

```
        movwf   ncount          ;to N counter
decn    decfsz  ncount,f        ;decrement N
        goto    decn            ;again
        decfsz  mcount,f        ;decrement M
        goto    loadn           ;again
        return                  ;done
;----------------------------------------------------------------
        end
;----------------------------------------------------------------
;at blast time, select:
;       memory unprotected
;       watchdog timer disabled (default is enabled)
;       standard crystal (using 4 MHz osc for test) XT
;       power-up timer on
;================================================================
```

Turn the pot and observe the port B LED's.

MATH ROUTINES

OK - some math is required for some PIC16 applications. No problem! It is easier than it appears at first (for 8-bit or 1-byte arithmetic at least). We will make some simplifying assumptions. The first is we will limit our scope to handling non-negative numbers in the range 0x0000 to 0xFFFF.

INSTRUCTIONS REQUIRED

```
----------------------------------------------------------------
MNEMONIC              DESCRIPTION
----------------------------------------------------------------
  ADDLW       Add literal to W
  ADDWF       Add W and f
  SUBLW       Subtract W from literal (not literal from W as name
                 suggests!)
  SUBWF       Subtract W from f
  RLF         Rotate bits in selected register one position to
                 left.
              Bits rotate through carry flag.
  RRF         Rotate bits in selected register one position to
                 right.
              Bits rotate through carry flag.
```

The PIC16 treats all 8-bit numbers as though they are non-negative numbers in the range 0-255. Negative numbers may be dealt with using 2's complement arithmetic, but that is beyond the scope of this book. Serious two-byte or double precision arithmetic is beyond the scope of this book as 2's complement arithmetic is required. We will do some simpler math and the result will be that you will know enough to be able to create some very useful microcontroller systems.

For 8-bit addition (non-negative values in the range 0-255):

```
Carry flag indicates whether or not the result fits in
      8 bits.

      Cleared to 0        Result fits in 8 bits
      Set to 1            Result is larger than 8 bits
```

For 8-bit subtraction (non-negative numbers in the range 0-255):

```
Carry flag indicates whether the result is non-negative
       or negative.

       Set to 1           Non-negative (in the range 0-255)
       Cleared to 0       Negative
```

Note that the carry flag isn't really a carry flag.

ARITHMETIC

Addition

Two single bytes may be added in two ways, add a literal to the W register contents or add the W register contents to the contents of a selected register (result in W or f).

```
       addlw   0x01     ;add 0x01 to W

       addwf   temp,f   ;add W to temp register
```

Examples of addition:

```
                0x05        0x01        0x02        0x03        0xff
       Plus     0x01        0xfe        0xfe        0xfe        0x01
       Result   0x06        0xff        0x00        0x01        0x00

       Carry flag   0          0           1           1           1
```

If the sum of the numbers is greater than 0xFF, an overflow will occur and the carry flag will be set to "1". We will see what to do if an overflow occurs later.

Subtraction

Two single bytes may be subtracted in two ways, subtract the contents of the W register from a literal or subtract the W register contents from the contents of a selected register (result in W or f).

If the subtraction clears the carry flag, the byte in the W register was larger than the byte it was subtracted from.

```
       sublw   0x--     ;subtract W from literal

       subwf   hold,f   ;subtract W from hold register
```

Examples of subtraction:

```
                 0x05        0x05        0x05
    Minus        0x06        0x05        0x04
    Result       0xff        0x00        0x01

    Carry flag     0           1           1

    Result negative      Result non-negative
```

Multiplication

Multiplication of a single byte by 2 is accomplished by using the rotate left 1 bit instruction (RLF). Bit 7 is moved into the carry flag when the instruction is executed. The carry flag contents is moved into bit 0 at the same time.

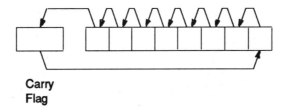

Carry
Flag

Since the carry flag will be in an unknown state (garbage) prior to the rotate operation, we must clear the carry flag first (clear bit 0 in the status register). To see how this works:

```
status   equ      0x03    ;status word register
c        equ      0       ;bit 0 is carry flag
mult     equ      0x0c    ;file register used for multiplication
;
;
         bcf      status,c ;clear carry flag
         rlf      mult,f   ;rotate bits left, result in mult
```

The contents of the file register labeled "mult" are, thus, multiplied by 2. Simple!

In binary, we can only multiply by 2 directly. One way to multiply a number by 10 is to multiply by 2 three times and add the original number multiplied by 2 to the result.

$$N \times 2 \times 2 \times 2 = 8N \qquad N = \text{Number}$$
$$N \times 2 \qquad\qquad = \underline{2N}$$
$$ 10N$$

As an example, we will devise a subroutine which will multiply a single byte binary number by 10 (decimal) and store the result. The subroutine must do the following:

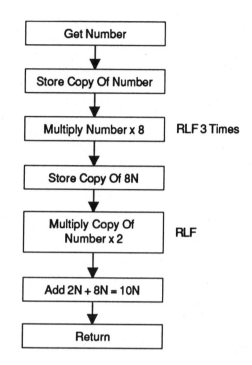

Note that some of the math program examples are designed to display a result via LED's at port B. Some example programs have no means for display (but could be easily modified) as they were tested using the simulator in MPLAB.

```
;=======PICM2.ASM===============================3/26/97==
;multiply by decimal 10 demo
;-----------------------------------------------------------
        list    p=16c84
        radix   hex
;-----------------------------------------------------------
;       cpu equates (memory map)
status  equ     0x03
portb   equ     0x06
test_n  equ     0x0c
math    equ     0x0d
copy_8xn equ    0x0e
;-----------------------------------------------------------
;       bit equates
c       equ     0
;-----------------------------------------------------------
        org     0x000
;
start   movlw   0x00            ;load w with 0x00
        tris    portb           ;copy w tristate, port B outputs
```

```
        movlw    0x03           ;test number
        call     decx10         ;to sub
        movwf    portb          ;display status via LED's
circle  goto     circle         ;done
;------------------------------------------------------------
;enter sub with number in w - exit with result in w
;------------------------------------------------------------
decx10  movwf    test_n         ;save copy of test number
        movwf    math           ;working register
        bcf      status,c       ;clear carry flag
        rlf      math,f         ;x2
        bcf      status,c       ;clear carry flag
        rlf      math,f         ;x2
        bcf      status,c       ;clear carry flag
        rlf      math,f         ;x2
        movf     math,w         ;get copy of 8xn
        movwf    copy_8xn       ;store copy of 8xn
        movf     test_n,w       ;get copy of n
        movwf    math
        bcf      status,c       ;clear carry flag
        rlf      math,f         ;x2
        movf     math,w         ;get copy of 2n
        addwf    copy_8xn,      ;add 2n and 8n
        return                  ;result in w
;------------------------------------------------------------
        end
;------------------------------------------------------------
;at blast time, select:
;        memory unprotected
;        watchdog timer disabled (default is enabled)
;        standard crystal (using 4 MHz osc for test)
;        power-up timer on
;============================================================
```

DOUBLE PRECISION

What happens if the numbers we need to use are larger than one byte = 0xFF = 256 decimal? We use two or more bytes to represent the number and make use of the carry flag to let the lower byte overflow into the higher byte.

We will use two bytes in our examples which is enough to represent 0 to 65,535 decimal. Arithmetic using two bytes is called double precision arithmetic and we will need double precision addition, subtraction and multiplication techniques for use in our decimal interface.

Double Precision Addition

Double precision addition is accomplished by adding the two least significant bytes followed by adding the two most significant bytes. If there is a carry resulting from the addition of the least significant bytes, it will be carried into the most significant byte addition process.

To demonstrate this, we can use the following routine to add the contents of lsb1 and msb1 into lsb2 and msb2:

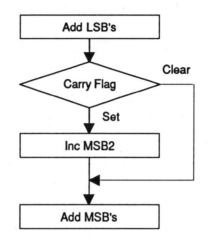

```
;=======PICM3.ASM====================================3/26/97==
;double precision addition demo
;-------------------------------------------------------------
        list    p=16c84
        radix   hex
;-------------------------------------------------------------
;       cpu equates (memory map)
status  equ     0x03
portb   equ     0x06
lsb1    equ     0x0c
msb1    equ     0x0d
lsb2    equ     0x0e
msb2    equ     0x0f
;-------------------------------------------------------------
;       bit equates
c       equ     0
;-------------------------------------------------------------
        org     0x000
;
start   movlw   0x00            ;load w with 0x00
        tris    portb           ;copy w tristate, port B outputs
        movlw   0xff            ;test number
        movwf   lsb1
        movlw   0x00            ;test number
        movwf   msb1
        movlw   0x02            ;test number
        movwf   lsb2
        movlw   0x00            ;test number
        movwf   msb2
        call    dblplus         ;to double precision addition
        movf    msb2,w          ;get msb2
        movwf   portb           ;display msb2 via LED's
```

```
circle   goto     circle       ;done
;-------------------------------------------------------------
dblplus  movf     lsb1,w       ;fetch lsb1
         addwf    lsb2,f       ;add low bytes, result in lsb2
         btfsc    status,c     ;carry set?
         incf     msb2,f       ;yes, add 1 to msb result
         movf     msb1,w       ;fetch msb1
         addwf    msb2,f       ;add high bytes, result in msb2
         return
;-------------------------------------------------------------
         end
;-------------------------------------------------------------
;at blast time, select:
;        memory unprotected
;        watchdog timer disabled (default is enabled)
;        standard crystal (using 4 MHz osc for test)
;        power-up timer on
;=============================================================
```

You can run this program in the MPLAB simulator. Open a watch window showing status, lsbi, msb1,lsb2, and msb2. Change the test numbers, run the program and check the results.

Double Precision Subtraction

Our (limited) objective for double precision subtraction is to be able to:

- Subtract a smaller number from a larger one.
- Subtract a larger number from a smaller one and know that that is
  the case, discard the result and take some action.

In our example, we will subtract the bytes labeled "1" (ie. lsb1) from the bytes labeled "2".

```
;=======PICM4.ASM===================================6/23/97==
;double precision subtraction demo
;-------------------------------------------------------------
         list     p=16c84
         radix    hex
;-------------------------------------------------------------
;        cpu equates (memory map)
status   equ      0x03
portb    equ      0x06
lsb1     equ      0x0c
msb1     equ      0x0d
lsb2     equ      0x0e
msb2     equ      0x0f
;-------------------------------------------------------------
;        bit equates
c        equ      0
;-------------------------------------------------------------
         org      0x000
;
```

```
start     movlw   0x00        ;load w with 0x00
          tris    portb       ;copy w tristate, port B
;                                     outputs
          movlw   0x01        ;test number
          movwf   lsb1
          movlw   0x00        ;test number
          movwf   msb1
          movlw   0xff        ;test number
          movwf   lsb2
          movlw   0xff        ;test number
          movwf   msb2
          call    dblsub      ;to double precision subtraction
          movf    status,w    ;get status to ck carry flag
          movwf   portb       ;display status via LED's
circle    goto    circle      ;done
;--------------------------------------------------------------
dblsub    movf    lsb1,w      ;fetch lsb1
          subwf   lsb2,f      ;subt low bytes, result in lsb2
          btfss   status,c    ;carry clear?
          decf    msb2,f      ;yes, subtract 1 from msb2
          movf    msb1,w      ;fetch msb1
          subwf   msb2,f      ;sub high bytes, result in msb2
          return
;--------------------------------------------------------------
          end
;--------------------------------------------------------------
;at blast time, select:
;       memory unprotected
;       watchdog timer disabled (default is enabled)
;       standard crystal (using 4 MHz osc for test)
;       power-up timer on
;==============================================================
```

Double Precision Multiplication

Double precision multiplication is carried out by shifting the low byte left (RLF) which moves the most significant bit into the carry flag followed by shifting the high byte left (RLF) which moves the carry flag contents into the least significant bit of the high byte.

```
Multiply (2-byte)
     Clear carry flag
     Use RLF (low byte) first
     Use RLF (high byte) next
```

Carry
Flag
Low Byte
RLF

Carry
Flag
High Byte
RLF

First, the carry flag is cleared. Using RLF multiplies the low byte by 2 and moves the most significant bit into the carry flag. It also moves the "0" from the carry flag into the low byte least significant position. Using RLF on the high byte multiplies it by 2 and moves the contents of the carry flag (which was the most significant bit in the low byte) into the high byte least significant bit position.

To test this concept:

```
;=======PICM5.ASM=================================3/27/97==
;double precision multiplication demo
;----------------------------------------------------------
        list    p=16c84
        radix   hex
;----------------------------------------------------------
;       cpu equates (memory map)
status  equ     0x03
portb   equ     0x06
lobyte  equ     0x0c
hibyte  equ     0x0d
;----------------------------------------------------------
;       bit equates
c       equ     0
;----------------------------------------------------------
        org     0x000
;
start   movlw   0x00        ;load w with 0x00
        tris    portb       ;copy w tristate, port B outputs
        movlw   0xff        ;test number
        movwf   lobyte
        movlw   0x00        ;test number
        movwf   hibyte
        call    dblmult     ;to double precision mult
        movf    hibyte,w    ;get hibyte
        movwf   portb       ;display hibyte via LED's
circle  goto    circle      ;done
;----------------------------------------------------------
dblmult bcf     status,c    ;clear carry flag
        rlf     lobyte,f    ;rotate low byte
        rlf     hibyte,f    ;rotate high byte
        return
;----------------------------------------------------------
        end
;----------------------------------------------------------
;at blast time, select:
;       memory unprotected
;       watchdog timer disabled (default is enabled)
;       standard crystal (using 4 MHz osc for test)
;       power-up timer on
;==========================================================
```

SUBROUTINE WHICH MULTIPLIES A 2-BYTE BINARY NUMBER BY DECIMAL 10
(For Use In Decimal Interface)

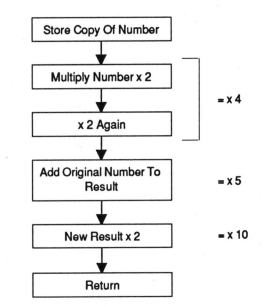

$$[(N \times 2 \times 2) + N] \times 2 = 10N$$

This could have been done using:

$$N \times 2 \times 2 \times 2 + 2N = 10N$$

$$= \times 8 \quad + 2$$

```
;======PICM6.ASM=================================3/27/97==
;multiply 2-byte binary by 10 decimal demo
;-----------------------------------------------------------
          list    p=16c84
          radix   hex
;-----------------------------------------------------------
;         cpu equates (memory map)
status    equ     0x03
portb     equ     0x06
lobyte    equ     0x0c
hibyte    equ     0x0d
copylo    equ     0x0e
copyhi    equ     0x0f
;-----------------------------------------------------------
;         bit equates
c         equ     0
;-----------------------------------------------------------
          org     0x000
;
start     movlw   0x00         ;load w with 0x00
          tris    portb        ;copy w tristate, port B outputs
          movlw   0x02         ;test number
          movwf   lobyte
          movlw   0x00         ;test number
          movwf   hibyte
          call    decmult      ;to 2-byte binary x 10 dec
          movf    hibyte,w     ;get hibyte
          movwf   portb        ;display hibyte via LED's
circle    goto    circle       ;done
;-----------------------------------------------------------
decmult   movf    lobyte,w     ;get low byte
          movwf   copylo       ;store copy
          movf    hibyte,w     ;get high byte
          movwf   copyhi       ;store copy
          bcf     status,c     ;clear carry flag
          rlf     lobyte,f     ;rotate low byte
          rlf     hibyte,f     ;rotate high byte
          bcf     status,c     ;clear carry flag
          rlf     lobyte,f     ;rotate low byte
          rlf     hibyte,f     ;rotate high byte
          movf    copylo,w     ;fetch low byte
          addwf   lobyte,f     ;add low bytes
          btfss   status,c     ;carry set?
          goto    contin       ;no, continue
          incf    hibyte,f     ;yes, add 1 to hi byte
contin    movf    copyhi,w     ;fetch high byte
          addwf   hibyte,f     ;add high bytes
          bcf     status,c     ;clear carry flag
          rlf     lobyte,f     ;rotate low byte
          rlf     hibyte,f     ;rotate high byte
          return
;-----------------------------------------------------------
          end
```

```
;-----------------------------------------------------------
;at blast time, select:
;        memory unprotected
;        watchdog timer disabled (default is enabled)
;        standard crystal (using 4 MHz osc for test)
;        power-up timer on
;===========================================================
```

8-BIT X 8-BIT MULTIPLY, 2-BYTE RESULT

An explanation of how this routine works is a little beyond the scope of this book, so we'll save that for another time. The numbers to be multiplied reside in the registers "number" and "multby".

```
;======PICM8.ASM=================================6/24/97==
;8-bit multiplication, 2-byte result demo
;-----------------------------------------------------------
        list    p=16c84
        radix   hex
;-----------------------------------------------------------
;       cpu equates (memory map)
status  equ     0x03
portb   equ     0x06
lobyte  equ     0x0c
hibyte  equ     0x0d
number  equ     0x0e
multby  equ     0x0f
;-----------------------------------------------------------
;       bit equates
c       equ     0
;-----------------------------------------------------------
        org     0x000
;
start   movlw   0x00            ;load w with 0x00
        tris    portb           ;copy w tristate, port B outputs
        movlw   0x02            ;test number
        movwf   number
        movlw   0x05            ;test number
        movwf   multby
        call    sglmult         ;to 8x8 multiply
        movf    hibyte,w        ;get hibyte
        movwf   portb           ;display hibyte via LED's
circle  goto    circle          ;done
;-----------------------------------------------------------
sglmult clrf    lobyte
        clrf    hibyte
        movf    number,w        ;get number to be multiplied into W
        bcf     status,c        ;clear carry flag
        btfsc   multby,0        ;bit 0
        addwf   hibyte,f
        rrf     hibyte,f
        rrf     lobyte,f
```

```
        btfsc    multby,1       ;bit 1
        addwf    hibyte,f
        rrf      hibyte,f
        rrf      lobyte,f
        btfsc    multby,2       ;bit 2
        addwf    hibyte,f
        rrf      hibyte,f
        rrf      lobyte,f
        btfsc    multby,3       ;bit 3
        addwf    hibyte,f
        rrf      hibyte,f
        rrf      lobyte,f
        btfsc    multby,4       ;bit 4
        addwf    hibyte,f
        rrf      hibyte,f
        rrf      lobyte,f
        btfsc    multby,5       ;bit 5
        addwf    hibyte,f
        rrf      hibyte,f
        rrf      lobyte,f
        btfsc    multby,6       ;bit 6
        addwf    hibyte,f
        rrf      hibyte,f
        rrf      lobyte,f
        btfsc    multby,7       ;bit 7
        addwf    hibyte,f
        rrf      hibyte,f
        rrf      lobyte,f
        return
;-------------------------------------------------------------
        end
;-------------------------------------------------------------
;at blast time, select:
;       memory unprotected
;       watchdog timer disabled (default is enabled)
;       standard crystal (using 4 MHz osc for test)
;       power-up timer on
;=============================================================
```

DECIMAL INTERFACE

People think in decimal and microcontrollers operate in binary. For control applications, operator inputs (temperature, pressure, flow rate, etc.) are in decimal form, usually entered via a keypad. Decimal to binary conversion is necessary. Conversely, operating parameters must be converted from binary to decimal for display. The purpose of this project is to develop the software to make these conversions.

3-DIGIT DECIMAL TO 8-BIT BINARY

The program does some setup and then gets each digit in succession, multiplies by its decimal weight (in binary) and adds it to a register which accumulates the total value of the number. The first digit entered is the 100's place digit so it is multiplied by 100 and added to the addition register named "numsum". The second digit entered is multiplied by 100, and so on, until the binary equivalent of the number has been assembled in the numsum location.

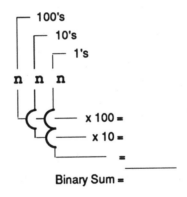

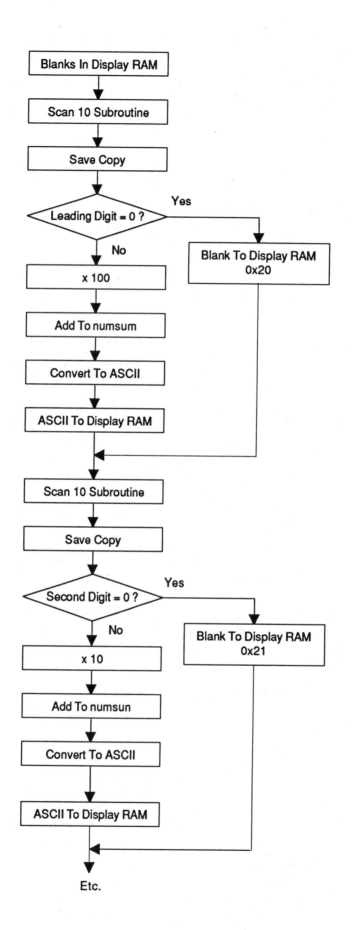

```
;=======DECENTRY.ASM===============================6/14/97==
        list    p=16c84
        radix   hex
;-------------------------------------------------------------
;       cpu equates (memory map)
tmr0    equ     0x01
status  equ     0x03
porta   equ     0x05
portb   equ     0x06
intcon  equ     0x0b
sendreg equ     0x0c
count   equ     0x0d
instr   equ     0x0e
char    equ     0x0f
addr    equ     0x10
digctr  equ     0x11
rowctr  equ     0x12
colctr  equ     0x13
rowbits equ     0x14
colbits equ     0x15
temp    equ     0x16
ncount  equ     0x17
mcount  equ     0x18
test_n  equ     0x19
math    equ     0x1a
copy_8xn equ    0x1b
numsum  equ     0x1c
hund    equ     0x1d
ten     equ     0x1e
hold    equ     0x1f
optreg  equ     0x81
trisa   equ     0x85
trisb   equ     0x86
;-------------------------------------------------------------
;       bit equates
c       equ     0
z       equ     2
rp0     equ     5
;-------------------------------------------------------------
        org     0x000
;
start   bsf     status,rp0   ;switch to bank 1
        movlw   b'00000000'  ;port A outputs
        movwf   trisa
        movlw   b'01110000'  ;port B inputs/outputs
        movwf   trisb
        bcf     status,rp0   ;switch back to bank 0
        bsf     porta,1      ;output mark, bit 1 (serial - LCD)
        bsf     portb,0      ;rows high
        bsf     portb,1
        bsf     portb,2
        bsf     portb,3
        bcf     portb,7      ;unused line low
```

```
          call      debounce
          call      debounce
          movlw     0x00              ;blanks to display RAM
          movwf     instr
          call      sndstf            ;send instruction to LCD module
          call      debounce
          movlw     0x01              ;send 16 characters to display
          movwf     instr
          call      sndstf            ;send instruction to LCD module
          call      debounce
          clrf      numsum            ;clean out
do100     call      scan10
          movf      digctr,w          ;get 100's digit
          movwf     hund              ;save copy
          sublw     0x00              ;compare - digit=0?
          btfsc     status,z
          goto      hzero             ;yes
          movf      hund,w
          call      decx10            ;times 10
          call      decx10            ;times 10, result = x100
          addwf     numsum,f          ;add 100's to num sum register
          movf      hund,w            ;get 100's digit
          call      hex2asc           ;convert binary digit to ascii
          movwf     char
          movlw     0x20              ;display RAM address
          movwf     addr
          movlw     0x03              ;ascii char follows, send to display RAM
          movwf     instr
          call      sndstf            ;send 100's digit to display RAM
          call      debounce          ;time delay - debounce switches
do10      call      scan10
          movf      digctr,w          ;get 10's digit
          movwf     ten               ;save copy
          sublw     0x00              ;compare - digit=0?
          btfsc     status,z
          goto      tzero             ;yes
          movf      ten,w
          call      decx10            ;times 10
          addwf     numsum,f          ;add 10's to num sum register
          movf      ten,w             ;get 10's digit
          call      hex2asc           ;convert binary digit to ascii
          movwf     char
          movlw     0x21              ;display RAM address
          movwf     addr
          movlw     0x03              ;ascii char follows, send to display RAM
          movwf     instr
          call      sndstf            ;send 10's digit to display RAM
          call      debounce          ;time delay - debounce switches
do1       call      scan10
          movf      digctr,w          ;get 1's digit
          addwf     numsum,f          ;add 1's to num sum register
          call      hex2asc           ;convert binary digit to ascii
          movwf     char
          movlw     0x22              ;display RAM address
```

```
            movwf    addr
            movlw    0x03        ;ascii char follows, send to display RAM
            movwf    instr
            call     sndstf      ;send 1's digit to display RAM
            call     debounce
send        movlw    0x01        ;send 16 characters to display
            movwf    instr
            call     sndstf      ;to LCD module
            call     debounce
;display numsum contents
            movf     numsum,w    ;get total
            movwf    char
            movlw    0x04        ;hex byte follows, convert and display
            movwf    instr
            call     sndstf
circle      goto     circle      ;done
;-----------------------------------------------------------
hzero       movlw    0x20        ;ascii blank
            movwf    char
            movlw    0x20        ;display RAM address
            movwf    addr
            movlw    0x03        ;ascii character to display RAM
            movwf    instr
            call     sndstf
            call     debounce
            goto     do10
;-----------------------------------------------------------
tzero       movlw    0x20        ;ascii blank
            movwf    char
            movlw    0x21        ;display RAM address
            movwf    addr
            movlw    0x03        ;ascii character to display RAM
            movwf    instr
            call     sndstf
            call     debounce
            goto     do1
;-----------------------------------------------------------
;returns with digit in digctr
;
scan10      bsf      portb,0     ;rows high
            bsf      portb,1
            bsf      portb,2
            bsf      portb,3
            clrf     digctr      ;digit counter=0
            bcf      portb,3     ;row=4
            btfss    portb,5     ;test column 2
            return               ;"0" key press
            bsf      portb,3     ;deselect row 4
            movlw    0x01
            movwf    digctr      ;digit counter=1
            movwf    rowctr      ;row counter=1
            movwf    rowbits     ;row bits = 0000 0001
rowout      movf     rowbits,w   ;get row bits
            xorlw    0x0f        ;complement row bits
```

```
        movwf   portb           ;output row bits
        movlw   0x01
        movwf   colctr          ;column counter=1
        movlw   0x10            ;0001 0000
        movwf   colbits         ;col=1
tstcol  movf    portb,w         ;read port B
        andlw   0x70            ;mask off rows and bit 7
        movwf   temp            ;columns
        movf    colbits,w       ;get column bits
        xorlw   0x70            ;complement column bits
        subwf   temp,w          ;compare with contents of temp
        btfsc   status,z
        return                  ;digit available
lastc   movf    colctr,w        ;get column count
        sublw   0x03
        btfsc   status,z        ;=3 ?
        goto    lastr
        rlf     colbits,f       ;shift column bits
        bcf     colbits,0       ;fix carry flag garbage
        incf    colctr,f
        incf    digctr,f
        goto    tstcol
lastr   movf    rowctr,w        ;get row count
        sublw   0x03
        btfsc   status,z        ;=3 ?
        goto    scan10          ;scan 10 digit keys again
        rlf     rowbits,f       ;shift row bits
        bcf     rowbits,0       ;fix carry flag garbage
        incf    rowctr,f
        incf    digctr,f
        goto    rowout
;-----------------------------------------------------------
debounce movlw  0x02            ;to counter
        movwf   count
dbloop  movlw   0xff            ;M
        movwf   mcount          ;to M counter
loadn   movlw   0xff            ;N
        movwf   ncount          ;to N counter
decn    decfsz  ncount,f        ;decrement N
        goto    decn            ;again
        decfsz  mcount,f        ;decrement M
        goto    loadn           ;again
        decfsz  count
        goto    dbloop          ;thru loop within a loop twice -
;                                   400 milliseconds
        return                  ;done
;-----------------------------------------------------------
sndstf  movf    instr,w         ;get instruction
        movwf   sendreg         ;to be sent
        call    ser_out         ;to serial out subroutine
        movf    char,w          ;get character or hex byte
        movwf   sendreg         ;to be sent
        call    ser_out         ;to serial out subroutine
        movf    addr,w          ;get address
```

```
           movwf     sendreg       ;to be sent
           call      ser_out       ;to serial out subroutine
           return
;-----------------------------------------------------------------
ser_out    bcf       intcon,5      ;disable tmr0 interrupts
           bcf       intcon,7      ;disable global interrupts
           clrf      tmr0          ;clear timer/counter
           clrwdt                  ;clear wdt prep prescaler assign
           bsf       status,rp0    ;to page 1
           movlw     b'11011000'   ;set up timer/counter
           movwf     optreg
           bcf       status,rp0    ;back to page 0
           movlw     0x08          ;init shift counter
           movwf     count
           bcf       porta,1       ;start bit
           clrf      tmr0          ;start timer/counter
           bcf       intcon,2      ;clear tmr0 overflow flag
time1      btfss     intcon,2      ;timer overflow?
           goto      time1         ;no
           bcf       intcon,2      ;yes, clear overflow flag
nxtbit     rlf       sendreg,f     ;rotate msb into carry flag
           bcf       porta,1       ;clear port A, bit 1
           btfsc     status,c      ;test carry flag
           bsf       porta,1       ;bit is set
time2      btfss     intcon,2      ;timer overflow?
           goto      time2         ;no
           bcf       intcon,2      ;clear overflow flag
           decfsz    count,f       ;shifted 8?
           goto      nxtbit        ;no
           bsf       porta,1       ;yes, output mark
time3      btfss     intcon,2      ;timer overflow?
           goto      time3         ;no
           return                  ;done
;-----------------------------------------------------------------
;enter sub with number in w - exit with result in w
;
decx10     movwf     test_n        ;save copy of test number
           movwf     math           ;working register
           bcf       status,c      ;clear carry flag
           rlf       math,f        ;x2
           bcf       status,c      ;clear carry flag
           rlf       math,f        ;x2
           bcf       status,c      ;clear carry flag
           rlf       math,f        ;x2
           movf      math,w        ;get copy of 8xn
           movwf     copy_8xn      ;store copy of 8xn
           movf      test_n,w      ;get copy of n
           movwf     math
           bcf       status,c      ;clear carry flag
           rlf       math,f         ;x2
           movf      math,w         ;get copy of 2n
           addwf     copy_8xn,w    ;add 2n and 8n
           return                  ;result in w

;-----------------------------------------------------------------
```

```
;enter with hex digit in w
;
hex2asc movwf     hold          ;store copy of hex digit
        sublw     0x09          ;subtract w from 1 less than 0x0a
        btfss     status,c      ;carry flag set if w < 0x0a
        goto      add37
        goto      add30
add37   movf      hold,w        ;get hex digit
        addlw     0x37
        return                  ;return with ascii in w
add30   movf      hold,w        ;get hex digit
        addlw     0x30
        return                  ;return with ascii in w
;---------------------------------------------------------------
        end
;---------------------------------------------------------------
;at blast time, select:
;       memory unprotected
;       watchdog timer disabled (default is enabled)
;       standard crystal (using 4 MHz osc for test) XT
;       power-up timer on
;===============================================================
```

USING THE 3-DIGIT DECIMAL TO 8-BIT BINARY DECIMAL ENTRY PROGRAM

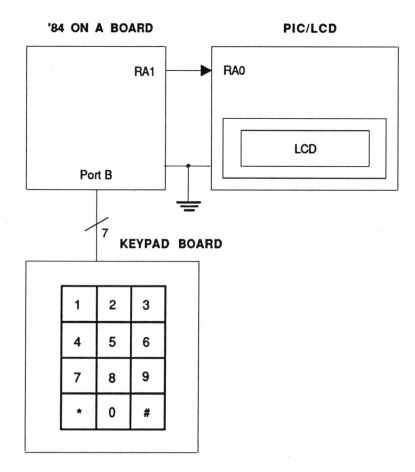

- Power up both PIC84 boards
- Key in 3 digits (including leading zeros)
- 0 - must key in 3 zeros
- Range of numbers is 0 to 255.

The resulting number will be in "numsum" and will be displayed on completion of the time delay ("debounce").

Examples:

```
------------------
Decimal     numsum
------------------
  000        0x00
  015        0x0F
  016        0x10
  127        0x7F
  128        0x80
  255        0xFF
```

The resulting number may be loaded into a counter or used for set point comparison or whatever.

8-BIT BINARY TO 3-DIGIT BCD

The magnitude of an unknown 3 digit decimal number can be determined by successive subtractions. First we test to see how many 100's the number contains. We count the number of times 100 can be subtracted without getting a negative result (subtracting too much). Actually, we will keep subtracting until we have done it one too many times (as determined by testing the carry flag) and then add 100 back into the number. The actual number of subtractions equals the 100's place decimal digit.

Next, we take the remainder and subtract 10 at a time until we have gone too far, add 10 back in and now we have the 10's place digit.

The 1's place can be displayed directly. As we go along, we will complete the testing for each decimal place and test to see if the remainder is 0. If it is, the remaining digits are 0's.

The decimal interface program makes use of looping and relative addressing. The index or offset is used to access a lookup table containing the binary equivalents of 100 and 10. The same index is used to address another table which is used to store the decimal digits as they are calculated.

The "index" file register is used to develop the offset or index for the two tables. A file register is used as a counter to count subtractions. The number of subtractions of a given value equals the corresponding decimal digit. Thus, the file register is the digit counter.

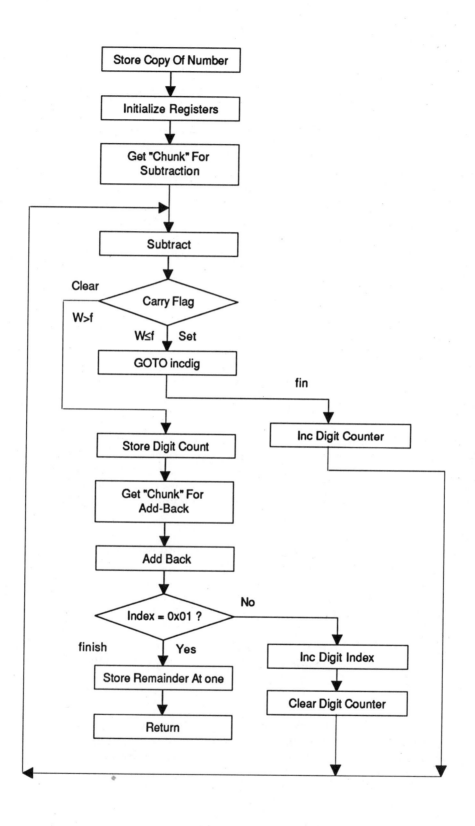

```
;=======BIN2DEC.ASM=========================6/25/97==
            list    p=16c84
            radix   hex
;-----------------------------------------------------
;           cpu equates (memory map)
indf        equ     0x00
pc          equ     0x02
status      equ     0x03
fsr         equ     0x04
number      equ     0x0c
index       equ     0x0d
dig_ctr     equ     0x0e
hund        equ     0x20
ten         equ     0x21
one         equ     0x22
;-----------------------------------------------------
;           bit equates
c           equ     0
z           equ     2
rp0         equ     5
;-----------------------------------------------------
            org     0x000
;
start       movlw   0x80        ;define test number
            call    bin2dec     ;call conversion subroutine
circle      goto    circle      ;done
;-----------------------------------------------------
table       addwf   pc,f        ;add index to program counter
            retlw   0x64        ;100 decimal
            retlw   0x0a        ;10 decimal
;-----------------------------------------------------
bin2dec     movwf   number      ;store copy of number
            clrf    hund
            clrf    ten
            clrf    one
            clrf    index
            clrf    dig_ctr
subtr       movf    index,w     ;get current index into W
            call    table       ;get chunk for subtraction
            subwf   number,f    ;test
            btfsc   status,c    ;test carry flag
            goto    incdig
            movlw   0x20        ;load base address of table
            movwf   fsr
            movf    index,w     ;get index
            addwf   fsr         ;add offset
            movf    dig_ctr,w   ;get digit counter contents
            movwf   indf        ;store at digit loc (indexed)
            movf    index,w     ;get index
            call    table       ;get chunk for addition
            addwf   number      ;add back
            movf    index,w     ;get index
            sublw   0x01        ;index=1?
            btfsc   status,z
```

```
        goto    finish
        incf    index           ;increment digit index
        clrf    dig_ctr
        goto    subtr
;------------------------------------------------------------
incdig  incf    dig_ctr         ;increment digit counter
        goto    subtr
;------------------------------------------------------------
finish  movf    number,w        ;get 1's=remainder
        movwf   one
        return
;------------------------------------------------------------
        end
;------------------------------------------------------------
;at blast time, select:
;       memory unprotected
;       watchdog timer disabled (default is enabled)
;       standard crystal (using 4 MHz osc for test)
;       power-up timer on
;============================================================
```

DISPLAY RESULT OF 8-BIT BINARY TO 3-DIGIT BCD

- Binary to decimal sub
        Results in hund, ten, one registers
- Leading zeros blanks
- Zero to one zero in one
- Uses indexed/indirect addressing
- Range 0x00 to 0xff   0 to 255 decimal

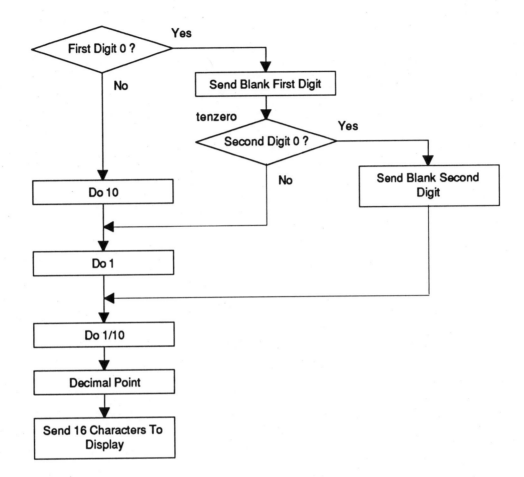

```
;======BINLCD.ASM==================================6/27/97==
        list    p=16c84
        radix   hex
;------------------------------------------------------------
;       cpu equates (memory map)
indf    equ     0x00
tmr0    equ     0x01
pc      equ     0x02
status  equ     0x03
fsr     equ     0x04
porta   equ     0x05
intcon  equ     0x0b
sendreg equ     0x0c
count   equ     0x0d
instr   equ     0x0e
char    equ     0x0f
addr    equ     0x10
number  equ     0x12
index   equ     0x13
dig_ctr equ     0x14
ncount  equ     0x15
```

```
mcount    equ       0x16
hold      equ       0x17
hund      equ       0x20
ten       equ       0x21
one       equ       0x22
optreg    equ       0x81
trisa     equ       0x85
;--------------------------------------------------------------
;         bit equates
c         equ       0
z         equ       2
rp0       equ       5
;--------------------------------------------------------------
          org       0x000
;
start     bsf       status,rp0   ;switch to bank 1
          movlw     b'00000000'  ;port A outputs
          movwf     trisa
          bcf       status,rp0   ;switch back to bank 0
          bsf       porta,1      ;output mark, bit 1 (serial - LCD)
          call      debounce
          call      debounce
          movlw     0x00         ;blanks to display RAM
          movwf     instr
          call      sndstf       ;send instruction to LCD module
          call      debounce
          movlw     0x01         ;send 16 characters to display
          movwf     instr
          call      sndstf       ;send instruction to LCD module
          call      debounce
          movlw     0x0f         ;define test number
          call      bin2dec      ;call conversion subroutine
zcheck    movf      hund,w       ;get 100's digit
          sublw     0x00         ;compare - digit=0?
          btfsc     status,z
          goto      hzero        ;yes
do100     movf      hund,w       ;get 100's digit
          call      hex2asc      ;convert binary digit to ascii
          movwf     char
          movlw     0x20         ;display RAM address
          movwf     addr
          movlw     0x03         ;ascii char follows, send to display RAM
          movwf     instr
          call      sndstf       ;send 100's digit to display RAM
          call      debounce     ;time delay
do10      movf      ten,w        ;get 10's digit
          call      hex2asc      ;convert binary digit to ascii
          movwf     char
          movlw     0x21         ;display RAM address
          movwf     addr
          movlw     0x03         ;ascii char follows, send to display RAM
          movwf     instr
          call      sndstf       ;send 10's digit to display RAM
          call      debounce     ;time delay
```

```
do1      movf     one,w         ;get 1's digit
         call     hex2asc       ;convert binary digit to ascii
         movwf    char
         movlw    0x22          ;display RAM address
         movwf    addr
         movlw    0x03          ;ascii char follows, send to display RAM
         movwf    instr
         call     sndstf        ;send 1's digit to display RAM
         call     debounce      ;time delay
send     movlw    0x01          ;send 16 characters to display
         movwf    instr
         call     sndstf        ;to LCD module
circle   goto     circle        ;done
;-------------------------------------------------------------
hzero    movlw    0x20          ;ascii blank
         movwf    char
         movlw    0x20          ;display RAM address
         movwf    addr
         movlw    0x03          ;ascii character to display RAM
         movwf    instr
         call     sndstf
         call     debounce
         movf     ten,w         ;get 10's digit
         sublw    0x00          ;compare - digit=0?
         btfss    status,z
         goto     do10
;-------------------------------------------------------------
tzero    movlw    0x20          ;ascii blank
         movwf    char
         movlw    0x21          ;display RAM address
         movwf    addr
         movlw    0x03          ;ascii character to display RAM
         movwf    instr
         call     sndstf
         call     debounce
         goto     do1
;-------------------------------------------------------------

table    addwf    pc,f          ;add index to program counter
         retlw    0x64          ;100 decimal
         retlw    0x0a          ;10 decimal
;-------------------------------------------------------------
bin2dec  movwf    number        ;store copy of number
         clrf     hund
         clrf     ten
         clrf     one
         clrf     index
         clrf     dig_ctr
subtr    movf     index,w       ;get current index into W
         call     table         ;get chunk for subtraction
         subwf    number,f      ;test
         btfsc    status,c      ;test carry flag
         goto     incdig
         movlw    0x20          ;load base address of table
```

```
        movwf    fsr
        movf     index,w      ;get index
        addwf    fsr          ;add offset
        movf     dig_ctr,w    ;get digit counter contents
        movwf    indf         ;store at digit loc (indexed)
        movf     index,w      ;get index
        call     table        ;get chunk for addition
        addwf    number       ;add back
        movf     index,w      ;get index
        sublw    0x01         ;index=1?
        btfsc    status,z
        goto     finish
        incf     index        ;increment digit index
        clrf     dig_ctr
        goto     subtr
;-----------------------------------------------------------
incdig  incf     dig_ctr      ;increment digit counter
        goto     subtr
;-----------------------------------------------------------
finish  movf     number,w     ;get 1's=remainder
        movwf    one
        return
;-----------------------------------------------------------
debounce movlw   0x02         ;to counter
        movwf    count
dbloop  movlw    0xff         ;M
        movwf    mcount       ;to M counter
loadn   movlw    0xff         ;N
        movwf    ncount       ;to N counter
decn    decfsz   ncount,f     ;decrement N
        goto     decn         ;again
        decfsz   mcount,f     ;decrement M
        goto     loadn        ;again
        decfsz   count
        goto     dbloop       ;thru loop within a loop twice -
;                                 400 milliseconds
        return                ;done
;-----------------------------------------------------------
sndstf  movf     instr,w      ;get instruction
        movwf    sendreg      ;to be sent
        call     ser_out      ;to serial out subroutine
        movf     char,w       ;get character or hex byte
        movwf    sendreg      ;to be sent
        call     ser_out      ;to serial out subroutine
        movf     addr,w       ;get address
        movwf    sendreg      ;to be sent
        call     ser_out      ;to serial out subroutine
        return
;-----------------------------------------------------------
ser_out bcf      intcon,5     ;disable tmr0 interrupts
        bcf      intcon,7     ;disable global interrupts
        clrf     tmr0         ;clear timer/counter
        clrwdt                ;clear wdt prep prescaler assign
        bsf      status,rp0   ;to page 1
```

```
        movlw   b'11011000' ;set up timer/counter
        movwf   optreg
        bcf     status,rp0  ;back to page 0
        movlw   0x08        ;init shift counter
        movwf   count
        bcf     porta,1     ;start bit
        clrf    tmr0        ;start timer/counter
        bcf     intcon,2    ;clear tmr0 overflow flag
time1   btfss   intcon,2    ;timer overflow?
        goto    time1       ;no
        bcf     intcon,2    ;yes, clear overflow flag
nxtbit  rlf     sendreg,f   ;rotate msb into carry flag
        bcf     porta,1     ;clear port A, bit 1
        btfsc   status,c    ;test carry flag
        bsf     porta,1     ;bit is set
time2   btfss   intcon,2    ;timer overflow?
        goto    time2       ;no
        bcf     intcon,2    ;clear overflow flag
        decfsz  count,f     ;shifted 8?
        goto    nxtbit      ;no
        bsf     porta,1     ;yes, output mark
time3   btfss   intcon,2    ;timer overflow?
        goto    time3       ;no
        return              ;done
;-----------------------------------------------------------
;enter with hex digit in w
;
hex2asc movwf   hold        ;store copy of hex digit
        sublw   0x09        ;subtract w from 1 less than 0x0a
        btfss   status,c    ;carry flag set if w < 0x0a
        goto    add37
        goto    add30
add37   movf    hold,w      ;get hex digit
        addlw   0x37
        return              ;return with ascii in w
add30   movf    hold,w      ;get hex digit
        addlw   0x30
        return              ;return with ascii in w
;-----------------------------------------------------------
        end
;-----------------------------------------------------------
;at blast time, select:
;       memory unprotected
;       watchdog timer disabled (default is enabled)
;       standard crystal (using 4 MHz osc for test) XT
;       power-up timer on
;===========================================================
```

16-BIT BINARY TO 5-DIGIT BCD - Range 0x0000 To 0x7FFF

This routine uses the simple but limited capability math described in the math chapter. It will handle 16-bit non-negative numbers in the range 0x0000 to 0x7FFF.

Short (much) more elegant routines are available to do this including one in Microchip's "Embedded Control Handbook". I am including this routine so you can see and try one that you can understand at this point in your learning experience. The neat short routines are based on some esoteric math which may (or may not) be beyond you. This is also true of the routine in the next section.

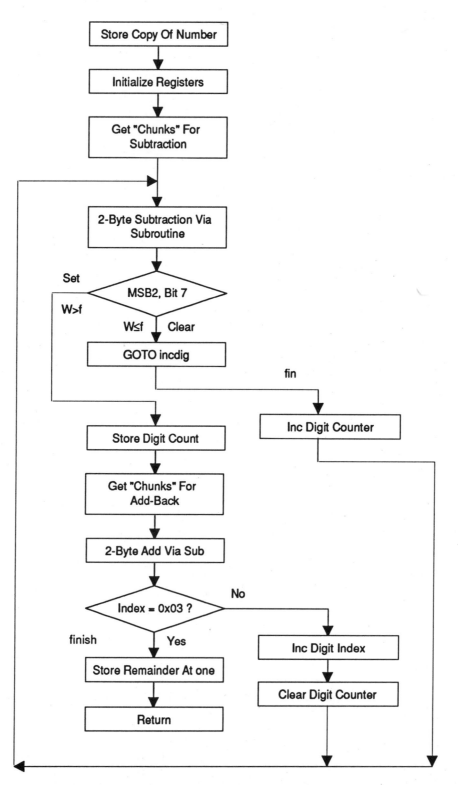

```
;=======DBLB2DZ.ASM=========================6/25/97==
;accepts 0x0000 through 7fff - 0 through 32767
;-------------------------------------------------
          list     p=16c84
          radix    hex
;-------------------------------------------------
;         cpu equates (memory map)
indf      equ      0x00
pc        equ      0x02
status    equ      0x03
fsr       equ      0x04
ms        equ      0x0c
ls        equ      0x0d
index     equ      0x0e
dig_ctr   equ      0x0f
lsb1      equ      0x10
msb1      equ      0x11
lsb2      equ      0x12
msb2      equ      0x13
tenk      equ      0x20
onek      equ      0x21
hund      equ      0x22
ten       equ      0x23
one       equ      0x24
;-------------------------------------------------
;         bit equates
c         equ      0
z         equ      2
rp0       equ      5
;-------------------------------------------------
          org      0x000
;
start     movlw    0x7f           ;define test number MS byte
          movwf    ms
          movlw    0xff           ;define test number LS byte
          movwf    ls
;prep for calling conversion subroutine
          movf     ms,w           ;get MS byte
          movwf    msb2
          movf     ls,w           ;get LS byte
          movwf    lsb2
          call     dblb2d         ;call conversion subroutine
circle    goto     circle         ;done
;-------------------------------------------------
tbl_lo    addwf    pc,f           ;add index to program counter
          retlw    0x10           ;10,000 decimal
          retlw    0xe8           ;1,000 decimal
          retlw    0x64           ;100 decimal
          retlw    0x0a           ;10 decimal
;-------------------------------------------------
tbl_hi    addwf    pc,f           ;add index to program counter
          retlw    0x27           ;10,000 decimal
          retlw    0x03           ;1,000 decimal
```

```
        retlw   0x00            ;100 decimal
        retlw   0x00            ;10 decimal
;----------------------------------------------------------
dblb2d  clrf    tenk
        clrf    onek
        clrf    hund
        clrf    ten
        clrf    one
        clrf    index
        clrf    dig_ctr
subtr   movf    index,w         ;get current index into W
        call    tbl_lo          ;get ls chunk for subtraction
        movwf   lsb1
        movf    index,w         ;get current index into W
        call    tbl_hi          ;get ms chunk for subtraction
        movwf   msb1
        call    dblsub          ;to double precision subtraction
        btfss   msb2,7          ;test bit 7, 1 means neg result
        goto    incdig
        movlw   0x20            ;load base address of table
        movwf   fsr
        movf    index,w         ;get index
        addwf   fsr,f           ;add offset
        movf    dig_ctr,w       ;get digit counter contents
        movwf   indf            ;store at digit loc (indexed)
        movf    index,w         ;get index
        call    tbl_lo          ;get ls chunk for addition
        movwf   lsb1
        movf    index,w         ;get index
        call    tbl_hi          ;get ms chunk for addition
        movwf   msb1
        call    dblplus         ;to double precision addition
        movf    index,w         ;get index
        sublw   0x03            ;index=3?
        btfsc   status,z
        goto    finish
        incf    index,f         ;increment digit index
        clrf    dig_ctr
        goto    subtr
;----------------------------------------------------------
incdig  incf    dig_ctr,f       ;increment digit counter
        goto    subtr
;----------------------------------------------------------
finish  movf    lsb2,w          ;get 1's=remainder
        movwf   one
        return                  ;done
;----------------------------------------------------------
dblsub  movf    lsb1,w          ;fetch lsb1
        subwf   lsb2,f          ;subt low bytes, result in lsb2
        btfss   status,c        ;carry clear?
        decf    msb2,f          ;yes, subtract 1 from msb2
        movf    msb1,w          ;fetch msb1
        subwf   msb2,f          ;sub high bytes, result in msb2
        return
```

```
;------------------------------------------------------
dblplus movf    lsb1,w          ;fetch lsb1
        addwf   lsb2,f          ;add low bytes, result in lsb2
        btfsc   status,c        ;carry set?
        incf    msb2,f          ;yes, add 1 to msb result
        movf    msb1,w          ;fetch msb1
        addwf   msb2,f          ;add high bytes, result in msb2
        return
;------------------------------------------------------
        end
;------------------------------------------------------
;at blast time, select:
;       memory unprotected
;       watchdog timer disabled (default is enabled)
;       standard crystal (using 4 MHz osc for test)
;       power-up timer on
;======================================================
```

16-BIT BINARY TO 5-DIGIT BCD - Range 0x0000 To 0xFFFF

The following routine is like the previous one except for the double add and double subtract routines plus a special purpose flag used to determine whether or not a negative result is generated in the subtraction process. The double subtraction routine uses 2's complement arithmetic which will not be explained here (advanced topic). You will have to take the fact that it works on faith and put the routine to work.

The routine has the full 16-bit bit range of 0x0000 to 0xFFFF.

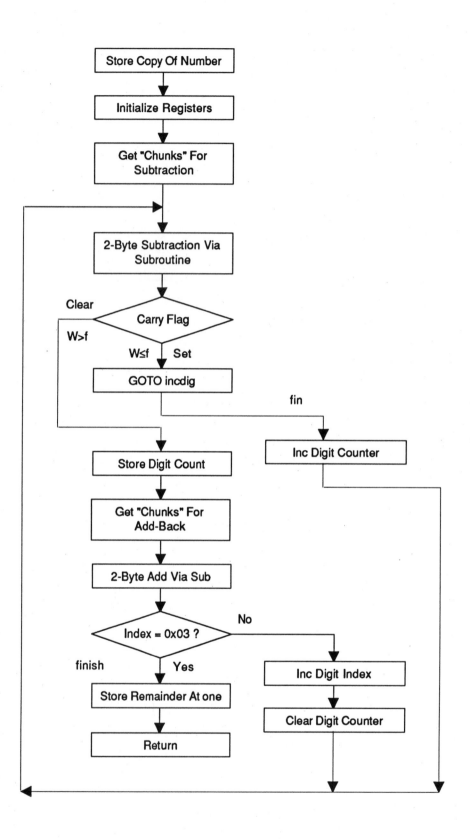

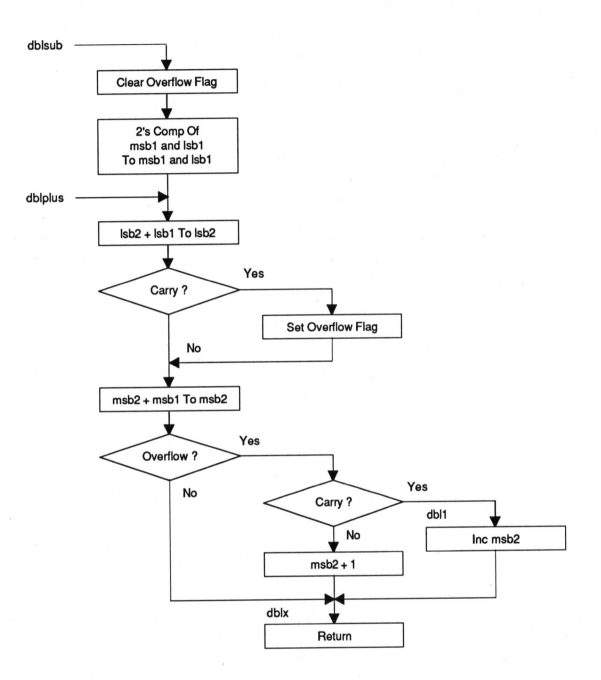

```
;=======DBLB2DY.ASM=========================6/27/97==
;accepts 0x0000 through ffff - 0 through 65535
;dblsub uses 2's comp plus flag
;----------------------------------------------------
        list    p=16c84
        radix   hex
;----------------------------------------------------
;       cpu equates (memory map)
indf    equ     0x00
pc      equ     0x02
status  equ     0x03
fsr     equ     0x04
ms      equ     0x0c
ls      equ     0x0d
index   equ     0x0e
dig_ctr equ     0x0f
lsb1    equ     0x10
msb1    equ     0x11
lsb2    equ     0x12
msb2    equ     0x13
flags   equ     0x14
tenk    equ     0x20
onek    equ     0x21
hund    equ     0x22
ten     equ     0x23
one     equ     0x24
;----------------------------------------------------
;       bit equates
c       equ     0
ovflw   equ     0
z       equ     2
rp0     equ     5
;----------------------------------------------------
        org     0x000
;
start   movlw   0xfa            ;define test number MS byte
        movwf   ms
        movlw   0x00            ;define test number LS byte
        movwf   ls
;prep for calling conversion subroutine
        movf    ms,w            ;get MS byte
        movwf   msb2
        movf    ls,w            ;get LS byte
        movwf   lsb2
        call    dblb2d          ;call conversion subroutine
circle  goto    circle          ;done
;----------------------------------------------------
tbl_lo  addwf   pc,f            ;add index to program counter
        retlw   0x10            ;10,000 decimal
        retlw   0xe8            ;1,000 decimal
        retlw   0x64            ;100 decimal
        retlw   0x0a            ;10 decimal
;----------------------------------------------------
```

236

```
tbl_hi  addwf   pc,f            ;add index to program counter
        retlw   0x27            ;10,000 decimal
        retlw   0x03            ;1,000 decimal
        retlw   0x00            ;100 decimal
        retlw   0x00            ;10 decimal
;------------------------------------------------
dblb2d  clrf    tenk
        clrf    onek
        clrf    hund
        clrf    ten
        clrf    one
        clrf    index
        clrf    dig_ctr
        bcf     flags,ovflw
subtr   movf    index,w         ;get current index into W
        call    tbl_lo          ;get ls chunk for subtraction
        movwf   lsb1
        movf    index,w         ;get current index into W
        call    tbl_hi          ;get ms chunk for subtraction
        movwf   msb1
        call    dblsub          ;to double precision subtraction
        btfsc   status,c        ;test carry flag
        goto    incdig
        movlw   0x20            ;load base address of table
        movwf   fsr
        movf    index,w         ;get index
        addwf   fsr,f           ;add offset
        movf    dig_ctr,w       ;get digit counter contents
        movwf   indf            ;store at digit loc (indexed)
        movf    index,w         ;get index
        call    tbl_lo          ;get ls chunk for addition
        movwf   lsb1
        movf    index,w         ;get index
        call    tbl_hi          ;get ms chunk for addition
        movwf   msb1
        bcf     flags,ovflw
        call    dblplus         ;to double precision addition
        movf    index,w         ;get index
        sublw   0x03            ;index=3?
        btfsc   status,z
        goto    finish
        incf    index,f         ;increment digit index
        clrf    dig_ctr
        goto    subtr
;------------------------------------------------
incdig  incf    dig_ctr,f       ;increment digit counter
        goto    subtr
;------------------------------------------------
finish  movf    lsb2,w          ;get 1's=remainder
        movwf   one
        return                  ;done
;------------------------------------------------
dblsub  bcf     flags,ovflw     ;clear overflow flag
        comf    lsb1,f          ;2's complement stuff
```

```
            comf     msb1,f
            movf     lsb1,w
            addlw    0x01
            movwf    lsb1
            btfsc    status,c
            incf     msb1,f
dblplus     movf     lsb1,w
            addwf    lsb2,f          ;add low bytes
            btfsc    status,c
            bsf      flags,ovflw ;indicate overflow occurred
            movf     msb1,w
            addwf    msb2,f          ;add high bytes
            btfss    flags,ovflw
            goto     dblx
            btfsc    status,c
            goto     dbl1
            movlw    0x01
            addwf    msb2,f
            goto     dblx
dbl1        incf     msb2,f
dblx        return
;-----------------------------------------------------------
            end
;-----------------------------------------------------------
;at blast time, select:
;       memory unprotected
;       watchdog timer disabled (default is enabled)
;       standard crystal (using 4 MHz osc for test)
;       power-up timer on
;===========================================================
```

Examples:

Hex	Decimal	tenk	onek	hund	ten	one
0XFA00	64,000	06	04	00	00	00
0XFA22	64,034	06	04	00	03	04
0X00FF	255	00	00	02	05	05
0X0002	2	00	00	00	00	02

So, what can be done with this stuff? A binary result can be displayed in decimal. A decimal temperature set point can be entered and converted to binary for comparison with a temperature brought into the microcontroller through an A to D converter. Humans think and communicate in decimal. Human numbers must be converted to the processor's language and back again.

DIGITAL THERMOMETER

BUILDING BLOCKS

The building blocks are are now available to build a digital thermometer with a 0°C to 50°C range.

- Temperature sensor - LM335
- Signal conditioning
- A/D (several methods)
- LCD interface
- Math
- Decimal interface

Offset and scaling are done by signal conditioning methods which provide a voltage range of 0 to 5 volts to the input of the A/D converter.

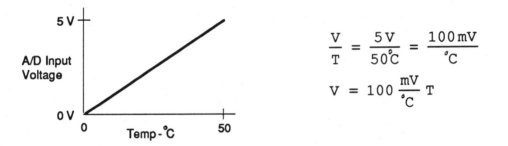

$$\frac{V}{T} = \frac{5\,V}{50°C} = \frac{100\,mV}{°C}$$

$$V = 100\,\frac{mV}{°C}\,T$$

The A/D counts up when it does a conversion. It's binary output represents temperature at 0.196 C°/ count.

$$0x00 = 0\ °C$$
$$0xFF = 49.98\ °C$$

$$\frac{50°C}{255\,counts} = 0.196\,\frac{°C}{count}$$

We want to multiply the A/D conversion value by 0.196 °C /count. That can't be done but we can multiply by 196 and worry about the decimal point later. Here is the plan:

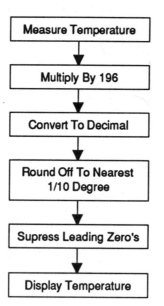

To multiply the data by 196, we need to find the hex equivalent.

$$\frac{196}{16} = 12.25$$

```
0xC4
    x1 =    4
  12x16 =  192
           196
```

We will multiply the data by 0xC4 using the 8x8 unsigned multiply, 16-bit result routine described in the chapter on math routines.

We already know how to convert a binary number to decimal. We will talk now about how to round off and suppress leading zeros. The decimal point is handled simply by displaying it in the correct position.

ROUNDING OFF

Once the temperature is in decimal form, it should be rounded off as the measurement is accurate to within approximately 0.1 C°.

Example: 49.980   50.0

We will round off the decimal result to the nearest tenth of a centigrade degree.

A little thought reveals that the rounding process can ripple back all the way to the most significant digit (see example above).

The round off routine rounds off the two least significant digits. It does not clean up trash left in their places because that information will not be displayed.

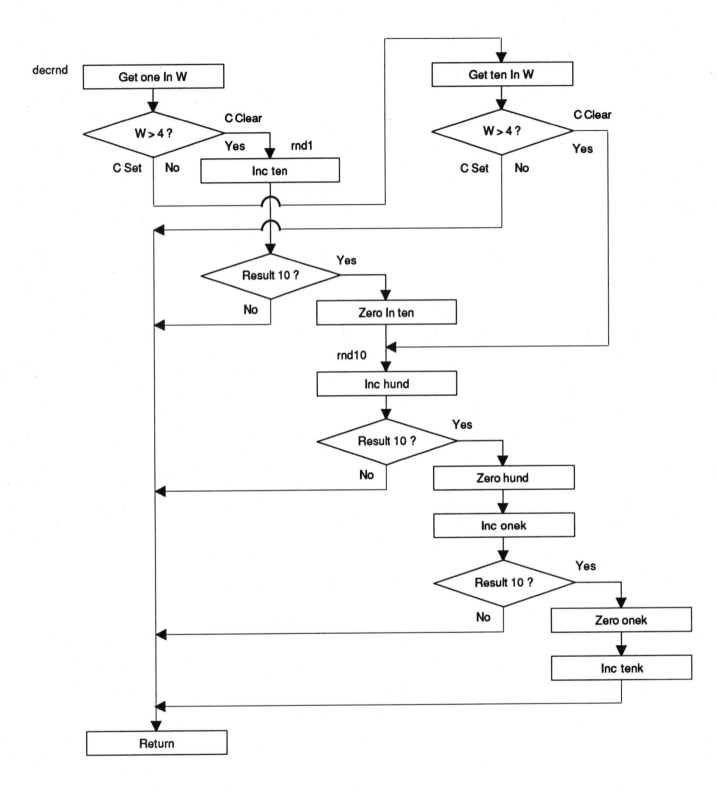

decrnd

Get one In W

W > 4 ?

C Clear

C Set   No   Yes   rnd1

Inc ten

Get ten In W

W > 4 ?

C Clear

C Set   No   Yes

Result 10 ?   Yes

No

Zero In ten

rnd10

Inc hund

Result 10 ?   Yes

No

Zero hund

Inc onek

Result 10 ?   Yes

No

Zero onek

Inc tenk

Return

```
;======DECRND.ASM==========================6/26/97==
;rounds off two least significant digits of a
;5-digit decimal number
;use only hund, onek and tenk in subsequent program as
;one and ten are left as trash
;----------------------------------------------------
        list    p=16c84
        radix   hex
;----------------------------------------------------
;       cpu equates (memory map)
status  equ     0x03
tenk    equ     0x20
onek    equ     0x21
hund    equ     0x22
ten     equ     0x23
one     equ     0x24
;----------------------------------------------------
;       bit equates
c       equ     0
z       equ     2
;----------------------------------------------------
        org     0x000
;
start   movlw   0x04            ;define 5 test digits
        movwf   tenk
        movlw   0x09
        movwf   onek
        movlw   0x09
        movwf   hund
        movlw   0x08
        movwf   ten
        movlw   0x00
        movwf   one
        call    decrnd          ;call round off subroutine
circle  goto    circle          ;done
;----------------------------------------------------
decrnd  movf    one,w           ;get one into W
        sublw   0x04            ;subtract W from 4, result in W
        btfss   status,c
        call    rnd1            ;if carry clear, round
        movf    ten,w           ;get ten into W
        sublw   0x04            ;subtract W from 4, result in W
        btfss   status,c
        call    rnd10           ;if carry clear, round
        return
;----------------------------------------------------
rnd1    incf    ten
        movf    ten,w           ;compare
        sublw   0x0a            ;result 10 decimal?
        btfss   status,z
        return                  ;not 10
        clrf    ten
rnd10   incf    hund
        movf    hund,w          ;compare
```

```
        sublw   0x0a            ;result 10 decimal?
        btfss   status,z
        return                  ;not 10
        clrf    hund
        incf    onek
        movf    onek,w          ;compare
        sublw   0x0a            ;result 10 decimal?
        btfss   status,z
        return                  ;not 10
        clrf    onek
        incf    tenk
        return
;-------------------------------------------------------
        end
;-------------------------------------------------------
;at blast time, select:
;       memory unprotected
;       watchdog timer disabled (default is enabled)
;       standard crystal (using 4 MHz osc for test)
;       power-up timer on
;=======================================================
```

DISPLAYING TEMPERATURE VIA A LCD

The next routine suppresses high order zeros as was done in the routine for displaying the result of 8-bit binary to 3-digit BCD conversion. The decimal point is displayed by sending the ASCII equivalent to the proper position in display RAM in the PIC16C84 which controls the LCD.

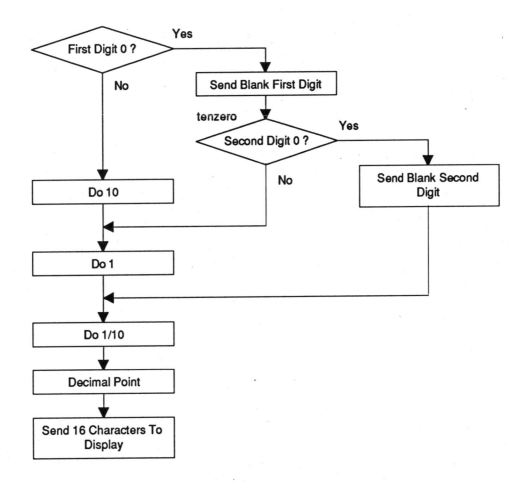

```
;=======TEMPLCD.ASM===============================6/27/97==
        list    p=16c84
        radix   hex
;------------------------------------------------------------
;       cpu equates (memory map)
tmr0    equ     0x01
status  equ     0x03
porta   equ     0x05
intcon  equ     0x0b
sendreg equ     0x0c
count   equ     0x0d
instr   equ     0x0e
char    equ     0x0f
addr    equ     0x10
number  equ     0x12
ncount  equ     0x15
mcount  equ     0x16
hold    equ     0x17
tenk    equ     0x20
onek    equ     0x21
hund    equ     0x22
tens    equ     0x25
```

```
ones      equ       0x26
tenths    equ       0x27
optreg    equ       0x81
trisa     equ       0x85
;---------------------------------------------------------
;         bit equates
c         equ       0
z         equ       2
rp0       equ       5
;---------------------------------------------------------
          org       0x000
;
start     bsf       status,rp0    ;switch to bank 1
          movlw     b'00000000'   ;port A outputs
          movwf     trisa
          bcf       status,rp0    ;switch back to bank 0
          bsf       porta,1       ;output mark, bit 1 (serial - LCD)
          call      debounce
          call      debounce
          movlw     0x00          ;blanks to display RAM
          movwf     instr
          call      sndstf        ;send instruction to LCD module
          call      debounce
          movlw     0x01          ;send 16 characters to display
          movwf     instr
          call      sndstf        ;send instruction to LCD module
          call      debounce
setup     movlw     0x00          ;test digits
          movwf     tenk
          movlw     0x05
          movwf     onek
          movlw     0x00
          movwf     hund
          movf      tenk,w        ;rename for easier comprehension
          movwf     tens          ;from round off to display
          movf      onek,w
          movwf     ones
          movf      hund,w
          movwf     tenths
zcheck    movf      tens,w        ;get 10's digit
          sublw     0x00          ;compare - digit=0?
          btfsc     status,z
          goto      tenzero       ;yes
do10      movf      tens,w        ;get 10's digit
          call      hex2asc       ;convert binary digit to ascii
          movwf     char
          movlw     0x20          ;display RAM address
          movwf     addr
          movlw     0x03          ;ascii char follows, send to display RAM
          movwf     instr
          call      sndstf        ;send 10's digit to display RAM
          call      debounce      ;time delay
do1       movf      ones,w        ;get 1's digit
          call      hex2asc       ;convert binary digit to ascii
```

246

```
        movwf    char
        movlw    0x21          ;display RAM address
        movwf    addr
        movlw    0x03          ;ascii char follows, send to display RAM
        movwf    instr
        call     sndstf        ;send 1's digit to display RAM
        call     debounce      ;time delay
do10ths movf     tenths,w      ;get 10ths digit
        call     hex2asc       ;convert binary digit to ascii
        movwf    char
        movlw    0x23          ;display RAM address
        movwf    addr
        movlw    0x03          ;ascii char follows, send to display RAM
        movwf    instr
        call     sndstf        ;send 10ths digit to display RAM
        call     debounce      ;time delay
decpt   movlw    0x2e          ;ascii "period", decimal point
        movwf    char
        movlw    0x22          ;display RAM address
        movwf    addr
        movlw    0x03          ;ascii char follows, send to display RAM
        movwf    instr
        call     sndstf        ;send decimal point to display RAM
        call     debounce      ;time delay
send    movlw    0x01          ;send 16 characters to display
        movwf    instr
        call     sndstf        ;to LCD module
circle  goto     circle        ;done
;----------------------------------------------------
tenzero movlw    0x20          ;ascii blank
        movwf    char
        movlw    0x20          ;display RAM address
        movwf    addr
        movlw    0x03          ;ascii character to display RAM
        movwf    instr
        call     sndstf
        call     debounce
        movf     ones,w        ;get 1's digit
        sublw    0x00          ;compare - digit=0?
        btfss    status,z
        goto     do1           ;if 0, fall thru to onezero
;----------------------------------------------------
onezero movlw    0x20          ;ascii blank
        movwf    char
        movlw    0x21          ;display RAM address
        movwf    addr
        movlw    0x03          ;ascii character to display RAM
        movwf    instr
        call     sndstf
        call     debounce
        goto     do10ths
;----------------------------------------------------
debounce movlw   0x02          ;to counter
        movwf    count
```

```
dbloop   movlw   0xff         ;M
         movwf   mcount       ;to M counter
loadn    movlw   0xff         ;N
         movwf   ncount       ;to N counter
decn     decfsz  ncount,f     ;decrement N
         goto    decn         ;again
         decfsz  mcount,f     ;decrement M
         goto    loadn        ;again
         decfsz  count
         goto    dbloop       ;thru loop within a loop twice -
;                                 400 milliseconds
         return               ;done
;-------------------------------------------------------------
sndstf   movf    instr,w      ;get instruction
         movwf   sendreg      ;to be sent
         call    ser_out      ;to serial out subroutine
         movf    char,w       ;get character or hex byte
         movwf   sendreg      ;to be sent
         call    ser_out      ;to serial out subroutine
         movf    addr,w       ;get address
         movwf   sendreg      ;to be sent
         call    ser_out      ;to serial out subroutine
         return
;-------------------------------------------------------------
ser_out  bcf     intcon,5     ;disable tmr0 interrupts
         bcf     intcon,7     ;disable global interrupts
         clrf    tmr0         ;clear timer/counter
         clrwdt               ;clear wdt prep prescaler assign
         bsf     status,rp0   ;to page 1
         movlw   b'11011000'  ;set up timer/counter
         movwf   optreg
         bcf     status,rp0   ;back to page 0
         movlw   0x08         ;init shift counter
         movwf   count
         bcf     porta,1      ;start bit
         clrf    tmr0         ;start timer/counter
         bcf     intcon,2     ;clear tmr0 overflow flag
time1    btfss   intcon,2     ;timer overflow?
         goto    time1        ;no
         bcf     intcon,2     ;yes, clear overflow flag
nxtbit   rlf     sendreg,f    ;rotate msb into carry flag
         bcf     porta,1      ;clear port A, bit 1
         btfsc   status,c     ;test carry flag
         bsf     porta,1      ;bit is set
time2    btfss   intcon,2     ;timer overflow?
         goto    time2        ;no
         bcf     intcon,2     ;clear overflow flag
         decfsz  count,f      ;shifted 8?
         goto    nxtbit       ;no
         bsf     porta,1      ;yes, output mark
time3    btfss   intcon,2     ;timer overflow?
         goto    time3        ;no
         return               ;done
;-------------------------------------------------------------
```

```
;enter with hex digit in w
;
hex2asc  movwf    hold          ;store copy of hex digit
         sublw    0x09          ;subtract w from 1 less than 0x0a
         btfss    status,c      ;carry flag set if w < 0x0a
         goto     add37
         goto     add30
add37    movf     hold,w        ;get hex digit
         addlw    0x37
         return                 ;return with ascii in w
add30    movf     hold,w        ;get hex digit
         addlw    0x30
         return                 ;return with ascii in w
;-------------------------------------------------------
         end
;-------------------------------------------------------
;at blast time, select:
;      memory unprotected
;      watchdog timer disabled (default is enabled)
;      standard crystal (using 4 MHz osc for test) XT
;      power-up timer on
;=======================================================
```

At last you have the modules to create a 0 to 50° digital thermometer good to one tenth C°. I leave it to you to "PIC" your favorite analog signal conditioning method and integrate the appropriate routines to create a working system.

Hint: Make sure you include all the equates required for each routine.

You can use the techniques you have learned to create other instruments or applications. You now know enough to display the binary contents of a counter register for example. Hmmmmmm.....

Have fun "PIC'n **Up the Pace**!"

PIC16C84/PIC16F84 DATA EEPROM MEMORY

The PIC16C84 and PIC16F84 microcontrollers have 64 bytes of data EEPROM which may be read or written to during program execution. This data memory is in a block completely separate from the program memory and file registers.

The data EEPROM memory may be used to store anything you want. Since EEPROM is nonvolitile, the data stored there will still be there when the power to the PIC16C84 is turned back on after being off.

The EEPROM data memory has an address range of 0x00 to 0x3F. This address space is accessed by placing the address in a special register (EEADR) and by passing data back and forth via another special register (EEDATA).

Data is read or written one byte at a time. A single bit cannot be read or written.

Four special function registers are used to read/write the data EEPROM.

```
Register     Address
-------------------
EEADR        0x09
EEDATA       0x08
EECON1       0x88
EECON2       0x89
```

The write time is about 10 milliseconds and is controlled by an on-chip timer.

Some PIC16C84 device programmers can program the data EEPROM memory. If the device is code-protected, only the CPU may access the data EEPROM.

EEADR

The EEADR register is capable of addressing a maximum of 256 locations, but only the first 64 are used. Only 6 of the 8 bits in the register are used. Bits 7 and 6 are not decoded. The usable address range is 0x00 to 0x3F.

EEDATA

EEDATA is an 8-bit register used to pass data into and out of data EEPROM memory.

EECON1

EECON1 is the control register and has the functions shown.

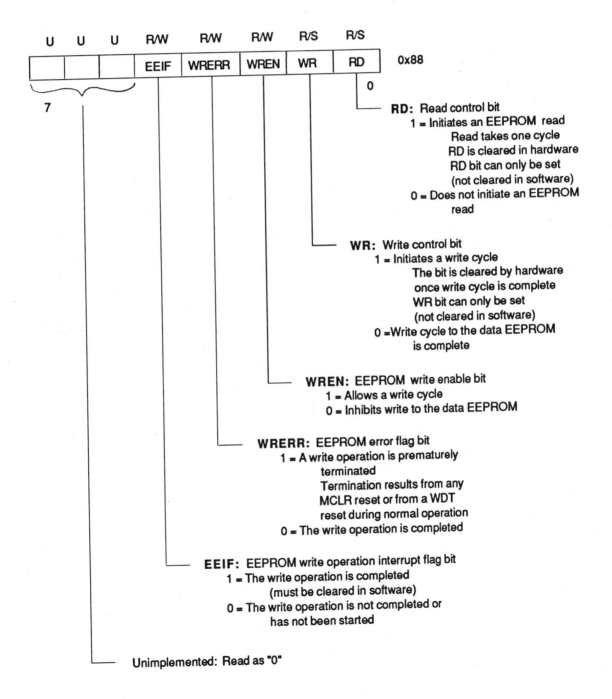

R = Readable bit
W = Writeable bit
S = Settable bit, read as "0"
U = Unimplemented bit, read as "0"
Power on reset - - - 0X000

0x88

RD: Read control bit
1 = Initiates an EEPROM read
Read takes one cycle
RD is cleared in hardware
RD bit can only be set
(not cleared in software)
0 = Does not initiate an EEPROM
read

WR: Write control bit
1 = Initiates a write cycle
The bit is cleared by hardware
once write cycle is complete
WR bit can only be set
(not cleared in software)
0 = Write cycle to the data EEPROM
is complete

WREN: EEPROM write enable bit
1 = Allows a write cycle
0 = Inhibits write to the data EEPROM

WRERR: EEPROM error flag bit
1 = A write operation is prematurely
terminated
Termination results from any
MCLR reset or from a WDT
reset during normal operation
0 = The write operation is completed

EEIF: EEPROM write operation interrupt flag bit
1 = The write operation is completed
(must be cleared in software)
0 = The write operation is not completed or
has not been started

Unimplemented: Read as "0"

The RD and WR control bits initiate read and write. These bits can only be set (not cleared) in software to initiate a read or write cycle. They are cleared automatically by completion of a read or write cycle.

A write operation is allowed when the WREN bit is set. WREN is cleared on power-up. The WRERR bit is set when a write cycle is interrupted by a MCLR reset or a WDT time-out reset. Following a reset, user software can be written to check the WRERR bit and start the (interrupted) write cycle over again. The address and data will remain unchanged in the EEADR and EEDATA registers.

Note that the EEIF interrupt flag is set on completion of a write cycle (after the required 10 milliseconds). It is must be cleared in software.

EECON2

EECON2 is not a physical register, but the address 0x89 is assigned to it. Two control words are written to it is as part of the write cycle.

READ CYCLE

To read the contents of a data EEPROM memory location, the address is presented to the EEPROM by writing it to the EEADR register followed by setting the RD control bit in EECON1 (bit 0). In the very next instruction cycle, the data will be available in the EEDATA register.

EEADR is in Bank 0 and EECON1 is in Bank 1, so file register bank switching is required.

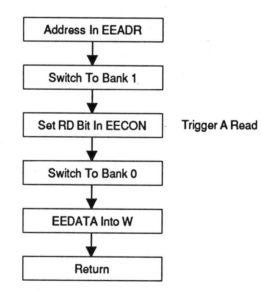

```
movlw      address     ;define address
movwf      eeadr       ;address to register
bsf        status,rp0  ;bank 1
bsf        eecon1,rd   ;read data EEPROM
bcf        status,rp0  ;return to bank 0
movf       eedata,w    ;data into W
```

WRITE CYCLE

To write to a data EEPROM memory location, the address is presented to the EEPROM by writing it to the EEADR register and the data is written to the EEDATA register. So far, so good. Next comes a specific sequence of instructions which initiates a WRITE. The timing of the steps is critical, so the prescribed sequence should be used. Interrupts must be disabled while this is going on so that the sequence timing won't be disrupted.

The WREN bit in EECON1 must be set to enable a WRITE. This prevents accidental writing to the data EEPROM when flawed programs go wild. The WREN bit should be clear at all times except when a WRITE is to take place.

On completion of the WRITE cycle, the WR bit is cleared automatically and the EE write complete interrupt flag (EEIF) is set. The program can detect completion of the WRITE cycle by enabling this interrupt, by polling the EEIF flag, or by polling the WR bit. The EEIF and WREN bits must be cleared by software.

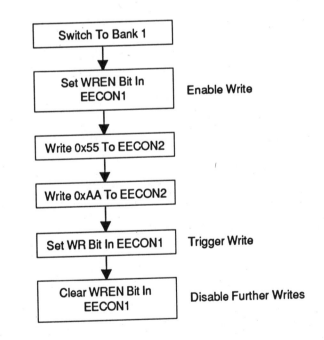

```
                address to EEADR
                data to EEDATA

        bsf     status,rp0   ;bank 1
        bsf     eecon1,wren  ;enable write
        movlw   0x55         ;define 0x55
        movwf   eecon2       ;to register
        movlw   0xaa         ;define0xAA
        movwf   eecon2       ;to register
        bsf     eecon1,wr    ;set WR bit to trigger write
        bcf     eecon1,wren  ;disable write (won't effect
;                                            this one)


;=======EEPROM.ASM===============================6/10/97==
        list    p=16c84
        radix   hex
;-----------------------------------------------------------
;       cpu equates (memory map)
status  equ     0x03
portb   equ     0x06
eedata  equ     0x08
eeadr   equ     0x09
address equ     0x0c
byte    equ     0x0d
trisb   equ     0x86
eecon1  equ     0x88
eecon2  equ     0x89
;-----------------------------------------------------------
;       bit equates
rd      equ     0
wr      equ     1
wren    equ     2
rp0     equ     5
;-----------------------------------------------------------
        org     0x000
;
start   bsf     status,rp0   ;switch to bank 1
        movlw   b'00000000'  ;outputs
        movwf   trisb
        bcf     status,rp0   ;switch back to bank 0
        clrf    portb        ;initialize, LED's off
        movlw   0x0f         ;test data
        movwf   byte
        movlw   0x00         ;test address
        movwf   address
        call    write        ;write test byte to data EEPROM
        bsf     status,rp0   ;to bank 1
wrcompl btfsc   eecon1,wr    ;test write complete?
        goto    wrcompl
        bcf     status,rp0   ;back to bank 0
        call    read         ;read test byte from data EEPROM
        movwf   portb        ;display test byte via LED's
circle  goto    circle
```

```
;-------------------------------------------------------------
read    movf    address,w   ;get address
        movwf   eeadr       ;address to register
        bsf     status,rp0  ;bank 1
        bsf     eecon1,rd   ;read data EEPROM (RD bit will
;                               be cleared in hardware)
        bcf     status,rp0  ;return to bank 0
        movf    eedata,w    ;data into W
        return              ;return with data in W
;-------------------------------------------------------------
write   movf    address,w   ;get address
        movwf   eeadr       ;address to register
        movf    byte,w      ;get data
        movwf   eedata      ;data to register
        bsf     status,rp0  ;to bank 1
        bsf     eecon1,wren ;enable write
        movlw   0x55        ;define 0x55 (per data book)
        movwf   eecon2      ;to register
        movlw   0xaa        ;define 0xaa (per data book)
        movwf   eecon2      ;to register
        bsf     eecon1,wr   ;set WR bit to trigger write
        bcf     eecon1,wren ;disable write (won't effect
;                               this one)
        bcf     status,rp0  ;back to bank 0
        return
;-------------------------------------------------------------
        end
;-------------------------------------------------------------
;at blast time, select:
;       memory unprotected
;       watchdog timer disabled (default is enabled)
;       standard crystal (using 4`MHz osc for test) XT
;       power-up timer on
;=============================================================
```

PROGRAMMING THE DATA EEPROM

Some device programmers are not capable of writing to or programming the PIC16C84's data EEPROM. If yours is, you are set. If you are using MPLAB, version 3.12.00 or greater is required (in my experience anyway).

The PICSTART plus has this capability. The data is included in the .ASM file as follows:

```
        org     2100
        de      0xaa, 0xbb
```

"de" is an assembler directive - define EEPROM data byte. Data bytes are separated by a coma followed by a space. The ORG statement places the data at address 0x2100 which corresponds to 0x00 in data EEPROM.

```
;======EEP2.ASM=====================================6/12/97==
        list    p=16c84
        radix   hex
;---------------------------------------------------------
;       cpu equates (memory map)
status  equ     0x03
portb   equ     0x06
eedata  equ     0x08
eeadr   equ     0x09
address equ     0x0c
trisb   equ     0x86
eecon1  equ     0x88
eecon2  equ     0x89
;---------------------------------------------------------
;       bit equates
rd      equ     0
wr      equ     1
wren    equ     2
rp0     equ     5
;---------------------------------------------------------
        org     0x000
;
start   bsf     status,rp0  ;switch to bank 1
        movlw   b'00000000' ;outputs
        movwf   trisb
        bcf     status,rp0  ;switch back to bank 0
        clrf    portb       ;initialize, LED's off
        movlw   0x01        ;test address
        movwf   address
        call    read        ;read test byte from data EEPROM
        movwf   portb       ;display test byte via LED's
circle  goto    circle
;---------------------------------------------------------
read    movf    address,w   ;get address
        movwf   eeadr       ;address to register
        bsf     status,rp0  ;bank 1
        bsf     eecon1,rd   ;read data EEPROM (RD bit will
;                                be cleared in hardware)
        bcf     status,rp0  ;return to bank 0
        movf    eedata,w    ;data into W
        return              ;return with data in W
;---------------------------------------------------------
        org     2100
        de      0xaa, 0xbb
;---------------------------------------------------------
        end
;---------------------------------------------------------
;at blast time, select:
;       memory unprotected
;       watchdog timer disabled (default is enabled)
;       standard crystal (using 4 MHz osc for test) XT
;       power-up timer on
;=========================================================
```

The sample program EEP2.ASM reads the byte at 0x01, and displays it via the LED's. The process of programming the device includes storing the two data bytes to be located at EEPROM addresses 0x00 and 0x01.

CODE PROTECTION

The PIC16C84 code protect bit only protects the code in program memory. Your program can still access and change the contents of data EEPROM memory with the code protection bit set.

PROGRAM MEMORY PAGING

PIC16/17 microcontroller program instructions include the address, or at least most of the address. There is only so much room in the instruction for address information. For parts with "smaller" program memory, the entire address fits in the instruction word. For parts with "larger" program memory, this is not be possible. In this situation, the rest of the address (high order bits) comes from somewhere else. If your base-line part programs require less than 512 memory locations or if your mid-range part programs require less than 2K memory locations, you will not need to concern yourself with program memory paging. Program memory paging becomes necessary when those upper limits are exceeded.

Program memory is divided into pages as follows:

	12-bit Core Base-line	14-bit Core Mid-range
Memory Locations Per Page	512	2K

Program memory page selection will be required if your part has more than one page of program memory and your program will occupy more than page 0. This is done by transferring page select bits held temporarily in a register to the program counter when program execution moves from one page to another. This can occur when CALL and GOTO instructions are executed as they alter the contents of the program counter to specify another page.

The primary considerations for the programmer here are:

- What happens when your code crosses a page boundary?

    Does MPASM let you know? If so, how do it know?! How do you know?

- Handling CALL and GOTO instructions.

    If you do a GOTO, how do you know what page the destination address is on? How do you tell the microcontroller to go there?

- Interrupts - 14-bit core parts only.

    What happens to the program counter?

How all this works depends on whether the part is a 12-bit core base-line part or a 14-bit core mid-range part, so we must treat them separately.

258

WHERE TO PUT THE CODE

The only way to control/know memory allocation is to use ORG statements to locate subroutine starting addresses and code destined for a specific memory page. You can verify this by looking at the "LOC" numbers = program memory locations in the .LST file generated by MPASM as past of the assembly process. The symbol table and the memory usage map in the .LST file will also help you figure out where you are and if things are ending up in the right place.

14-BIT CORE MID-RANGE PARTS

The specs for some popular mid-range parts are:

Device	Program Memory Pages	Size	Number Of High Bits To Mess With (Live In PCLATH)
PIC16C554	1/4	512	0
C61	1/2	1K	0
C62	1/2	1K	0
C71	1/2	1K	0
C74	2	4K	1
C84	1/2	1K	0
F84	1/2	1K	0

The good news here is that you will have to graduate to using a PIC16C74 (in this group) before you need to worry about program memory paging.

For all the parts in this family, the program counter is 13 bits wide. The CALL and GOTO instruction address range is 11 bits, enough to handle 2K of program memory address space. Our task, then, is to learn what to do with the high order 2 bits when your part has 4K or 8K of program memory.

Program counter bits 11 and 12 are used to select memory pages in parts having 4K or 8K program memory.

The program counter is in two sections, program counter low (PCL) and program counter high (PCH).

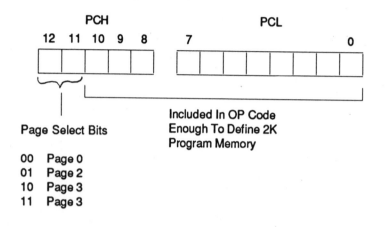

PCH

| 12 | 11 | 10 | 9 | 8 |

PCL

| 7 | | | | | | | 0 |

Page Select Bits

Included In OP Code
Enough To Define 2K
Program Memory

00 Page 0
01 Page 2
10 Page 3
11 Page 3

The program counter high (PCH) cannot be read or written to directly. It is loaded from a 5-bit latch called program counter latch high or PCLATH.

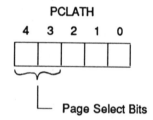

PCLATH

| 4 | 3 | 2 | 1 | 0 |

Page Select Bits

When a CALL or GOTO instruction is used in a program for a 14-bit core mid-range device with two program memory pages (4K), the page bit in PCLATH (bit 3) must be programmed to select the desired destination program memory page prior to executing the CALL or GOTO instruction. The write to PCLATH bit 3 should immediately proceed the CALL or GOTO instruction in your program. Bit 4 must be 0.

For 8K parts, two PCLATH bits (3 and 4) are used.

After returning from a subroutine, the page bits should be restored to the current page via program instructions to prevent confusion.

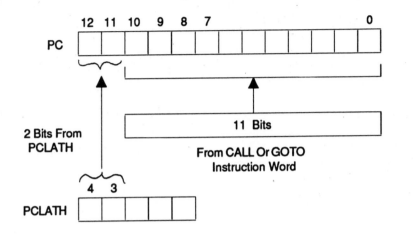

2 Bits From
PCLATH

From CALL Or GOTO
Instruction Word

GOTO - 14-bit core (example)

```
PIC16C74          From code on page 0 to code on page 1

        org       0x0000
        ----
        bsf       pclath,3      ;select page 1
        goto      job           ;to code on page 1
        ----
        org       0x0800
        ----
job
```

Subroutine CALL - 14-bit core (example)

```
PIC16C74          From code on page 0 to subroutine on page 1 and
                      return

        ----
        bsf       pclath,3      ;select page 1
        call      do_it         ;to subroutine on page 1
        bcf       pclath,3      ;select page 0 on return
        ----
        org       0x0800
        ----
do_it   ----
        ----
        return
```

Interrupts and Program Memory Paging

In the event of an interrupt, the program counter contents (all 13 bits) is saved on the hardware stack automatically. Manipulation of PCLATH is not required prior to a return instruction. The return address is handled automatically including the page (comes from stack).

When you are using a device which has more than one page of program memory and your program uses interrupts, you will need to save and restore the contents of PCLATH as part of your interrupt service routine. This is in case PCLATH was written to just prior to the interrupt. You will need its contents after the return from interrupt.

12-BIT CORE BASE-LINE PARTS

The specs for some popular mid-range parts are:

	PROGRAM MEMORY		Number Of High Bits To Mess With - Bits Live In Status
DEVICE	Pages	Size	Register (bits 6 & 7)
PIC16C54	1	512	0
56	2	1K	1
57	4	2K	2

For 12-bit core devices with more than one page of program memory, the status register contains two bits used for page selection (status register bits 6,5). The two status register page select bits are loaded into the upper two bits of the program counter (PC 10,9) on execution of a CALL or GOTO instruction.

GOTO instructions provide the lower 9 bits (bits 0 to 8) of the address to the program counter. Bits 9 and 10 come from the status register. GOTO's allow jumping to any location in any page.

A CALL loads the lower 8 bits of the program counter. The 9th bit (bit 8) is cleared to "0". This dictates that the first instruction of a subroutine must be in the first 256 locations of a program memory page. The upper 2 bits of the program counter are loaded with the page select bits from the status register if there is more than one page of program memory.

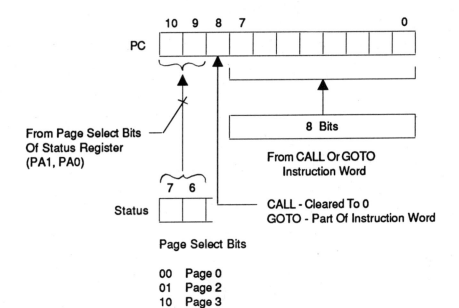

Page Select Bits

```
00   Page 0
01   Page 2
10   Page 3
11   Page 3
```

GOTO - 12-bit core (example)

PIC16C57   From code on page 0 to code on page 3

```
        org    0x000
        ----
        bsf    status,5    ;select page 3
        bsf    status,6
        goto   task            ;to code on page 3
        ----
        org    0x600
task
```

Subroutine CALL - 12-bit core (example)

PIC16C56   From code on page 0 to subroutine on page 1 and
                 return

```
        ----
        bsf    status,5    ;select page 1
        call   do_work       ;to subroutine on page 1
        bcf    status,5    ;select page 0 on return
        ----
        org    0x200
do_it   ----
        ----
        return
```

Again, the page select bits are made the same as the page the code is on immediately after a return from subroutine to prevent confusion.

SUMMARY

CALL Subroutine

12-Bit Base-Line

First instruction of subroutine must be in first 256
locations of any program memory page because 9th bit
(bit 8) of PC is cleared by execution of CALL
instruction. If program memory is larger
than one page (512), you must deal with the upper 2 bits
of the PC.

14-Bit Mid-Range

First instruction of subroutine may be anywhere as long
as PCLATH is programmed first when there is more than
one program memory page.

GOTO

12-Bit Base-Line

Any location on any page. If program memory is larger
than one page (512), you must deal with the upper 2 bits
of the PC.

14-Bit Mid-Range

Any location on any page. If program memory is larger
than one page (2K), you must deal with PCLATH.

LOCATING TABLES IN PROGRAM MEMORY

Tables are very important because they are the only means by which data can be included in a program. Their use is introduced in **Easy** PIC'n. Some more advanced issues are discussed here.

The only way to control/know memory allocation is to use an ORG statement to locate the subroutine which contains the table.

The rules for locating tables in program memory depend on device core size.

TABLE LOCATION FOR 14-BIT MID-RANGE PARTS

As we said in the previous chapter, 14-bit core, mid-range parts may have as much as 8K of program memory. Each 1K of memory has four 256-location segments. Tables should be located entirely within a 256 location segment of program memory. This can be any segment on any page. When the ADDWF instruction is used to jump into the table, the PCL contains the computed destination address and it is 8 bits wide. This is the reason for the 256 location limit. Actually, tables can straddle 256 segment boundaries, but that is beyond the scope of this book (see Microchip AN556).

For the PIC16C84, the 1K of program memory (half page) contains four 256-location segments which have the following address ranges:

Page 0	0x000	- 0x0FF
Page 1	0x100	- 0x1FF
Page 2	0x200	- 0x2FF
Page 3	0x300	- 0x3FF

TABLE LOCATION FOR 12-BIT BASE-LINE PARTS

When the ADDWF instruction is used to jump into a table (computed address), the computed 8-bit result is loaded into the lower 8 bits of the program counter. The 9th bit (bit 8) of the PC is cleared. The upper 2 bits of the program counter are loaded with the page select bits from the status register.

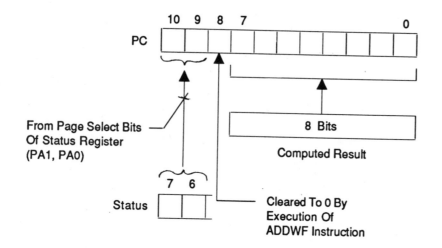

Tables are limited to the first 256 locations of any program memory page because the computed result is 8 bits and execution of the ADDWF instruction clears bit 8 of the PC.

SUMMARY

12-Bit Base-Line

Table must be in first 256 locations of any program memory page because 9th bit (bit 8) of PC is cleared by execution of ADDWF instruction.

14-Bit Mid-Range

Table may be in any 256 address program memory segment. The result of a computed address (ADDWF   PC) is limited to the 8-bit PCL which limits the number of possible addresses to 256 (unless you want to get really serious - see Microchip AN556).

APPENDIX A
SOURCES

Following is a list of sources for PIC16/17 parts, information and tools.

Digi-Key Corporation
701 Brooks Ave. South
Thief River Falls, MN 56701-0677   USA
(800)344-4539
http://www.digikey.com

Parts/Programmers

DonTronics
P.O. Box 595 Tullamarine 3043 Australia
Int+ 613 9338-6286
Int+ 613 9338-2935 FAX
http://www.dontronics.com

SimmStick $^{(tm)}$ Protyping Boards for PIC16/17

ITU Technologies
3704 Cheviot Ave. Suite 3
Cincinnati, OH 45211
(513)661-7523
http://www.itutech.com

Programmers and Software

JDR Microdevices
1850 South 10th Street
San Jose, CA 95112-4108
(800)538-5000

Parts/Programmers

JAMECO
1355 Shoreway Road
Belmont, CA 94002-4100
(800)831-4242
http://www.jameco.com

Parts/Programmers

Marlin P. Jones
P.O. Box 12685
Lake Park FL 33403-0685
(800)652-6733

Programmers

Microchip Technology Inc.
2355 West Chandler Blvd.
Chandler, AX 85224-6199   USA
(602) 786-7200
http://www.microchip.com

Manufacturer of PIC16/17

microEngineering Labs, Inc.
Box 7532
Colorado Springs, CO 80933   USA
(719)520-5323
http://www.melabs.com

Programmers, software
    and prototyping PCB's

Wirz Electronics
P.O. Box 457
Littleton MA 01460-0457
1-888-289-9479
http://www.wirz.com

SimmStick $^{(tm)}$ Protyping
Boards for PIC16/17

APPENDIX B
HEXADECIMAL NUMBERS

Binary numbers which are two bytes long are difficult to recognize, remember and write without errors, so the hexadecimal numbering system is used instead. Think of hex as a kind of shorthand notation to make life easier rather than some kind of terrible math.

```
------------------------------------
Hexadecimal     Binary     Decimal
------------------------------------
     0           0000          0
     1           0001          1
     2           0010          2
     3           0011          3
     4           0100          4
     5           0101          5
     6           0110          6
     7           0111          7
     8           1000          8
     9           1001          9
     A           1010         10
     B           1011         11
     C           1100         12
     D           1101         13
     E           1110         14
     F           1111         15
```

Hexadecimal is the language used in this book. It will seem awkward at first, but working with binary is time consuming and will result in errors which would quickly force you to learn hexadecimal. Using hexadecimal is not difficult. All you need is a little practice.

One byte requires two hex digits. Note that the bits representing a byte are sometimes shown in groups of four. Note, also, that the most significant binary digit is on the left.

Hex numbers are denoted by "0x" in this book.

Subject: Re: Continious delay
Date: Fri, 6 Mar 1998 02:00:49 -0800
From: Andrew Warren <fastfwd@IX.NETCOM.COM>
Reply-To: pic microcontroller discussion list <PICLIST@MITVMA.MIT.EDU>
Organization: Fast Forward Engineering
To: PICLIST@MITVMA.MIT.EDU

Gennady Palitsky <PICLIST@MITVMA.MIT.EDU> wrote:

> *I believe this should be simple, but don't have an idea as of right*
> *now. To generate delay I am using standard procedure:*
>
> *LOOP*
> *   decfsz   COUNTER,1*
> *   goto   LOOP*
> *------------------*
> *As far as I understand, both DECFSZ and GOTO are 2 cycle*
> *instructions, so 1 point change in COUNTER value gives me 4 cycles*
> *change in delay time (am I wrong?).*

     Gennady:

     Yes, you're wrong... The DECFSZ only takes two cycles on the
     FINAL iteration of the loop (when the GOTO is skipped); every
     other time through the loop, it takes just one cycle.

     The GOTO is a two-cycle instruction, so the total delay is X*3-1,
     where X is the value loaded into the counter before the loop.

> *Is there any way to generate delay which will give me 1:1 ratio (1*
> *point change in COUNTER value : 1 cycle change in delay time). Or*
> *do I want too much?*

     Try this; it generates delays with a resolution of one cycle,
     although it's limited to the range [20-271].

```
         MOVLW    X
         CALL     DELAY

         ....

; This routine delays X cycles.  Enter with X (in the range
; [20-271]) in the W register.
;
; Note that the delay is inclusive of the "MOVLW X", "CALL
; DELAY", and "RETURN" overhead, so a sequence like:
;
;        MOVLW    100
;        CALL     DELAY
;        MOVLW    200
;        CALL     DELAY
;
; will delay EXACTLY 300 cycles.

DELAY:

         MOVWF    COUNTER

         BTFSC    COUNTER, 0
         GOTO     $+1
```

```
        BTFSS   COUNTER, 1
        GOTO    SKIP
        NOP
        GOTO    $+1

SKIP:

        RRF     COUNTER
        RRF     COUNTER

        MOVLW   4
        SUBWF   COUNTER

        BCF     COUNTER, 6
        BCF     COUNTER, 7

LOOP:

        NOP
        DECFSZ  COUNTER
        GOTO    LOOP

        RETURN
```

As is always the case with code that I write online, this code
has neither been tested nor even assembled.

-Andy

=== Andrew Warren - fastfwd@ix.netcom.com
=== Fast Forward Engineering - Vista, California
=== http://www.geocities.com/SiliconValley/2499

Subject: Re: Continious delay
Date: Fri, 6 Mar 1998 09:39:55 +0100
From: Caisson <caisson@TELEBYTE.NL>
Reply-To: pic microcontroller discussion list <PICLIST@MITVMA.MIT.EDU>
To: PICLIST@MITVMA.MIT.EDU

> Van: Gennady Palitsky <gennadyp@MAINLINK.NET>
> Aan: PICLIST@MITVMA.MIT.EDU
> Onderwerp: Continious delay
> Datum: vrijdag 6 maart 1998 9:16
>
> I believe this should be simple, but don't have an idea as of right now.
> To generate delay I am using standard procedure:
>
> LOOP
>   decfsz   COUNTER,1
>   goto   LOOP
> -----------------
> As far as I understand, both DECFSZ and GOTO are 2 cycle instructions, so
1
> point change in COUNTER value gives me 4 cycles change in delay time (am
I
> wrong?).

I do not like to be the one to tell you, but yes, you're wrong. So there
:-)

A conditional command is a 1 -OR- 2 cycle command, depending on the
outcome of the compare.

Explanation:
If you don't skip the next command you can continue with the _pre-fetched_
next
command.
If you skip the next command (or perform a 'goto') , you'll have to ignore
the
pre-fetched next command (and lose a cycle), and get a new command.

Your delay-routine has a delay of 3 * (COUNT-1) +2 cycles
- When COUNT <> 1 -> Decfsz := 1 cycle, Goto := 2 cycles
- When COUNT == 1 -> Decfsz := 2 cycles, goto := <skipped>

> Is there any way to generate delay which will give me 1:1 ratio (1 point
> change in COUNTER value : 1 cycle change in delay time). Or do I want too
> much?

You could try to use the Timer-module, if your PIC has got one.

> Gennady Palitsky
> Jefferson Audio Video Systems
> gennadyp@mainlink.net

Greetz,
  Rudy Wieser